Military Professionalism and Humanitarian Law

Military Professionalism and Humanitarian Law

The Struggle to Reduce the Hazards of War

YISHAI BEER

OXFORD
UNIVERSITY PRESS

OXFORD
UNIVERSITY PRESS

Oxford University Press is a department of the University of Oxford. It furthers the University's objective of excellence in research, scholarship, and education by publishing worldwide. Oxford is a registered trademark of Oxford University Press in the UK and certain other countries.

Published in the United States of America by Oxford University Press
198 Madison Avenue, New York, NY 10016, United States of America.

Library of Congress Cataloging-in-Publication Data

Names: Beer, Yishai, author.
Title: Military professionalism and humanitarian law : the struggle to reduce the hazards of war / Yishai Beer.
Description: Oxford [UK] ; New York, NY : Oxford University Press, [2018] | Includes bibliographical references and index.
Identifiers: LCCN 2017046073 | ISBN 9780190881146 ((hardback) : alk. paper)
Subjects: LCSH: War (International law) | Self-defense (International law) | Just war doctrine. | Humanitarian law.
Classification: LCC KZ6396 .B44 2018 | DDC 341.6/7—dc23
LC record available at https://lccn.loc.gov/2017046073

1 3 5 7 9 8 6 4 2

Printed by Edwards Brothers Malloy, United States of America

Note to Readers

This publication is designed to provide accurate and authoritative information in regard to the subject matter covered. It is based upon sources believed to be accurate and reliable and is intended to be current as of the time it was written. It is sold with the understanding that the publisher is not engaged in rendering legal, accounting, or other professional services. If legal advice or other expert assistance is required, the services of a competent professional person should be sought. Also, to confirm that the information has not been affected or changed by recent developments, traditional legal research techniques should be used, including checking primary sources where appropriate.

(Based on the Declaration of Principles jointly adopted by a Committee of the American Bar Association and a Committee of Publishers and Associations.)

For Hagit, my soulmate

Contents

Preface xi

Introduction 1

1. Revitalizing the Concept of Military Necessity 31
   Introduction 31
   1.1 Military Professionalism: Constraining Brute Force Enhances Military Effectiveness 35
   1.2 The Prevailing Necessity Principle: A Hollow Rule and Its Effects 38
   1.3 The Effects of Transforming Professional Military Standards into Legal Norms 40
      1.3.1 "If It Ain't Broke Don't Fix It": Why Transform Self-Imposed and Voluntarily Respected Professional Standards into Legal Norms? 40
      1.3.2 The Institutional and Substantive Challenges 41
      1.3.3 The Suggested Effect upon Combatants: Soldiers' Lives Should Matter 45
      1.3.4 The Suggested Effect upon Noncombatants: Reducing the Lawful Collateral Damage 52
      1.3.5 Imposing Political Leaders' *in bello* Responsibility 55
      1.3.6 Constraining Brutal Militaries and Vicious Soldiers 58
   1.4 Why Now? Has the Time Come for Revised Military Necessity? 60
   1.5 Concluding Remarks 64

2. Lawful War of Self-Defense: When Not to Be a Sitting Duck 69
Introduction 69
2.1 Self-Defense: The Prevailing Law 72
2.2 The Practice of States and Its Justification 75
Introduction 75
2.2.1 The Six Day War 77
2.2.2 Prevention in the Guise of an Anticipatory Strike: The American Lessons 79
2.3 Lawful Self-Defense against an "Occurring" Armed Attack: A Suggested Operational Standard 84
2.3.1 Normative Introduction: A Self-Defendant Is Not Doomed to Be a Sitting Duck 84
2.3.2 Military Professionalism: Learning Its Objectives and Subjective Variants 87
2.3.3 Operational Last Resort: A Professional Standard 96
2.3.4 Military Necessity of the Self-Defendant in Case of an Imminent Threat: The Special Attributes of the Operational Last Resort 100
2.3.5 The Operational Last-Resort Standard Is Consistent with the UN Charter 108
2.4 Challenges to the Operational Last Resort Standard: A Normative Balance 108
2.5 Concluding Remarks 113

3. Military Strategy: The Blind Spot of International Humanitarian Law 117
Introduction—Thinking Strategically to Reduce War's Hazards 117
3.1 Strategy Determines War's Patterns and Scope 122
3.2 The Strategic Change: The Rise and Decline of Total War 125
3.2.1 A Pendulum Movement: The Evolution of "Total War" 125
3.2.2 Napoleon's Practice and Clausewitz's Theory Do Not Hold a Monopoly on Military Thinking and Practice 128
3.2.3 The Effectiveness of the Total Destruction of an Adversary's Military: The American Lesson 132

3.2.4 Internalization of the Limitations of Force by Law-Abiding States 134
3.3 Turning a Blind Eye to Military War Aims: The Silence of the Law Promotes the Roar of the Cannons 139
3.4. Tactical "Military Advantage" or Strategic? 145
3.4.1 The Two Dichotomist Schools 145
3.4.2 The Prevailing Schools' Mistakes and the Suggested Hybrid Approach 149
3.4.3 Adapting Lawful Targets to Limited Wars: The Shrinking of the Potential Targets Bank 152
3.4.4 Reasoned Declaration of War: Revisiting an Old Neglected Practice 154
3.5 The Required Nexus—Connecting Targeting to Strategy 156
3.5.1 The Prevailing Nexus: "Effective Contribution to Military Action" 156
3.5.2 The Vertical Nexus 158
3.5.3 Losing Strategic Ambiguity: Costs and Benefits 162
3.6 Concluding Remarks 167
4. Defensive Deterrence: Legalizing the Stepchild of International Law 171
4.1 Deterrence: An Essential—yet Problematic—Strategy 174
4.2 The Rejection of Reciprocal Deterrence Considerations by the Prevailing Law 178
4.3 The Potential Benefits of Introducing Defensive Deterrence Considerations into Lawful Self-Defense 183
4.3.1 Deterrence—An Efficient Tool to Enforce Compliance with the Law 183
4.3.2 Introducing Defensive Deterrence Considerations into the *ad Bellum* Proportionality: Challenging Its Quantitative Basis 184
4.4 Tailoring an Appropriate Defensive Deterrent Suit 189
4.4.1 Proportional Deterrence—Limited to the Specific Conflict 194
4.4.2 Deterrence-Oriented Proportionality in a Changing Reality—A Self-Adjustment Challenge 195

4.5 Defensive Deterrence: A Tool for Evaluating the Legality of a War's Aims 197
Introduction: Revitalizing the *ad Bellum* Proportionality 197
4.5.1 "Halt and Repel"—the Minimal In-Scale Response 199
4.5.2 Deterring a Repeat Aggressor 200
4.5.3 When Deterrence Fails: Incapacitation or Regime Change 203
4.6 Defensive Deterrence: Advantages and Disadvantages—An Interim Balance 206
4.7 Concluding Remarks 210

5. Conclusions 213

Index 219

Preface

THIS BOOK REFLECTS my own journey through the legal and moral labyrinth related to war. My frustration with this body of law, as a lawyer and as a military commander, might have driven me to the therapist's sofa, but instead it has motivated me, at a relatively late stage of my academic career, to explore this field. The tensions and challenges this book deals with are, however, universal, and they have spurred me upon this writing adventure.

I was born in Israel: a state that serves as an experimental laboratory for international law related to war. Indeed, the biblical state of milk and honey has become the Promised Land to international law experts. Israel is a state whose very existence is not accepted by an entire segment of the international community, including some of its bordering neighbors; a state whose own citizens are divided with regard to the substance of its constitutional definition as a Jewish-democratic state, and whose geographical borders are disputed; a state that is often criticized for its military practices.

I am a Jew. I belong to a nation that has suffered and been humiliated and oppressed for thousands of years. This suffering is part of my "moral DNA." My father was a Holocaust survivor, the only one of his family who was not murdered by the Nazis. It is probably my own family history, then, that has begotten my sensitivity toward human suffering, just as it has triggered my commitment to fighting for the survival of my nation, prompting me to serve a long career in the Israeli Defense Forces (IDF).

I have had two simultaneous lifetime careers, as a military officer and as a law professor. I served as a major general in the IDF. During most of my military career (33 out of 38 years), I was a combat soldier, mainly as a reservist. In my last military position (2007–2012), I served as an Army Corps commander. Before that, I commanded a paratroopers brigade and a division. Though I was never part of the Judge Advocate General Corps,

I did have one judicial role in the IDF, having been appointed to serve as president of the Israeli Military Court of Appeals. In parallel to this long military career, I always had an academic position. For the past 30 years, after earning my PhD from the Hebrew University of Jerusalem, I have been teaching tax law; for more than 20 years as a member of the law faculty at the Hebrew University, and currently as a faculty member at the Radzyner Law School, at the Interdisciplinary Center in Herzliya.

In recent years, my main research focus has shifted from tax law to war-related issues. My desire to contribute to the welfare of society as a whole—an idea represented in Jewish culture by the Hebrew concept of *tikkun olam* (literally, "repairing the world")—and my intellectual curiosity both stimulated me to combine my military experience with my academic interest in writing this book. My own personal background and identity—an Israeli, a Jew, a law professor, a retired general, and a humanist—are reflected in this project. Its core argument is that military professionalism should be leveraged to reduce war's hazards, while allowing militaries a lawful way to fight and win wars. In-depth academic research was required to establish this insight, and this book is its product. Throughout my military career, I tried to strike a balance between military necessities and humanity; now the time has come to write about these issues.

This book challenges the unacceptable gap between the positive rules of the international law governing armed hostilities and actual state practice. It aims at reducing the human suffering caused by this reality. The current law does not seem to be optimal in balancing the different interests of states' militaries and the humanitarian agenda. In response to this challenge, this book offers a new paradigm based on reality that may, in appropriate cases, elevate the humanitarian threshold by replacing those currently unsustainable or doubtful imperatives imposed upon militaries with professionally-based, therefore attainable, requirements. The suggested paradigm has two aims: first, to create an environment in which full abidance by the law becomes a realistic norm, thus facilitating the second and more important aim, namely reducing human suffering. It calls for the acknowledgment of the core interests of law-abiding states fighting in their own self-defense—those that, from their militaries' professional perspective, are essential in order to exercise their defense. Under the suggested approach, military necessity should not be perceived as a black box; rather, internalizing that not all security interests are existential and prioritizing only the essential ones allows more room for the humanitarian arena.

Militaries function in a professional manner; they develop and respect their doctrine, operational principles, fighting techniques, and values. Their performances are not random or incidental. The suggested paradigm calls for leveraging the constraining elements that are latent in military professionalism. Talking professional language and adopting the professional way of thinking that underlies militaries' conduct makes it possible to identify and focus upon the core interests of a military in any given lawful war—those that ought to be taken into consideration—alongside those that can be sacrificed for the sake of the humanitarian concerns, while still allowing the military mission to be achieved. Indeed, leveraging professional standards and norms would establish a reasonable modus vivendi for a military, while allowing substantial new space for the humanitarian mission of the law.

Military professionalism does not endorse excessive use of force, above the amount reasonably necessary to achieve a given, lawful military advantage. In performing a given military mission, a professional and well-trained military will exercise its force with care and precision. From a utilitarian perspective, efficient exercise of military force is in the self-interest of a professional trained military, and this utilitarian concern is buoyed by legal and ethical ones. This book sheds light upon the internal constraining forces within military professionalism, and calls for the utilization of this internal brake. Under the suggested paradigm, military necessity and humanity are not always polar opposites, as usually perceived; rather, the message of this book is to discover and leverage their complementary attributes.

Now that this book is completed, the time has come to express my gratitude. This project would not have been possible without the hospitality and challenging research environment of leading academic law schools—among them Harvard University, the Hebrew University, and Columbia University—which I have enjoyed over the years and where I have found stimulating colleagues to whom I am indebted. In 2009–2010 I was a Tikvah Fellow at NYU Law School, and it was mainly in that year that I began my research in international law governing armed hostilities. I am grateful to the Tikvah Center and to its directors Moshe Halbertal and Joseph Weiler for providing me this opportunity. This book was written at my current academic home, the Radziner Law School, in an enabling and inspiring academic environment. I am indebted to the Interdisciplinary Center in Herzliya, and to Uriel Reichman its president, for providing such an immensely supportive research atmosphere.

I have been blessed with the friendship of two fine scholars: Eyal Benvenisti and Moshe Halbertal. It is their unique intellectual skills and enduring patience, as demonstrated over countless cups of coffee with me, that have brought me to the finish line of this project. I have also enjoyed the wisdom and generosity of colleagues who read parts of this book, and I would like to thank Eyal Benvenisti, Gabriella Blum, Moshe Halbertal, David Kretzmer, Eliav Lieblich, David Luban, and Kenneth Watkin for their useful comments. I am grateful to Ruvik Danieli for his professional editing and to Ohad Abrahami for his research assistance. I would like to thank the editorial team at Oxford University Press: Blake Ratcliff, Alden W. Domizio, Balamurugan Rajendran and Brooke Smith for their dedicated and professional work.

Last but not least, of course, are my wife Hagit and our family. Our children: Shachar and his spouse, Michal; Omer and his spouse, Yael; Netta and her spouse, Micha; Gal; Nitzan; and Roni, are our source of inspiration and the joy of our lives. This book is dedicated to the most precious of all, Hagit; whatever I have is hers.

Yishai Beer
Jerusalem
August 2017

Introduction

THIS BOOK CHALLENGES the contemporary paradigm of the international law governing armed hostilities. It focuses on the currently huge gap between its positive rules and actual state practice, and on the damage caused by this reality. The law as it stands today is perceived as a compromise reached, in an evolutionary process, between two competing camps interested in regulating war's arena, each with its own prism, emphases, and priorities. Whereas the military camp focuses upon regulating the belligerency, allowing first enough room for military necessities and only afterward some space for reducing human suffering, the humanitarian camp's priority is the reduction of war's horrors and hazards. Currently, the humanitarian camp seems to have prevailed on some core issues. Paradoxically, though, this is a pyrrhic victory, most effectual only when it is least relevant, during peacetime. But when the cannons roar, it is the military camp that usually assumes the reins. What we see, then, even in law-abiding democracies, is a wide gap between the rhetoric of peacetime, as reflected in the positive law, and actual state practice. This reality has a devastating effect, primarily as regards human suffering. Given the humanitarian mission of this body of law, which is not disputed by either camp, this book suggests a new paradigm and calls for redefining and reshaping its legal contours in a more effective way.

The modern law of armed conflict[1] was developed in Europe during the nineteenth century. Its early stages reflect the belligerent reality and

---

1. Currently, nongovernmental organizations and most academic writers prefer the alternative name of international humanitarian law (IHL) over the law of armed conflict—the term usually referred to by militaries. *See, e.g.*, YORAM DINSTEIN, THE CONDUCT OF HOSTILITIES UNDER THE LAW OF INTERNATIONAL ARMED CONFLICT 18–21 (2d ed. 2010).

Military Professionalism and Humanitarian Law. Yishai Beer.

states' interests of that period. Armed conflicts in those days were mainly between state armies that shared similar principles and means. The main norms of the law—the protection of noncombatants and the elimination of unnecessary suffering of combatants—were agreed by states, as they reflected their shared concerns and interests. This consensus was consolidated in mutual agreements and enforced through the promise of reciprocity.[2] Indeed, consent between two parties is a precondition for reaching an agreement in general, in international law (between two or more states) in particular.[3] However, the horrible experience of the titanic wars of the nineteenth century, compounded by the trauma of the two World Wars in the twentieth, led to a substantial change—the abandonment of the reciprocity precondition. This consensual rejection of mutuality took place in both the *ad bellum* ("the right to fight")[4] and the *in bello* ("how to fight right") segments of international law related to war.

The *in bello* rules, the law of armed conflict, changed dramatically with the introduction of the Geneva Conventions of 1949[5] and the 1977 Additional Protocols.[6] Absolute norms were introduced at the expense of the contingent ones. Following this shift, the prevailing rules have come to be generally applied equally and symmetrically in all circumstances, regardless of what the other side may have done. For example, the Geneva Conventions start with the explicit declaration in Common Article 1: "The High Contracting Parties undertake to respect and to ensure respect for

---

2. *See, e.g.*, JEAN PICTET, THE DEVELOPMENT AND PRINCIPLES OF INTERNATIONAL HUMANITARIAN LAW 18–26 (1985); Eyal Benvenisti, *The Legal Battle to Define the Transnational Asymmetric Warfare*, 20 DUKE J. COMP. & INT'L L. 339, 340 (2009).

3. *See, e.g.*, LASSA OPPENHEIM, INTERNATIONAL LAW—A TREATISE, VOL. I—PEACE 20 (Ronald F. Roxburgh ed., 3d ed. 2005) 20.

4. The *ad bellum* rules determine whether the use of military force is legal. As to the rejection of reciprocity in this sphere, *see, e.g.*, the discussion below, and text accompanying notes 66–68, relating to the prohibition of reprisals.

5. Geneva Convention (I) for the Amelioration of the Condition of Wounded and Sick in Armed Forces in the Field, Aug. 12, 1949, 75 U.N.T.S. 31; Geneva Convention (II) for the Amelioration of the Condition of Wounded, Sick and Shipwrecked Members of Armed Forces at Sea, Aug.12, 1949, 75 U.N.T.S. 85; Geneva Convention (III) Relative to the Treatment of Prisoners of War, Aug.12, 1949, 75 U.N.T.S. 135; Geneva Convention (IV) relative to the Protection of Civilian Persons in Time of War, Aug. 12, 1949, 75 U.N.T.S. 287 (GCIV).

6. Protocol Additional to the Geneva Conventions of 12 August 1949, and relating to the Protection of Victims of International Armed Conflicts (Protocol I), June 8, 1977, 1125 U.N.T.S. 3 (API); Protocol Additional to the Geneva Conventions of 12 August 1949, and relating to the Protection of Victims of Non-International Armed Conflict (Protocol II), June 8, 1977, 1125 U.N.T.S. 609 (APII).

the present Convention in all circumstances."[7] This well-established principle has also been codified in the preamble to the first Protocol (API), granting the protection of the Geneva Conventions "to all persons who are protected by those instruments, without any adverse distinction based on the nature or origin of the armed conflict or on the causes espoused by or attributed to the Parties to the conflict." Thus the aggressor's combatants[8] must be accorded similar treatment to the defendant's; the law of armed conflict grants similar benefits (and obligations) to the aggressor and defendant alike. Under the *in bello* rules, the aggressor's soldiers and civilians are not penalized for the aggression, even though their war is neither just nor lawful.

As the law of armed conflict shifted from the contractual model to a regulatory one,[9] various states reacted differently to this dramatic change. Indeed, there are countries that have signed the Conventions and also the Additional Protocols[10] and have abided, or intended to abide, by their rules. Others, for whom the new prevailing model of the law is inconsistent with their will and interests, distanced themselves from its full implementation, as reflected in their behavior. Their reactions range from formal disagreement, relating to those segments of the law that are not binding as customary law,[11] to practical measures. De jure disagreement[12] is manifested through practices ranging from persistent objection,[13] through reserved

7. Geneva Conventions of 1949, *supra* note 5, at common art. 1.

8. As to what constitutes aggression, *see infra* Chapter 4 note 7.

9. Samuel Estreicher, *Privileging Asymmetric Warfare (Part II): The "Proportionality" Principle Under International Humanitarian Law*, 12 CHI. J. INT'L L. 143, 144–46 (2011).

10. *See, e.g.*, the list of signatory and party states to the API at: https://www.icrc.org/ihl/INTRO/470 (last visited Aug. 16, 2017); and the list of state parties to the Fourth Geneva Convention at: https://www.icrc.org/applic/ihl/ihl.nsf/States.xsp?xp_viewStates=XPages_NORMStatesParties&xp_treatySelected=380 (last visited Aug. 16, 2017).

11. On the concept and formation of customary law, *see* MALCOLM SHAW, INTERNATIONAL LAW 72–76 (6th ed. 2008). With regard to the scope of customary humanitarian law, *see, e.g.*, the ICRC's customary law database, reflecting the humanitarian camp's view of this body of laws. https://www.icrc.org/customary-ihl/eng/docs/home (last visited Aug. 16, 2017).

12. De facto evasion will be dealt with later; *see infra* text accompanying notes 17–22, 57–79.

13. A persistent objector is a country that continuously and persistently expresses its objection to a certain law being customary. As such, it is exempt from it; however, said objection can only apply to rules that have become customary after the establishment of the state, and not to rules that became customary before the state's establishment. *See, e.g.*, Olufemi Elias, *Persistent Objector*, *in* MAX PLANCK ENCYCLOPEDIA OF PUBLIC INTERNATIONAL LAW (Rudiger Wolfrum ed. 2006), opil.ouplaw.com/home/EPIL (last visited Aug. 16, 2017).

consent to parts of the Additional Protocols,[14] to downright refusal to sign them.[15]

The ambivalence of states toward the regulatory model can clearly be seen in the case of the restrictions imposed upon wartime reprisals ("belligerent reprisals"), codified in the API, art. 51(6). The "traditional" rule is relatively permissive, allowing "acts of retaliation in the form of conduct which would otherwise be unlawful, resorted to by one belligerent against enemy personnel or property for acts of warfare committed by the other belligerent in violation of the law of war, for the purpose of enforcing future compliance with the recognized rules of civilized warfare."[16] The current API rule, however, is much more restrictive: reprisal in wartime is very limited in scope. It can only be aimed against combatants and, in any case, is not allowed as a retaliatory or penal measure. Countries signatory to the API that are ambivalent with respect to this Article can be roughly divided into three groups. The first group consists of countries that have agreed to the ban on reprisals with no reservation, but are not known for their respect of international law (including its human rights segment) in general and the laws of war in particular. These include, for example, Afghanistan,[17] Lebanon,[18]

---

14. Reservation allows states to exclude or modify the application of specific parts of treaties to themselves. *See, e.g.*, Jutta Brunnee, *Consent*, in MAX PLANCK ENCYCLOPEDIA OF PUBLIC INTERNATIONAL LAW (Rudiger Wolfrum ed. 2006), opil.ouplaw.com/home/EPIL (last visited Aug. 16, 2017).

15. For example, in a letter transmitted to the American Congress urging ratification of the APII, President Ronald Reagan wrote that at the same time, ratifying the API would not be recommended, as it was "fundamentally and irreconcilably flawed." *Letter of Transmittal from President Ronald Reagan, Protocol II Additional to the 1949 Geneva Conventions, and Relating to the Protection of Victims of Non international Armed Conflicts, reprinted in full in* 81 AM. J. INT'L L. 910 (1987).

16. DEP'T OF THE ARMY, FIELD MANUAL 27–10, THE LAW OF LAND WARFARE, para. 497 (July 1956) [hereinafter FM 27-10]. However, certain reprisals—that is, against prisoners of war, the wounded, or the sick—are specifically prohibited by the Geneva Conventions. *See, e.g.*, DINSTEIN, THE CONDUCT OF HOSTILITIES, *supra* note 1, at 257–61.

17. The ICC was inspecting possible allegations of war crimes by Afghan forces, including torture and child soldier recruitment, in the years preceding the country's accession to the API on 10 November 2009. *See* ICC Office of the Prosecutor, *Report on Preliminary Examination Activities* 7–8 (Dec. 13, 2011), https://www.icc-cpi.int/NR/rdonlyres/63682F4E-49C8-445D-8C13-F310A4F3AEC2/284116/OTPReportonPreliminaryExaminations13December2011.pdf (last visited Apr. 24, 2016).

18. Lebanon, just prior to the ratification of the API on July 23, 1997, acquiesced in Hezbollah's deliberate launching of rockets into civilian population centers in Israel. *See, e.g.*, Human Rights Watch, *Military Operations by Lebanese Guerilla Forces* (Sept. 1997), https://www.hrw.org/reports/1997/isrleb/Isrleb-02.htm#P635_149465 (last visited Apr. 24, 2016).

Libya,[19] Syria,[20] Yemen,[21] and Saudi Arabia.[22] The second group of countries is comprised of several leading Western democracies that have announced their reservation with regard to the ban on reprisals in case the enemy does not abide by it—making their formal consent to this API provision a contingent one. The third group is comprised of countries signatory to the Protocol, but who have not ratified it, most prominent among them the United States.[23]

Indeed, leading Western democracies that have signed the API have reserved the right not to be bound by the norm prohibiting reprisals against civilians to varying degree, in case the *in bello* rules are violated by the enemy in the form of deliberate and serious attacks mounted against civilians; prominent among them are France, Germany, Italy, and the UK.[24] Whereas the first three have allowed themselves to use whatever

---

19. On June 7, 1978, Libya was one of the first states to ratify the API. But just two years later, in 1980, its leader Muammar Ghaddafi was involved in serious human rights violations, for example, by using hit squads against dissidents abroad. David Blundy, Ghaddafi and the Libyan Revolution 138 (1987).

20. Syria, in 1982, just one year prior to ratifying the API on November 14, 1983, with a reservation regarding its application towards Israel, committed the Hama Massacre. *See, e.g.*, Jason Rodrigues, *1982: Syria's President Hafez al-Assad crushes rebellion in Hama*, Guardian, Aug. 1, 2011, http://www.theguardian.com/theguardian/from-the-archive-blog/2011/aug/01/hama-syria-massacre-1982-archive (last visited Apr. 24, 2016).

21. Yemen, soon after ratifying the API on April 17, 1990, became embroiled in the destruction of civilian objects in the context of the civil war that took place in the country between 1990 and 1994. *See* Human Rights Watch, *Yemen—Human Rights in Yemen During and After the 1994 Civil War*, Oct. 1994, at 17, https://www.hrw.org/sites/default/files/reports/YEMEN94O.PDF (last visited Apr. 24, 2016).

22. A month prior to ratifying the API on August 21, 1987, Saudi Arabia engaged in serious human rights violations by firing at Iranian rioters during the 1987 Mecca incident—a charge Saudi Arabia denied. *See, e.g.*, John Kifner, *400 Die as Iranian Marchers Battle Saudi Police in Mecca; Embassies Smashed in Tehran*, N.Y. Times, Aug. 2, 1987, http://www.nytimes.com/1987/08/02/world/400-die-iranian-marchers-battle-saudi-police-mecca-embassies-smashed-teheran.html?pagewanted=all (last visited Apr. 24, 2016).

23. Though the United States signed the API the day it was opened for signature, to date it has not ratified it. The main reasons behind this refusal included, inter alia, the ban on reprisals and art. 1(4) applying the API to wars of national liberation. *See* Abraham D. Sofaer, *Agora: The US Decision Not to Ratify Protocol I to the Geneva Conventions on the Protection of War Victims*, 82 Am. J. Int'l L. 784, 785 (1988). *See* also President Reagan's letter, *supra* note 15.

24. *See, inter alia*, Germany, *Reservation to API*, at para. 6, http://www.icrc.org/applic/ihl/ihl.nsf/Notification.xsp?action=openDocument&documentId=3F4D8706B6B7EA40C1256402003FB3C7 (last visited Apr. 24, 2016); France, *Reservation to API*, at para. 11, http://www.icrc.org/applic/ihl/ihl.nsf/Notification.xsp?action=openDocument&documentId=D8041036B40EBC44C1256A34004897B2 (last visited Apr. 24, 2016); Italy, *Reservation to API*,

means permissible under international law (pre-API) without specifying,[25] the UK has gone a step further, releasing itself of said obligations under the API while still adhering to the original Geneva Conventions:

> If an adverse party makes serious and deliberate attacks, in violation of Article 51 or Article 52 against the civilian population or civilians or against civilian objects, . . . the United Kingdom will regard itself as entitled to take measures otherwise prohibited by the Articles in question to the extent that it considers such measures necessary for the sole purpose of compelling the adverse party to cease committing violations under those Articles, but only after formal warning to the adverse party requiring cessation of the violations has been disregarded and then only after a decision taken at the highest level of government.[26]

Similarly, the United States limits the ban on reprisals strictly to the Geneva rules. Thus, the U.S. Navy states that as a last resort and in a limited way, "Reprisals may be taken against enemy armed forces, enemy civilians other than those in occupied territory, and enemy property."[27] Indeed, this state of affairs, with Western democracies having either not ratified or stated their reservation with regard to the ban on reprisals, reflects a reality in which states formally insist upon maintaining their core security interests—for example, protection of their own citizens—in the international arena.

The rejection of the API ban on reprisals against civilians by Western democracies demonstrates the unilateral erosion of the wide consensual basis of the law of armed conflict, or at least creates cracks in its apparent consensus. An opposite phenomenon can be seen on the other side

---

http://www.icrc.org/applic/ihl/ihl.nsf/Notification.xsp?action=openDocument&documentId=E2F248CE54CF09B5C1256402003FB443 (last visited Apr. 24, 2016). For the UK, *see* UK, *Reservation to API on arts. 51–55*, at para. m, http://www.icrc.org/ihl.nsf/NORM/0A9E03F0F2EE757CC1256402003FB6D2?OpenDocument (last visited Apr. 24, 2016).

25. As to reprisals specifically prohibited by the Geneva Conventions, *see supra* note 16.

26. UK, Reservation to API, *supra* note 24.

27. United States Navy, The Commander's Handbook of Naval Operations, Naval War Pub. 1–14, ¶ 6.2.4 (2007). "The United States has expressed the view that API's provisions on reprisal are counterproductive and that they remove a significant deterrent that protects civilians and war victims on all sides of a conflict." U.S. Dep't of Defense, DOD Law of War Manual 1098 (June 12, 2015).

of the spectrum: its unilateral extension. In recent times, international courts and leading nongovernmental organizations (NGOs) as well as international organizations have been pushing the envelope of the regulatory model through judicial legislation or public pressure. Under this expansionist approach, the regulatory model—formally agreed upon by consenting states—is subject to unilateral changes, or threat of changes, in two ways: certain rules may be declared customary, mainly in the course of the development of international criminal law, and public pressure may be exerted on states by NGOs.

First, international criminal law tribunals have increasingly been making declarations of customary law. As Eyal Benvenisti notes, the substantial development of international criminal law, and its applicability to internal armed conflict, "must be attributed to the jurisprudence of the International Criminal Tribunal of the former Yugoslavia ('ICTY'), which has in only a few years of adjudicating crimes in the former Yugoslavia virtually rewritten the law on internal armed conflicts."[28] Indeed, by asserting the law's customary status, "the ICTY overcame years of governmental resistance to regulating methods for fighting insurgents."[29] In fact, both the ICTY and the International Criminal Tribunal for Rwanda (ICTR) granted this developing law status as customary and binding.[30] For example, former ICTY president, Judge Theodor Meron, describes how it was in fact an ICTY judgment by Judge Cassese in 2000 that proclaimed the API's ban on reprisals as customary and binding upon powers not signatory to the API, based on the Marten's Clause and *opinio juris* and despite a lack of state practice at the time.[31]

---

28. Benvenisti, *The Legal Battle*, *supra* note 2, at 347.

29. *Id. See also*, Allison Marston Danner, *When Courts Make Law: How the International Criminal Tribunals Recast the Laws of War*, 59 VAND. L. REV. 1, 25–33 (2006).

30. *See* THEODOR MERON, THE HUMANIZATION OF INTERNATIONAL LAW, 100–01, 177–81 (2006). Judge Meron also describes how some of the ICTY's rulings with regard to certain clauses of the APII being customary were later relied upon by the ICTR in determining their customary status. *Id.* at 108–10.

31. *Id.* at 13. The practical, proactive—perhaps even aggressive—steps taken toward achieving this humanization of the war arena by stretching the contours of customary law were described by Judge Meron: "Judges, scholars, governments, and nongovernmental organizations are often prepared to accept a rather large gap between practice and the norms concerned without questioning their binding character. In many cases, gradual and partial compliance has been accepted as fulfilling the requirements for the formation of customary law, and contrary practice downplayed. Courts and tribunals have frequently ignored operational or battlefield practice. Without formally abandoning the dual requirements (practice

Second, public pressure can be harnessed to attack the consensual basis of the law. A good example is the International Committee of the Red Cross (ICRC)'s Guide on direct participation in hostilities, specifically in the case of non-international armed conflicts.[32] Under the prevailing distinction rule, civilians are entitled to protection in times of conflict; they lose that right, however, when they take a "direct part in hostilities" (DPH).[33] Clarifying what constitutes DPH was the subject of the ICRC Guide.[34] It answers several questions arising in connection with DPH, including the classification of membership in armed forces in international and non-international armed conflict, the establishment of tests for that purpose, and the determination of the time period that such membership lasts.[35] The Guide, however, is very controversial.[36] Indeed, prominent military lawyers—reflecting the opinion of Western democracies' militaries—dispute it.[37] For the sake of the current discussion, some of the main points of contention will be elaborated on to demonstrate how pressure is exerted on states to deviate from their common practice by expanding humanitarian rules.

The first issue is what acts constitute DPH and, particularly, what standing preparatory acts toward a combative operation should have. Whereas the commentary to API Article 44(3) declares that DPH includes "actions carried out with a view to combat," the Guide argues that actions carried out for the sake of general combat readiness—"general capacity to carry out unspecified hostile acts"—shall not constitute

---

and *opinion juris)* for the formation of customary international law, they have tended to weigh statements both as evidence of practice and as articulations of *opinion juris*." Theodor Meron, *The Humanization of Humanitarian Law*, 94 AM. J. INT'L L. 239, 244 (2000).

32. International Committee of the Red Cross [ICRC], *Interpretive Guidance on the Notion of Direct Participation in Hostilities Under International Humanitarian Law* (2009) [hereinafter ICRC Guide] https://www.icrc.org/eng/assets/files/other/icrc-002-0990.pdf (last visited Apr. 24, 2016).

33. "Civilians shall enjoy the protection afforded by this Section, unless and for such time as they take a direct part in hostilities." API, *supra* note 6, at art. 51(3).

34. The Guide established three criteria constituting DPH: threshold of harm, direct causation, and belligerent nexus. *See* ICRC Guide, *supra* note 32, at part V.

35. *Id.*, part VI.

36. *See, e.g.*, Kenneth Watkin, *Opportunity Lost: Organized Armed Groups and the ICRC "Direct Participation in Hostilities" Interpretive Guidance*, 42 N.Y.U. J. INT'L L. & POL. 641 (2009).

37. *See, e.g.*, W. Hays Parks, *Part IX of the ICRC "Direct Participation in Hostilities" Study: No Mandate, No Expertise, and Legally Incorrect*, 42 N.Y.U. J. INT'L L. & POL. 769 (2009).

DPH.[38] States insist upon following the wider definition, which includes such preparatory actions as well.[39] This issue also concerns another prerequisite set by the Guide—direct causation—requiring that only specific acts with direct causation regarding the belligerency ("one causal step")[40] be considered DPH. The suggested causality means that "[a]nything that simply builds up the capacity of a party to inflict harm is 'excluded from the concept of DPH,' " and that the Guide limits DPH activities only to those that are part of the tactical level.[41] Finally, there is a dispute regarding the Guide's "belligerent nexus" prerequisite,[42] and its restricted approach toward the deployment and return from the execution of a hostile act[43] is contested as well.[44] Indeed, another point of dispute in this context, related to the temporal dimension of DPH, is "the revolving door" phenomenon. Although the Guide argues that once civilians are no longer engaged in DPH, they regain their protection as civilians,[45] states and military-law experts disagree. They argue that this will allow civilians to step in and out of protection at will, to the detriment of other combatants.[46] Yoram Dinstein, for example, disputes the Guide's claim "that civilian protection is restored each time

38. Jean de Preux, *Protocol I Article 44—Combatants and Prisoners of War, in* Commentary on the Additional Protocols of 8 June 1977 to the Geneva Conventions of 12 August 1949, para. 1692 (Claude Pilloud et al. eds., 1987); ICRC Guide, *supra* note 32, at 66 (respectively).

39. Bill Boothby, *"And for Such Time As": The Time Dimension to Direct Participation in Hostilities*, 42 N.Y.U. J. Int'l L. & Pol. 741, 746–50 (2009). Michael N. Schmitt, *Deconstructing Direct Participation in Hostilities: The Constitutive Elements*, 42 N.Y.U. J. Int'l L. & Pol. 697, 739 (2009). *See also* HCJ 769/02, *The Public Committee Against Torture and Others v. The Government of Israel and Others* (2005), 62(1) PD 507, [33] (Isr.) (discussed below circa note 49).

40. ICRC Guide, *supra* note 32, at 53.

41. Watkin, *Opportunity Lost, supra* note 36, at 658, 659, footnotes omitted. Watkin demonstrates how this requirement in the case of improvised explosive devices, for example, would mean that the placing of devices might be considered DPH, but not the manufacturing, selling, smuggling, and maintaining of such explosives. He therefore argues for an extension of the causation requirement beyond the first direct step.

42. *See* ICRC Guide, *supra* note 32, at part V. *Cf.* Yoram Dinstein, Non-international Armed Conflicts in International Law 62–63, 13–15 (2014) (the nexus between a war crime and non-international armed conflict).

43. ICRC Guide, *supra* note 32, at 67.

44. Boothby, *"And for Such Time As," supra* note 39, at 750–52.

45. ICRC Guide, *supra* note 32, at 70.

46. Boothby, *"And for Such Time As," supra* note 39, at 753–58.

that a segment of participation in hostilities is ended."[47] In his opinion, a civilian involved in "revolving door" activities "loses his civilian protection on a 24/7 basis: he can be targeted in any location, even during respites when he is engaged in innocent chores."[48] Similarly, in the Israeli High Court of Justice's "targeted killings" case, President Aaron Barak rejected granting immunity to "part-time" combatants, engaged in "revolving door" activities. "On the one hand, a civilian who took a direct part in hostilities once, or sporadically, but detached himself from them (entirely, or for a long period) is not to be harmed. On the other hand, the 'revolving door' phenomenon, by which each terrorist has 'horns of the altar' (1 Kings 1:50) to grasp or a 'city of refuge' (Numbers 35:11) to flee to, to which he turns in order to rest and prepare while they grant him immunity from attack, is to be avoided."[49]

The DPH controversy reflects the humanitarian expansionist approach—in this example spearheaded by the ICRC—and its struggle, in real time, with the conflicting camp. This dispute is further exacerbated by the transition in recent decades from conventional international conflicts between states to asymmetric conflicts of a non-international character between states on the one hand and nonstate organizations on the other.[50]

It is this new evolving legal environment—in which the wide consensual basis of the law of armed conflict is being eroded, partly due to its rejection by states and partly due to its unilateral extension by tribunals and NGOs—that led Eyal Benvenisti to conclude, with regard to the latter factor, that "[t]hus, the intensified involvement of third parties creates a new conflict between the conventional armies that fight insurgents or terrorists and seek more discretion and fewer constraints and the third parties who insist on maintaining and even increasing constraints in warfare. We might call it a conflict between the 'IHL camp' that emphasizes the humanitarian aim of the *jus in bello*, which they refer to as International Humanitarian Law, and the 'LOAC camp,' that wishes to point out that the Law of Armed Conflict is primarily designed to regulate the relations between fighting armies and therefore must take military concerns

---

47. Dinstein, Non-international Armed Conflicts in International Law, *supra* note 42, at 63.

48. *Id.*

49. HCJ 769/02, *The Public Committee Against Torture v. Israel, supra* note 39, at [40].

50. Schmitt, *Deconstructing Direct Participation in Hostilities, supra* note 39, at 735.

seriously into account."[51] Similarly, the same phenomenon—the division that has evolved between states and armies on the one hand and NGOs and civil societies on the other—has been characterized by David Luban as a division between the IHL and LOAC visions of international law.[52] The IHL vision, represented by NGOs and others, is primarily concerned with humanitarianism—it assigns human dignity and human rights primary status—and war, whenever justified and necessary, has to adjust itself to that end. Although not devoid of humanitarian considerations, the LOAC vision, which is endorsed by states and military professionals, prioritizes military necessities, with the law's role in that context being confined to mitigating war's horrors.[53]

Indeed, this kind of legal dispute—dependent upon the beholder's perspective—is not unique. Tension between interest groups arguing about positive versus normative rules stimulates legal discussion in all of its aspects. Furthermore, the tension between utopianism and apologetics stands at the heart of international law in general, and international law related to war in particular.[54] Indeed, in terms of interests, states operating under the regulatory model had a lesser interest and motivation in unilaterally enforcing the laws of war upon themselves to their detriment. Yet the contemporary gap between the positive rules and legal rhetoric on the one hand and states' actual practice on the other seems to be unacceptable. This gap might reflect either states' strategic shortsightedness

---

51. Benvenisti, *The Legal Battle, supra* note 2, at 348. Benvenisti argues further that "the LOAC camp insists that this 'lawfare' is not only hypocritical but also perilous: that the IHL camp is being manipulated by the terrorists, who endanger the population on whose behalf they ostensibly fight by their abuse of civilian immunities. In a sense, and certainly unwillingly, the IHL camp becomes a strategic ally of the terrorists because the terrorists benefit indirectly from whatever constraints the IHL camp would impose." *Id.*

52. David Luban, *Military Necessity and the Cultures of Military Law*, 26 LEIDEN J. INT'L L. 315, 315–16 (2013).

53. *Id.* at 316. *Cf.* Monica Hakimi & Jacob Katz Cogan, *The Two Codes on the Use of Force*, 27 EUR. J. INT'L L. 257 (2016) (explaining the actual operation of the *jus ad bellum* regime as a site of ongoing contestation and compromise between two "codes": one a state code, the other an institutional one).

54. Martti Koskenniemi explains this tension, and the risks involved in leaning one way or the other, as follows: "A law which would lack distance from State behaviour, will or interest would amount to a non-Normative apology, a mere sociological description. A law which would base itself on principles which are unrelated to State behaviour, will or interest would seem utopian. . . . It is not difficult to see that law is continuously in danger of lapsing into an apology for politics." MARTTI KOSKENNIEMI, FROM APOLOGY TO UTOPIA: THE STRUCTURE OF INTERNATIONAL LEGAL ARGUMENT 17 (reissue, 2005).

or, alternatively, their deliberate manipulation. If the former, the strategic myopia occurs when states bona fide declare that they are willing to accept and abide by all the humanitarian legal rules, but, in real time, when faced with belligerency with all its difficulties, follow their core interests, especially existential ones, whenever those collide with humanitarian rules.[55] This shortsightedness yields a de facto evasion, the product of the difference between the ex-ante declaration (and expectation) of states and their ex-post actual performance.

Alternatively, the other, more cynical explanation suggests that the positive law merely reflects some states' lip service to the humanitarian camp. The consent given—for example, to all of the API rules—is no more than declaratory, with states expressing their consent by way of ratification with no intention of backing that consent, either in whole or in part, in their own state practice. Given the lack of an effective enforcement mechanism for the law,[56] which is well known in advance, states in general are not deterred from breaching its rules, whenever it is convenient to them. The gap between the law and reality is perceived, under this approach, as a conscious, declarative premium paid for the regulatory model. From both perspectives, though, the humanitarian camp appears to prevail in peacetime, introducing some utopian norms to the positive law, but retreats before the military camp whenever belligerency actually takes place. States faced with security threats act opportunistically and might prefer the apologetic position. The more substantial the threat, the more regression from the law might be expected, depending, of course, upon each state's specific circumstances and preferences.

---

55. Michael Schmitt opines a more extreme view, not restricted to core interests, when it comes to this conflict of interest: "States are generally only willing to accept those humanitarian limitations on their conduct of hostilities that neither enfeeble them militarily nor give their opponents a measurable advantage." Michael N. Schmitt, *Asymmetrical Warfare and International Humanitarian Law*, *in* INTERNATIONAL HUMANITARIAN LAW: FACING NEW CHALLENGES 22 (Wolff Heintschel von Heinegg & Volker Epping eds., 2007).

56. Nor do the *ad bellum* rules enjoy an effective enforcement mechanism. Chapter VII of the UN Charter entrusts the Security Council with a twofold duty: first, to investigate any international conflict and determine whether it constitutes a breach of or threat to peace, and whether an act of *ad bellum* aggression has occurred; and second, to take collective action against an aggressor. However, the veto right of the five permanent members, combined with the inability to establish a formal mechanism for the collective use of force, usually paralyzes the ability to exercise it. One exception in which the UN did exercise its authority for collective enforcement action occurred on July 7, 1950, when the Security Council came to the defense of South Korea and issued a resolution authorizing collective action against North Korea's armed attack, under the flag of the United Nations and the joint command of the United States. S.C. Res. 84 (July 7, 1950) and see *infra* Chapter 4 note 39.

Earlier we dealt with concrete de jure objections to the law; now we turn to demonstrating the de facto evasion of abidance by its rules with examples from both the *ad bellum* and the *in bello* segments of the law. These examples will show that the conflict between the humanitarian vision and the actual practice of states' militaries (led, or substantially influenced, by the military camp) is not over, even in cases where the former has apparently prevailed, as reflected formally in positive law. Indeed, compliance with formal law can never be taken for granted; however, when it comes to international law related to war, breaches of the law seem to be, in some issues, almost the norm rather than an exception. This evasive, common practice of states in turn might have a special meaning in customary international law.[57]

Let us start with the *ad bellum* breaches of the law. One of the main achievements of the humanitarian vision is the UN Charter's general prohibition upon the exercise of military force in the international arena,[58] which allows only two exceptions: individual or collective self-defense against an armed attack,[59] or pursuant to a Security Council authorization.[60] Looking at the bright side, in the post-Charter era there have been no World Wars and less inter-state wars (indeed, we have seen a shift from inter-state wars to intra-state belligerencies and conflicts with nonstate actors).[61] However, although the rhetoric of the prevailing law is impressive, banning any UN member from threatening or using force against another, its effectiveness definitely is not. Yoram Dinstein relates to the huge gap between the peace rhetoric of the Charter and states' actual belligerent practice: "[o]ne may say . . . [that] so far the legal abolition of war has stamped out not wars but declarations of war. This lip-service to the cause of peace may be hypocritical."[62] Similarly, Michael Walzer, relating

---

57. State practice is considered the objective element required to establish customary law; the subjective element is an *opinio juris* supporting this practice by leading international law experts. *See* Sir Michael Wood & Omri Sender, *State Practice*, *in* Max Planck Encyclopedia of Public International Law, para. 2 (Rudiger Wolfrum ed., 2014) opil.ouplaw.com/home/EPIL.

58. U.N. Charter art. 2, ¶4.

59. U.N. Charter art. 51.

60. U.N. Charter art. 42.

61. *See, e.g.*, The Correlates of War Project, http://www.correlatesofwar.org/data-sets (last visited Apr. 24, 2016).

62. Yoram Dinstein, War, Aggression and Self-Defence 351 (5th ed. 2011).

to legal positivism in the post-UN Charter age, describes this contrasting reality, noting that "[t]he lawyers have constructed a paper world, which fails at crucial points to correspond to the world the rest of us still live in."[63] Indeed, Michael Glennon, drawing up an interim balance of the UN's performance and the effect of Article 2(4), 55 years after the establishment of the UN in 1945, concluded:

> . . . international "rules" concerning use of force are no longer regarded as obligatory by states. Between 1945 and 1999, two-thirds of the members of the United Nations—126 states out of 189—fought 291 interstate conflicts in which over 22 million people were killed. This series of conflicts was capped by the Kosovo campaign in which nineteen NATO democracies representing 780 million people flagrantly violated the Charter. The international system has come to subsist in a parallel universe of two systems, one *de jure*, the other *de facto*.[64]

Thirty years earlier, Thomas Franck, in an article titled "Who Killed Article 2(4)? or: Changing Norms Governing the Use of Force by States," pointed to the same gap, noting that "[i]n the twenty-five years since the San Francisco Conference, there have been some one hundred separate outbreaks of hostility between states."[65]

Another example of the unacceptable gap between the legal *ad bellum* imperatives and actual state practice is the current war-peace dichotomy. The prevailing law disallows, under the self-defense exception of UN Charter Article 51,[66] a military response "short of war" in response to a "modest" attack—a single, small-scale armed action—that does not reach the legal threshold of an armed attack.[67] In reality, however, life is not

---

63. Michael Walzer, Just and Unjust Wars, at xxi (4th ed. 2006).

64. Michael J. Glennon, *The Fog of Law: Self-Defense, Inherence, and Incoherence in Article 51 of the United Nations Charter*, 25 Harv. J.L. & Pub. Pol'y 539, 540 (2001–2002).

65. Thomas M. Franck, *Who Killed Article 2(4)? or: Changing Norms Governing the Use of Force by States*, 64 Am. J. Int'l L. 809, 810–11 (1970).

66. The Article states that "Nothing in the present Charter shall impair the inherent right of individual or collective self-defence if an armed attack occurs against a Member of the United Nations, until the Security Council has taken measures necessary to maintain international peace and security." U.N. Charter, art. 51.

67. Under the ICJ's ruling, a state is restricted in its own self-defense by a quantitative threshold scaled to fit the aggression aimed against it. In the Nicaragua case, the court decided

colored with the black-and-white dichotomy of war and peace. States may be attacked by an "insignificant" aggression, as well. The Charter's formal response to such an attack is to refer the attacked state to the Security Council.[68] In actuality, however, this organ of the UN is paralyzed in many cases and cannot fulfill its mission effectively. In the absence of an effective solution, the attacked state's security is actually damaged due to, inter alia, a lack of genuine military deterrence vis-à-vis its attacker. In addition, its leaders, who are obliged to protect the sovereignty of their state and the safety of its citizens,[69] are faced with huge pressures from their own constituents, and in many cases have no other *realpolitik* alternative but to respond militarily. Law-abiding states usually design and justify their military reaction to such an aggression as a proportional self-defense reprisal, subject to the *in bello* limits (including the distinction,[70] proportionality,[71] and necessity[72] rules). The common strategic justification for such repris al, in the appropriate circumstances, is to stop the aggression while still in its preliminary stages;[73] and to prevent, or at least reduce, the risk of

---

to allow the right of self-defense only against armed attacks of "significant scale." Military and Paramilitary Activities in and Against Nicaragua (Nicar. v. U.S.), Judgment, 1986 I.C.J. Rep. 14, ¶195 (June 27). "Insignificant" aggression against a defendant state does not, in the court's opinion, amount to an "armed attack," and a law-abiding defendant is therefore prohibited from exercising its "inherent right of individual or collective self-defense." Similarly, in the Oil Platforms case, the Court stated: "The question is therefore whether that incident [the mining of the USS *Samuel B. Roberts* by Iran] sufficed in itself to justify action in self defence, as amounting to an 'armed attack.'" Oil Platforms (Islamic Republic of Iran v. U.S.), Judgment, 2003 I.C.J. Rep. 161, ¶72 (Nov. 6). It should be noted, however, that the "scale and effects," or gravity of harm criteria, have not been universally accepted. *See, e.g.*, David Kretzmer, *The Inherent Right to Self-Defence and Proportionality in Jus Ad Bellum*, 24 Eur. J. Int'l L. 235, 243 (2013).

68. U.N. Charter, art. 37. Of course, the victim state might respond in non-military countermeasures—for example, economic—following, inter alia, the law of State Responsibility. G.A. Res. 56/83, annex, Responsibility of States for internationally wrongful acts, part III ch. II (Jan. 28, 2002).

69. *See, e.g.*, White House, National Security Strategy 4 (May 2010), http://nssarchive.us/NSSR/2010.pdf (last visited Aug. 16, 2017) [hereinafter White House 2010 National Security Strategy].

70. The distinction rule outlaws the intended targeting of civilians (including their objects) and minimizes the collateral damage that can lawfully occur to them.

71. *See infra* Chapter 1 note 59.

72. *See infra* text accompanying notes 80–83.

73. For example, the United States attacked Libya on April 14, 1986, in response to a bombing, in a West Berlin disco, that killed an American soldier and wounded others. This attack however, has been criticized due to its punitive connotation. *See, e.g.*, Antonio Cassese, International Law 356 (2nd ed. 2005).

escalation, thus containing the belligerency before it explodes into a full-scale war. Typically, the self-defensive response is limited and concrete and focused on a military target. This practice is so widespread that it has become almost a natural response. "Since the entry into force of the UN Charter, the record is replete with measures of defensive armed reprisals implemented by many countries (including all Permanent Members of the Security Council), although statesmen frequently shy away from the expression 'reprisals.'"[74] Formally, however, this common practice is usually considered illegal.[75] The current law seems to have adopted an "all or nothing" approach, legitimizing a full-scale self-defensive war or prohibiting it entirely; turning a blind eye to the prevailing—potentially moderate, if regulated—tool of self-defense, namely, armed reprisal short of war.[76] The war-peace dichotomy is therefore a legal fiction that does not exist in reality; in many cases, it is rather War and Peace, correlating to Tolstoy's famous book title,[77] that corresponds with actuality.

There is a wide gap between state practice and the prevailing legal rules in the *in bello* sphere as well. An important mission of the law of armed conflict is to humanize war's environment for combatants and noncombatants alike.[78] Its core interest is to spare the lives and property

---

74. DINSTEIN, WAR, AGGRESSION AND SELF-DEFENCE, *supra* note 62, at 252. Indeed, the 1993 U.S. bombing campaign in Baghdad, in response to Saddam Hussein's failed attempt to assassinate U.S. president George H.W. Bush, was justified by the United States as self-defense and approved by many (if not most) states. *See* W. Michael Reisman, *The Raid on Baghdad: Some Reflections on Its Lawfulness and Implications*, 5 EUR. J. INT'L L. 120, 120–25 (1994).

75. *See, e.g.*, CASSESE, INTERNATIONAL LAW, *supra* note 73, at 371–72 (pointing, inter alia, at the hypocrisy of Western states, which have engaged in armed reprisals but criticized resort to such reprisals by other states. *See also* his endorsement of the "on-the-spot-reaction," which should be distinguished from a delayed response. *Id.*). The International Court of Justice, in its *Nuclear Weapons Advisory Opinion*, has stated—albeit in what might be regarded as a dictum—that "[t]he Court does not have to examine, in this context, the question of armed reprisals in time of peace, which are considered to be unlawful." Legality of the Threat or Use of Nuclear Weapons, Advisory Opinion, 1996 I.C.J. Rep. 226, ¶ 46 (July 8).

76. Oscar Schachter challenges this conventional wisdom. *See infra* text accompanying Chapter 4 note 97.

77. LEO TOLSTOY, WAR AND PEACE (1968).

78. The early modern law of armed conflict focused on protecting combatants, dealing with the means and ways in which wars were to be fought between professional armies. However, the horrors that surfaced after the Second World War proved that a change was required to strengthen the protection of civilians in the context of IHL, as reflected by the creation of the fourth Geneva Convention. *See generally* GEOFFREY BEST, HUMANITY IN WARFARE: THE MODERN HISTORY OF THE INTERNATIONAL LAW OF ARMED CONFLICT (1983).

of noncombatants and to eliminate the unnecessary suffering of combatants. Its success should be examined in light of this criterion. In reality, however, this noble mission has a problematic record, due, inter alia, to the huge gap between the law's imperatives and actual practice by belligerents. Indeed, in the fulfillment of its most important mission the law does not succeed: the "treatment of civilians has the worst record" of compliance in the entire law of armed conflict.[79]

Although our previous examples related to the gap between the legal rules and their actual application by states, we can now turn to another *in bello* practical gap: the "interpretative" gap between the stated aim of a legal rule and its current actual legal validity. This gap will be demonstrated by the *in bello* necessity principle. Theoretically, this principle, which is one of the pillars of the law of armed conflict, imposes a de jure restraint upon the exercise of military power, forbidding the use of power unnecessary for attaining a military goal.[80] Indeed necessity, in theory, has the dual legal function of being both an enabling and constraining principle,[81] as it permits only that degree of force required in order to achieve a legitimate military objective.[82] Practically, however, the necessity principle does not currently function as a substantial constraining standard on militaries,

---

79. An empirical study, which examined compliance with eight segments of the law of armed conflict through the twentieth century, concluded that the prohibition upon the use of chemical weapons has the best record. The other six components of the law of armed conflict are: aerial bombardment, armistice/ceasefire, protection of cultural property, conduct on the high seas, prisoners of war, and treatment of wounded. *See, e.g.*, James D. Morrow, *When Do States Follow the Laws of War?*, 101 Am. Pol. Sci. Rev. 559, 562, 567 (2007).

80. The other pillar of the law of armed conflict is the humanity principle, which forbids the use of means and methods of warfare that cause superfluous injury or unnecessary suffering. "The principle of humanity is based on the notion that once a military purpose has been achieved, the further infliction of suffering is unnecessary." U.K. Ministry of Defence, The Manual of the Law of Armed Conflict 23 (2005). Under art. 23(e) of the 1907 Hague Regulations, it is forbidden "to employ arms, projectiles, or material calculated to cause unnecessary suffering." Hague Convention (IV) Respecting the Laws and Customs of War and its Annex: Regulations concerning the Laws and Customs of War on Land, Oct. 18, 1907, 187 C.T.S. 227 [hereinafter 1907 Hague Regulations].

81. *See, e.g.*, Gabriella Blum, *The Laws of War and the "Lesser Evil"*, 35 Yale J. Int'l L. 1, 3, at note 5 (2010) (referring to Antonio Cassese, International Criminal Law 280–84 (2d ed. 2008)); and *see generally* Jens David Ohlin & Larry May, Necessity in International Law (2016).

82. This rule's modern roots were established in the Lieber Code, which stated in art. 14: "Military necessity, as understood by modern civilized nations, consists in the necessity of those measures which are indispensable for securing the ends of the war, and which are lawful according to the modern law and usages of war." U.S. War Dep't, General Order No. 100: Instructions for the Government of Armies of the United States in the Field, Apr. 24,

as originally expected.[83] States' practice has turned it into a hollow principle, and its current impotency and weakness demonstrate the huge gap between this rule's stated aim and actual state practice.

The above-mentioned examples, from both the *ad bellum* and *in bello* segments of the law, illustrate the huge gap between the positive law and its actual implementation in states' practice. Besides this common form of de facto evasion, I presented earlier the practice of *de jure* objections to the law and reservations from it. What can be done to narrow this huge gap? In particular, how can the challenge of reducing war's hazards and human suffering be met less rhetorically and more effectively?

This book suggests a new paradigm in balancing the different interests of states' militaries and the humanitarian agenda. Although the struggle between the military and humanitarian camps may never end, due to the different prisms through which they inspect conflict, this book proposes to reduce the scope of the division between the two. In that, it follows former successful precedents of bridging legal gaps within the law of armed conflict.[84] Rather than that the law should be dictated by the strongest camp, even if with states' consent, it calls for a dialogue between them. This dialogue should recognize that total abrogation of militaries' freedom of action on issues crucial to them is counterproductive, while simultaneously internalizing the core humanitarian requests. Therefore this book, instead of introducing declarative humanitarian provisions, seeks to phrase effective rules to guide actual performance, which in turn will lead to a reduction in war's hazards. It tries to replace visionary, but in some cases impractical, rules with more workable ones based on a professional examination of what militaries can realistically—yet maximally—do to reduce human suffering. In order to elevate the humanitarian threshold,

---

1863, http://avalon.law.yale.edu/19th_century/lieber.asp (last visited Aug. 16, 2017) [hereinafter Lieber Code].

83. The effect of this rule's weakness will be at the focus of a substantial part of the coming discussion in Chapter 1 of this book.

84. In the past, it was common to distinguish between "Hague law" (the law governing the conduct of hostilities) and "Geneva law" (the law protecting the victims of armed conflict). Today, however, "these two branches of the law applicable in armed conflict have become so closely interrelated that they are considered to have gradually formed one single complex system, known today as international humanitarian law." Legality of the Threat or Use of Nuclear Weapons, Advisory Opinion, *supra* note 75, at ¶ 75, and *see above* note 78. Furthermore, the Hague rules too were "inspired by the desire to diminish the evils of war, as far as military requirements permit." 1907 Hague Regulations, *supra* note 80, at the preamble.

it calls for the replacement of some unsustainable imperatives imposed upon militaries—rules that largely pay lip service to the humanitarian agenda—with professionally-based, and thus attainable, requirements. Instead of utopian standards it offers challenging yet practical ones, reducing the need for apologetic argumentation.

The suggested paradigm has two aims. The first is to narrow the gap between the two camps by creating an environment in which full abidance by the law becomes an attainable norm. The second, more important aim, which to a large extent derives from the first, is to reduce human suffering. To achieve these aims, the first step is to face reality. *Realpolitik* considerations dictate that in real time, when states, including law-abiding ones, are fighting in their own self-defense, their militaries' interests—those that, from their professional perspective, are essential in order to exercise their defense—will prevail. An existential threat affects states' behavior, and this reality should have legal effect. Indeed, it has been admitted by the International Court of Justice that it "cannot conclude definitively whether the threat or use of nuclear weapons would be lawful or unlawful in an extreme circumstance of self-defence, in which the very survival of a State would be at stake."[85] This reality, however, does not mean giving up humanitarian considerations and allowing the military a free hand as regards every interest, but rather the opposite. Indeed, a precondition for drafting and implementing humanitarian rules is to internalize the importance of existential security interests when drawing the contours of the law. Humanitarian considerations are serious and important, and their legal effect should be prominent, as long as states can obey the law and still win wars. Indeed, the humanitarian rules too have their core values—for example, distinguishing between combatants and noncombatants—that should be prioritized. A delicate balance is required. To that end, the core existential interests of states should be given substantial consideration, whereas the convenient interests of militaries ought to be discounted in favor of humanitarian concerns. The suggested paradigm is based upon a sincere dialogue between the two camps, reflecting both sides' core interests, while balancing between them. Its outcome would be an improved equilibrium at the "maximal humanitarian point," the restraints imposed being those that militaries can live with, albeit with difficulties and risks (including to their own soldiers' lives), and yet still win a war. The question

85. Legality of the Threat or Use of Nuclear Weapons, Advisory Opinion, *supra* note 75, at ¶ 105.

is how to identify this point of "maximum humanism" that will still be acceptable to militaries.

Reflected in the way militaries think, function, and fight, military professionalism in its wider sense, including the strategic dimension, is the suggested key to identifying the core military interest of law-abiding states; its recognition would make it possible to elevate the humanitarian threshold in a sustainable way. In any given war, this professionalism defines the contour of military advantages required to win it and analyses its essential components. Inherent to this professional analysis is a reflection upon the actual tension between achieving a given military mission and the humanitarian issues related to it: core interests are taken into consideration, along with less essential ones—those that can be sacrificed for the sake of the humanitarian interests, while still achieving the mission. Furthermore, military professionalism by definition requires inherent self-constraining standards and allows for a variety of options in terms of military force used at all levels of war—strategic, operational, and tactical[86]—to achieve a given military aim or advantage. Leveraging this professionalism, while concurrently signaling and prioritizing its core interests, might create a reasonable modus vivendi for a military and still allow substantial space for the humanitarian mission of the law.

Indeed, wars are conducted in light of military professionalism. Militaries—especially well-trained and disciplined ones—adhere to their doctrine, operational principles, fighting techniques, and values. Their performances are not random or incidental, and their results do not resemble a lottery. Rather, these performances are mainly contingent, at the strategic level, on the competence of both the civilian and military leaders of the campaign, and at the operational and tactical levels, on officers' and soldiers' knowledge, professional skills, and virtues. The complexity of the battlefield arises due to the "fog" of war,[87] and its surprising potential and inherent ambiguity—indeed a crucial factor in understanding military reality—make it all the more necessary to face and manage this phenomenon professionally. Commanders—as well as civilian leaders who instruct their militaries, whether formally defined as their "commander

86. It is common practice for militaries to distinguish between three levels of war: strategic, operational, and tactical. These levels of war will be discussed *infra* text accompanying Chapter 3 notes 20–27.

87. Carl Von Clausewitz, On War 101 (Michael Eliot Howard & Peter Paret trans., indexed ed. 1984) ("a fog of greater or lesser uncertainty").

in chief"[88] or such who actually possess the ultimate authority over their states' militaries—and soldiers are required to operate their skills under harsh circumstances in a domain of knowledge, and to exercise their profession in light of a set of standards, norms, and rules.

Certainly, military professionalism is about killing and damaging. Wars, including just wars, are not humanitarian projects, and are destructive by their very nature. Yet this professionalism does not endorse excessive use of force, above what is reasonably necessary to achieve a given, lawful military advantage. Despite the common saying, from a professional perspective, not all is fair in war! On utilitarian grounds, only that amount of force required to achieve the military mission is desirable. Though the exercise of ruthless force by militaries is a common phenomenon in warfare, it usually derives from professional incompetency and lack of discipline, or is the result of political, psychological, and cultural pressures (or a combination thereof). The latter are external forces to military professionalism. In performing a given military mission and attaining specific advantages, the more professional and well-trained a military is, the more precise it is in exercising its force with the minimal amount of brutality. Such efficient exercise of military force is in the self-interest of a professional trained military, and it is motivated not only by utilitarian but also by moral and ethical concerns.[89] A military thus demonstrates its competency and signals its high discipline and concern for domestic and international public opinion; in counterinsurgency operations, it also signals an explicit wish to "win hearts and minds."[90] Indeed, there are brutal militaries that intentionally target civilians and damage their property. But when they

---

88. In the United States, for example, the commander in chief of the armed forces is the U.S. president. This is pursuant to U.S. CONST. art. II, § 2, cl. I, which states that the president " . . . shall be Commander in Chief of the Army and Navy of the United States. . . ."

89. The adaption of ends to the means and the conservation of military energy for its designated purposes requires the exercise of military force in measured dosage so as not to waste it by using excessive force for unrelated (or secondary) purposes. The "economy of force" is, indeed, a common principle of war. *See* U.S. DEP'T OF THE ARMY, FIELD MANUAL 3-0, OPERATIONS (Feb. 27, 2008) appendix A, para. A-10 [hereinafter FM 3-0]. In other militaries it is dubbed by different names. See the discussion *infra* text accompanying Chapter 1 note 14 and Chapter 2 notes 109–112.

90. "The phrase 'hearts and minds' is generally associated with a less coercive approach to counterinsurgency which emphasizes the importance of using 'minimum force' in order to win the 'hearts and minds' of the people." Paul Dixon, *"Hearts and Minds"? British Counter-Insurgency from Malaya to Iraq*, 32 J. STRATEGIC STUD. 353 (2009).

engage in activity aimed intentionally, and not collaterally, at civilians,[91] they are no longer acting in their military capacity, but as an organized terrorist group (headed by their government).[92] Typically, terrorists do not aim at military targets; rather, they usually avoid them. By intentionally going after civilian targets, their goal is to elicit extreme horror, panic, and demoralization in all echelons of their adversary's civil society, in order to affect their behavior. The mere fact that they use military tools—for example, guns and explosives—does not make their activities military, but rather the opposite: although their intentions may be more complex, their activities are more akin to those of civilian criminals, for example robbers and pirates. Indeed, the suggested call for the adoption of military professionalism as a legal tool relates only to the professional military capacity, per se, as reflected when militaries fight to achieve military advantages.

Furthermore, military professionalism has a moderating effect at all levels of war, including the strategic one. The current legal discourse with regard to this level of war is very poor, and this in turn affects the limited menu of lawful war aims. Due to this legal shortsightedness, the legality of war aims selected in real time by a belligerent will be, in many cases, doubtful and their effectiveness less than optimal. Indeed, the strategic preferences selected largely determine the scope and magnitude of a given war and the damage caused by it to both life and property. Turning a blind eye to the strategic level of war triggers a counter-effect to the law's

---

91. The discussion above relates to the prevailing distinction rule, which outlaws the intended targeting of civilians (including their objects) and minimizes the collateral damage that can lawfully occur to them, as a given. In the past, however, targeting civilians was indeed part of the legacy of decisive war. *See* the discussion *infra* text accompanying Chapter 1 notes 38–39. Furthermore, the supporters of the decisive battle in that period went even further by humanizing it, arguing that in order to minimize human suffering in times of war the desired goal should be to shorten its duration. The most efficient way to conclude a war in a short time and thereby minimize the human suffering caused by it is, according to this approach, through a decisive battle, in all dimensions. This rationale was accepted, for example, by the Lieber Code (*see infra* Chapter 3 note 86) and was advocated by Field-Marshal Moltke and other Prussian generals who insisted, in a somewhat Clausewitzian manner, that no substantial humanitarian boundaries apply to the conduct of war, for a short war ultimately minimizes the violation of humanitarianism. *See infra* text accompanying Chapter 3 notes 41–44 and 86.

92. Legally speaking, the argument that sovereign government violence might be classified as state terrorism was rejected (during the Cold War) by most Western states. *See, e.g.*, Tal Becker, Terrorism and the State: Rethinking the Rules of State Responsibility 91 (2006). Morally however, it's a different story. For example, the indiscriminate bombing of German cities in the Second World War, especially in its later stages, was problematic; indeed, Michael Walzer dubbed it "terror bombing." *See* Walzer, Just and Unjust Wars, *supra* note 63, at 261; and *see infra* Chapter 5 note 5.

mission of reducing war's hazards. If it were to be introduced into the legal discourse—while recognizing the practical limits to how far the humanitarian envelope can be pushed—it could, to a large extent, bridge the gap between the law and reality, facilitating an environment that promotes the law's humanitarian mission. It would dictate to a law-abiding belligerent the adoption of a strategy that allows it to win its war with lesser humanitarian harms.

In sum, it is military professionalism that, to a large extent, prescribes the way wars are conducted. Acknowledging the reality, however, does not mean yielding to brutality, but rather the opposite. Although military professionalism allows the use of lethal force, it should also at the same time constrain it and protect combatants and noncombatants alike from excessive violence, at all levels of war. Adopting this professionalism as a tool can bridge the law-reality gap, while directly serving, in many cases, the vision of reducing human suffering. Indeed, merely adapting the law to the reality, while retaining its core values (e.g., sparing the innocent), would change the atmosphere of the belligerent environment and improve the law's chances of being more respected and abided by.

Calling for the adoption of military professionalism as a tool to bridge the gap between two competing worlds invites the following question: Is it not an amorphous criterion? Though not simple, the answer is clear. Although armies differ in their individual war methods, they still share common attributes in terms of planning, functioning, and fighting, while relating to all levels of war. Their professional pillars, as reflected in their war principles, are to a large extent common. These are the principles that substantially affect their conduct of operations. In this Introduction, then, I regard military professionalism as an objective-generic concept, based on the wide common denominator of developed states' militaries' mode of operations. Nonetheless, the subjective variance that exists between militaries, in their own professionalism, and between them and less developed ones allows for a normative discussion. These differences allow a margin of appreciation as regards the suggested humanitarian threshold: where the equilibrium between military core interests and humanitarian ones should be set.

Adopting professionalism to bridge the gap between the law and reality (or between the two perceptions of the law) and, in many cases, to consequently achieve, whether directly or indirectly, the vision of reducing human suffering requires substantial steps, indeed concessions, from both the humanitarian and military camps. This should be the product of the suggested dialogue between the two and the mutual effect they have upon each other. The humanitarian camp has to recognize the presence and validity of military professionalism and to internalize that wars are and ought to be conducted in light of these professional standards and norms. Furthermore, it has to accept that it does not have a monopoly over humanitarian considerations, nor can humanitarian considerations alone substantially reduce war's hazards. The military camp, on the other hand, has to defer to the core norms and values of the humanitarian camp—for example, the distinction rule—as well as to the constraining effects of military professionalism. It has to give up the convenient zone of military operations that it currently enjoys, which imposes relatively few legal-humanitarian requirements upon it, especially in conventional wars. Indeed, it will be suggested that the current humanitarian threshold should be elevated to a more demanding level. It should create a belligerent sphere for militaries in which they can still fight and win a war, though subject to more humanitarian constraints and exposed to greater risk.

This book calls for a reassessment of the underlying assumptions of the contemporary law. It challenges the prevailing equilibrium between military necessities and humanitarian considerations. It aims at rethinking the prevailing principles and focuses upon the legal standards rather than the concrete rules deriving from them.[93] It does not offer a detailed draft of a new Protocol. Rather, it examines the suggested standards in selected test cases and focuses upon their efficacy in contending with contemporary challenges that are undermining the current legal regime. It deals with substantial macro challenges to this regime in order to change the direction of the prevailing law; indeed, the suggested paradigm requires further elaboration to deal with its micro details.

This book proceeds as follows. Chapter 1 revisits the *in bello* necessity principle. It challenges the current dichotomy between the two pillars—mistakenly assumed to be polar opposites—of the law of armed conflict: necessity and humanity. It embraces the idea that a well-trained military has an inherent interest in enhancing its operational effectiveness and constraining unnecessary brutality. The exercise of brute force by militaries, though common, reflects professional incompetency. The prevailing law of armed conflict, however, generally ignores the constraining

93. For the distinction between rules and standards, *see, e.g.*, Kathleen M. Sullivan, *The Justices of Rules and Standards*, 106 HARV. L. REV. 22, 57–59 (1992); Ronald Dworkin, *The Model of Rules*, 35 U. CHI. L. REV. 14, 22 (1967) (and the discussion therein).

effect of the necessity principle, which was originally intended to allow only the minimally necessary use of force on the battlefield. Consequently, the prevailing law places the burden of restricting the exercise of brute military force upon humanitarian considerations (and the specific norms derived from them). Humanitarianism alone, however, cannot deliver the goods and substantially reduce war's hazards. This chapter therefore calls for the transformation of the military's actual or potential self-imposed professional constraining standards into a revised legal standard of necessity. Although the necessity principle justifies the mere use of lethal force, it should not only facilitate wielding the military sword but also function simultaneously as a shield, protecting combatants and noncombatants alike from excessive brutality. The suggested transformation would bind and restrain the prospective exercisers of excessive force, political and military alike, and restrict the potential damage that might be caused both intentionally (to combatants) and collaterally (to noncombatants). The combined effect of the current changes in war's pattern and the law of armed conflict, in the military and social thinking of recent decades, and the new strategies available due to the development of new military technologies have all created a new war environment—one that may be ready to leverage the constraining potential of military professionalism, turning it into binding legal standards and norms. This chapter advances an argument of broad application, relevant to the entire suggested paradigm; if accepted it would narrow the gap between the law and its actual implementation in states' practice, while reducing human suffering. That explains why this book does not follow a linear-chronological axis and why this chapter, which deals with an *in bello* issue, precedes a chapter dealing with the *ad bellum* aspect: the mere recourse to war.

Chapter 2 deals with the application of the suggested professionalism criterion in the other segment of the law, the *ad bellum* sphere. An unresolved legal issue in the self-defense context concerns its timing: when can a self-defendant state be proactive in its defense and strike preemptively? In the face of an armed attack, a self-defendant state is not restricted to an ex-post military response delivered only after absorbing the aggressor's blow. Lawful self-defense allows proactivity against either an actual "armed attack" or, according to the prevailing view, an imminent one, as well. However, the ambiguity of the positive law regarding the legality of an anticipatory strike by a potential victim, as well as the disputed actual practice of states, invites a normative discussion. On the assumption that a self-defendant is not obliged to remain a sitting duck when confronted by an imminent threat against it, this chapter suggests that the criterion to be used in defining the legal-timing threshold, vindicating the right of self-defense, be taken from the toolbox of military professionalism. It should be the last reasonable point, according to the self-defendant's military circumstances, at which it can, according to its military doctrine, successfully face the aggressor's threat and still operationally defend itself—including, when necessary, by taking the initiative in its own self-defense.

Indeed, the suggested standard, allowing a first strike by a self-defendant when appropriate, has its disadvantages; it could be abused, whenever preemption is used as a pretext for aggression, and might be counter-effective. The answer to the challenges of potential abuse and manipulation should be based mainly on military professionalism and transparency requirements. The burden of proof lies with the self-defender who is actually the first to use force. It has to convince both the public (domestic and international) and the international community (and, if necessary, its organs) that it was justified to attack in light of its last-resort defensive alternatives, in what it considers to be the relevant circumstances. Allowing a necessary last-resort self-defense is not only consistent with strategic considerations and reality (thus narrowing the gap between the law and reality), but in many cases it would have a direct moderating effect, as well. Legalizing proactivity, when appropriate, would provide a self-defendant with the tools—and indeed, place upon it the obligation—to minimize the collateral damage caused by it to its adversary's noncombatants.[94] Although it was dragged into the fighting in the first place, it should limit its first strike to the belligerent arena, as compared to a totally reactive self-defense scenario in which the time, place, pattern, magnitude, and focus of the aggression are all selected by the attacker. The development of new technology, allowing both accurate intelligence and precise targeting, might minimize the potential unnecessary suffering, to both combatants and noncombatants, caused by a self-defendant's first strike.

Although the first two chapters preserve the traditional *ad bellum* and *in bello* dichotomy, Chapter 3 challenges this common separation. It points at a paradox related to the gap between law and reality. As it is the strategic level of war that mostly affects war's conduct, one might have expected that the law of armed conflict—whose stated agenda is to humanize war's arena—would focus upon it. The current law, however, generally

94. *See* the *in bello* proportionality equation, *infra* Chapter 1, note 59.

ignores the strategic discourse and prefers to scrutinize the conduct of war through a tactical lens. This chapter challenges the current blind spot of the law: its disregard of the direct consequences of war strategy and the war aims derived from it. Ignoring reality by disregarding military strategy, which is originally decided at the *ad bellum* stage and adapted during the evolution of the *in bello* belligerency, carries a humanitarian price that will be demonstrated in the prevailing law of targeting. The chapter asks of those who want to comprehensively reduce war's hazards to think strategically—indeed, to face reality—and to leverage military strategy as a constraining tool. Under the suggested approach, the law of armed conflict would require militaries to operate coherently when it comes to targeting by, in fact, adhering to their own professional standards. (Though coherency in targeting is professionally desired by militaries, the need to turn autonomously working and effective internal norms into mandatory ones will be explained by the tension between the grand strategy ("policy") considerations of a state and its military strategy.) Requiring adherence in targeting to strict and definite war aims, as strategically selected by a belligerent, might substantially moderate the scope of lawful targets and reduce humanitarian damage, especially in limited wars.

Chapter 4 deals with the lack of coherency between strategic reality—which uses deterrence as an essential strategic tool—and the prevailing law. Currently the notion of deterrence in both *ad bellum* and *in bello* situations challenges the prevailing legal paradigm because of its duality. Deterrence is a tool for enforcing compliance with the law and promotes the containment of potential conflicts. It is pivotal in strategic thinking and, in many cases, an essential component of the national-defense strategy of law-abiding states. Indeed, deterrence could be perceived as appealing to the prevailing legal system—which was shaped by the UN Charter and is characterized by the absence of a well-functioning central law-enforcement body—due to being aimed at preserving the international status quo. But although deterrence is central to the management of global security, in current international law deterrence considerations are perceived with suspicion and mistrust. Its bad reputation may stem in part from its inherent limitations as a strategy—indeed, the mere notion of manipulating or even controlling an adversary's will is very problematic—and in part from its being perceived as an unlawful punitive measure. The lack of consensus on lawful deterrence, however, might create a vacuum that invites aggressors (who breach the *ad bellum* rules) and transgressors (who breach the *in bello* rules). In all too many cases, the lack of effective deterrence might incentivize aggression and transgression of the law instead of discouraging it, and consequentially promote bloodshed.

This chapter offers normative suggestions for introducing defensive deterrence and overcoming the practical problem of putting it into practice within the current contours of the law, by using the military professionalism criterion. Although deterrence is not a magic formula, it might be effective in some strategic scenarios. This discussion therefore deals with four generic war aims and outlines the scope of potential lawful deterrence as a moderating alternative between them.[95] It starts with the minimal war aim of "halt and repel," currently perceived as an optimal generic lawful response by a self-defendant to an armed attack. However, this war aim is strategically suitable mainly against an isolated armed attack, limited in its scope and intentions, with a low probability of recurrence. At the other end of the strategic spectrum, though legally disputed, are wars aimed at either incapacitation—eliminating the aggressor's substantial military capabilities—or, in extreme cases, a regime change, where only the uprooting of the entire ruling system can promote peace and security for the international community. The legality of these two war aims at the extremes is currently disputed, leaving a strategic vacuum in terms of legitimate action where, as in typical contemporary wars, there is a repeat offender, as reflected by its actions and declarations, who should be deterred from further acts of *ad bellum* aggression or *in bello* transgression. However, adopting the "halt and repel" strategy against such a raging bull might only drive it to further escalation, and incapacitation carries, in too many cases, too heavy a humanitarian price. This strategic arena invites, in appropriate cases, the introduction of a median war aim of creating a credible threat (and if necessary, exercising it) that is highly likely to moderate the aggressor's belligerent intentions and activities. Legalizing this delicate strategy of defensive deterrence—which aims to keep the important assets of the aggressor-transgressor under threat, yet untouched (either in whole or in part), in order to create a "losing premium" and the incentive attached to it—might offer a relatively moderate alternative, which is consistent with the contemporary strategic arena. Indeed, introducing defensive deterrence invites criticism regarding a possible slippery slope. But self-defense, per se, can be abused and manipulated too by an ostensible defendant. Both can be used as a pretext for the illegal use of

95. The four generic war aims will be introduced first, at the text accompanying Chapter 3, notes 94–97.

force—especially due to subjective variables and in the absence of an effective international central law-enforcement mechanism. The suggested answers to these challenges will be based, inter alia, on the principles of transparency and military professionalism. They would minimize bona fide reckless mistakes and reduce any opportunistic misuse of deterrence, or any other proactive measure suggested in this book, as a pretext for aggression.

This book suggests a new stage in the evolution of the international law governing armed hostilities. It calls for the adoption of military professionalism as a tool to bridge the unacceptable gap between the law and reality and consequently, in most cases, to achieve, whether directly or indirectly, the vision of reducing human suffering. It challenges the prevailing legal paradigm, including the traditional role of the necessity and proportionality principles and the *ad bellum* and *in bello* dichotomy. It further challenges the prevailing *in bello* distinction rule, which currently grants carte blanche in regard to killing soldiers by indiscriminately classifying all of them as legitimate targets. The suggested paradigm calls for reducing the scope of lawful intentional targeting of combatants and collateral targeting of civilians. It does not accept the binary choice between the utopian and apologetic approaches toward the entire body of laws related to war, but rather suggests adopting the middle, more realistic road, by challenging the military comfort zone. When it comes to their interests, militaries, like other bureaucratic organizations, will go to great lengths to defend them. The suggested way to convince them to sacrifice their convenience for the sake of the humanitarian mission is to distinguish, using their own professional prism, between their core and relatively peripheral interests. This can be achieved, as will be suggested, by a revision of both principles of military necessity and *ad bellum* proportionality combined with the introduction of a lawful defensive deterrence. This, in turn, would create a new strategic balance that better correlates the risks and rewards granted to law-abiding states and their adversaries, either actual or potential. The use of military logic and ethics, including its utilitarian rationale—indeed, the very principles of military professionalism—is a way to enable militaries to give up their peripheral interests for the sake of the humanitarian mission of the law. All they are being asked to do is to extend the maximal humanitarian point that might still be acceptable to them in practice.

The potential for reform is there. The nature of many contemporary wars, as well as the social attitudes toward them, has changed dramatically in recent decades. The development of the humanistic approach and the introduction of new weapons and intelligence technology have had a substantial effect upon current military thinking and practice. All of these changes, which will be elaborated upon later in this book, have created a new environment—one that may be ready to absorb the suggested new paradigm.

1

*Revitalizing the Concept of Military Necessity**

Introduction

The noble mission of the law of armed conflict—to humanize war's environment for both combatants and noncombatants—has a mixed record, due either to the law's shortcomings or to the huge gap between the law's rhetoric and actual practice by belligerents.[1] In the face of a combat reality full of hazards, an important humanitarian challenge—to be dealt with in this chapter—is to substantially reduce the scope of brutality in both international and non-international armed conflicts.[2]

On the prevailing perception, the task of the law of armed conflict is to balance the demands of military necessity against humanitarian concerns.[3]

---

* This chapter is based mainly on, Yishai Beer, *Humanity Considerations Cannot Reduce War's Hazards Alone: Revitalizing the Concept of Military Necessity*, 26 Eur. J. Int'l L. 801 (2015).

1. *See, e.g.*, James D. Morrow, *When Do States Follow the Laws of War?*, 101 Am. Pol. Sci. Rev. 559, 567 (2007).

2. The law of armed conflict applies in every case of armed conflict, namely '"whenever there is a resort to armed force between States or protracted armed violence between governmental authorities and organized armed groups or between such groups within a State." Prosecutor v. Tadić, Case No. IT-94-1-I, Decision on the Defence Motion for Interlocutory Appeal on Jurisdiction ¶70 (Int'l Crim. Trib. for the former Yugoslavia Oct. 2, 1995), http://www.icty.org/x/cases/tadic/acdec/en/51002.htm.

3. *E.g.*, the commentary on Additional Protocol I to the Geneva Conventions states: "The entire law of armed conflict is, of course, the result of an equitable balance between the necessities of war and humanitarian requirements." Claude Pilloud & Jean Pictet, *Protocol I Article 57—Precautions in Attack*, *in* Commentary on the Additional Protocols of 8 June 1977 to the Geneva Conventions of 12 August 1949, at 683 (Claude Pilloud et al. eds., 1987).

Military Professionalism and Humanitarian Law. Yishai Beer.

This traditional agenda might have been efficacious had it not preferred to place all (or most) of the brutality-restricting burden upon the thin shoulders of humanitarian considerations and norms. The military necessity requirement is currently perceived as being entirely opposed to humanity, enabling, in fact, almost any belligerent activity. This perception explicitly ignores existing professional military standards that might also effectively restrict war's hazards. It will be argued that humanitarian considerations and the specific norms derived from them, per se, should not carry the burden of effectively restricting the exercise of brute military force alone.[4] The equilibrium is not currently at its optimum, and the law of armed conflict cannot fully accomplish its mission in the international arena. For example, under the prevailing law, combatants' lives are the cheapest commodity on the battlefield,[5] and the evidence related to civilians reflects the "worst record" of compliance in the entire law of armed conflict.[6]

Theoretically, the necessity principle imposes a restraint upon the exercise of military power—forbidding the use of power unnecessary to attain the military goal—whereas the humanity principle forbids the use of means and methods of warfare that cause superfluous injury or unnecessary suffering.[7] Indeed necessity should have permitted only that degree of force required in order to achieve the legitimate military purpose of the conflict.[8] Legally, however, it has failed to function as a substantial constraining standard, as originally expected. Its current impotency and the effects of its weakness will be at the focus of the coming discussion. Consequently, humanitarian considerations and specific positive norms

---

4. Furthermore, the contemporary reinforcement they have received from the infusion of human rights into the humanitarian scale required in a battle-zone does not change the picture: "[H]umanitarian law has become less geared to military necessity and increasingly impregnated with human rights values . . . The most conspicuous development of modern humanitarian law was that it had been strongly influenced by human rights doctrines." ANTONIO CASSESE, INTERNATIONAL LAW 404 (2d ed. 2005). It should be noted, however, that even in a period in which the role of human rights law in wartime has become significant, it is the law of armed conflict that dominates the war arena: "The [human rights] test of what is an arbitrary deprivation of life, however, then falls to be determined by the applicable lex specialis, namely, the law applicable in armed conflict which is designed to regulate the conduct of hostilities." Legality of the Threat or Use of Nuclear Weapons, Advisory Opinion, 1996 I.C.J. Rep. 226, 240 (July 8).

5. *See, e.g.*, Gabriella Blum, *The Dispensable Lives of Soldiers*, 2 J. LEGAL ANALYSIS 115 (2010).

6. *See* Morrow, *supra* note 1.

7. *See supra* Introduction note 80.

8. *See, e.g.*, Gabriella Blum, *The Laws of War and the "Lesser Evil"*, 35 YALE J. INT'L L. 1 (2010).

derived from them (distinction, proportionality, and the forbiddance of unnecessary suffering) must currently carry most, if not all, of the humanitarian weight. They actually function as the only substantial brake against war's hazards in general, but their capacity to limit the use of excessive military force in particular is restricted.

The principle of humanity was given prominent expression in modern times by the Martens Clause of the 1899 Hague Regulations.[9] The clause grants protection to "populations and belligerents" by "the principles of international law, as they result from the usage established between civilized nations, from the laws of humanity and the requirements of public conscience."[10] Today, the principle of humanity in the conduct of hostilities manifests itself, according to some, by independent substance.[11] Yoram Dinstein, by contrast, claims that humanity in the conduct of hostilities is not a positive law in the sense that it does not determine concrete operational obligations on the battlefield; rather, it is more of an abstract, "meta-juridical" consideration triggering the legal norms to follow.[12] Whatever the status granted to humanity—independent principle or abstract considerations leading to concrete norms—it could be sustained by way of military necessity if the latter had any substantial constraining merit of its own. Unfortunately, currently (and paradoxically) it does not.

This chapter seeks to revisit the prevailing paradigm and to challenge the current dichotomy between the two basic principles of the law of armed conflict: necessity and humanity. Indeed, military necessity is used to vindicate war and the hazards deriving from it; however, it is not entirely an opposite force to humanity when it comes to restricting excessive military force. Rather, in many cases, if exercised professionally, military necessity

---

9. *See, e.g.*, Theodor Meron, *The Martens Clause, Principles of Humanity, and Dictates of Public Conscience*, 94 Am. J. Int'l L. 78 (2000).

10. Hague Convention (II) with Respect to the Laws and Customs of War on Land, at the preamble, July 29, 1899, 32 Stat. 1803. *See also* Protocol Additional to the Geneva Conventions of 12 August 1949, and relating to the Protection of Victims of International Armed Conflicts (Protocol I), art. 1(2), June 8, 1977, 1125 U.N.T.S. 3 (API); Jean Pictet, *The Fundamental Principles of the Red Cross*, 19 Int'l Rev. Red Cross 130 (1979).

11. *E.g.*, in the principles of human rights law, which they see serving as a sort of principle of humanity for IHL. *See* Larsen K. Mujezinović, *A "Principle of Humanity" or a "Principle of Human-Rightism"?*, *in* Searching for a 'Principle of Humanity' in International Humanitarian Law 124 (Larsen K. Mujezinović et al. eds., 2013).

12. Yoram Dinstein, *The Principle of Proportionality*, *in* Searching for a 'Principle of Humanity' in International Humanitarian Law 72–74 (Larsen K. Mujezinović et al. eds., 2013).

could be a complementary force in fulfilling the humanitarian quest. Necessity, per se, can and should restrict brutality in the exercise of military force. Excessive use of force is not a professional requirement of a military, and the mere fact that it happens in many wars does not mean that it has any military substance or basis; however common the phenomenon may be, it is not professionally oriented, but rather derives from a combination of external forces, political, psychological, or cultural. It will also be argued that the inherent interest of a trained military is to constrain and contain these unnecessary—indeed, unprofessional—forces. Vitalizing the necessity principle, by infusing acceptable professional military standards into it, would create an additional level of restraints above the specific prohibiting norms of the law of armed conflict. Furthermore, it would challenge specific norms, regarding which compromise has currently been reached in light of the principles of humanity and military necessity,[13] and it would relieve the humanity principle of part of the burden of preventing unnecessary suffering to combatants.

This chapter proceeds as follows. Part 1.1 introduces the self-interest of a military in constraining brute force and argues that the humanitarian requisite to prevent unnecessary suffering to an adversary's combatants and civilians might be derived, to a large extent, from the justification of military (un)necessity. Part 1.2 presents the prevailing legal necessity principle as a hollow rule and suggests strengthening it by infusing substantial professional military standards into it, as originally intended but currently lacking. Part 1.3 discusses both the institutional and substantive effects that follow from the transformation of professional military standards into legal norms. These relate to war's casualties, restricting the potential damage caused to combatants and noncombatants and to the exercisers of military force, leaders, and "old-school" soldiers, whose potential brutality would be restricted if professional standards became legal norms. Even if one is convinced that the suggested transformation is desirable, it invites

13. Indeed, according to the view that the prevailing law reflects the current balance between the "opposing" principles, humanity and military necessity, and that necessity cannot operate as an extra general prohibiting layer, which applies above the present rules that have already been infused into it, this chapter represents a primarily normative discussion rather than a combination of positive and normative. *See, e.g.*, Michel N. Schmitt, *Military Necessity and Humanity in International Humanitarian Law: Preserving the Delicate Balance*, 50 VA. J. INT'L L. 795, 798 (2010) (arguing that "IHL represents a carefully thought out balance between the principles of military necessity and humanity. Every one of its rules constitutes a dialectical compromise between these two opposing forces").

a timing question: Has the time come for a revised military necessity? The discussion in Part 1.4 answers positively, arguing that the combined effects of the changes in the pattern of modern wars and in the social attitudes toward them, the development of the humanistic approach to the laws of war and the introduction of new weapons and intelligence technology can all lead currently to new constraining paradigms in military thinking. Part 1.5 offers concluding remarks related to the new suggested equilibrium between humanity and military necessity.

1.1 Military Professionalism: Constraining Brute Force Enhances Military Effectiveness

Constraining the brute force of a military is in its own self-interest and enhances its operational effectiveness. Effectiveness and efficiency in operation is a recognized professional military requirement. All belligerent activities ought to be professionally necessary or otherwise avoided. The military requirement of operational effectiveness, as demonstrated in the targeting process and priorities, will be used to demonstrate the inherent constraining effects of military professionalism. Indeed, this is mainly a utilitarian requirement, not contingent upon reciprocity, as military resources will always be scarce. For example, the limited amount of ammunition in general, of sophisticated precise ammunition in particular—which is even scarcer due to its relatively high price—requires a trained soldier to choose his or her targets carefully. Professionally speaking, there is no room for "wasted" shots or carelessness in targeting. Only precise shooting, consistent with targeting priorities, can be considered professionally "legitimate," and there can be no tolerance of ineffective use of military resources. The adaption of ends to the means and the conservation of military energy for its designated purposes requires the exercise of military force in measured dosage so as not to waste it by using excessive force for unrelated (or secondary) purposes:

> Rational and effective military organizations recognize proportionality not only as part of the laws of war but also as part of their own combat doctrine—except it is called economy of force . . . Economy of force is defined in US Army Field Manual 3-0, Operations . . . The British and Commonwealth armies call this principle economy of effort. The Soviet Union defined it as adapting the end to the means. However identified, the principle holds that military forces should

> concentrate effort in the most rational, economic, and limited way, to free up resources for other undertakings. As such, it makes little military sense to use force or effort out of proportion to the objective sought, or beyond military necessity.[14]

The effectiveness requirement applies at all levels of battle: tactical, operational, and strategic. The U.S. armed forces, for example, have nine professional principles of war,[15] requiring effective and coordinated military operations. For example, the objective principle stipulates "direct[ing] every military operation toward a clearly defined, decisive, and attainable objective"; the offensive principle states that "offensive action is the most effective and decisive way to achieve a clearly defined objective"; mass requires concentrating "the effects of combat power at the decisive place and time"; and the economy of force dictates employing all combat power available in the most effective way, noting that the "[e]ffective Maneuver keeps enemy forces off balance."[16] Indeed, there are no universally agreed principles of war.[17] As trained militaries are utilitarian and mission-oriented, however, effectiveness and efficiency are essentially expected of them.[18]

The effectiveness requirement rationalizes, for example, the American military's effects-based operational doctrine. This doctrine calls for achieving the strategic goals of a military campaign by applying military levers not for the sake of destruction per se, but rather to create (indirect and cascading) effects that break the "enemy as a system."[19] The desire for a coherent and effective operational approach has led the American military

---

14. Jonathan F. Keiler, *The End of Proportionality*, 39 PARAMETERS 53, 58–59 (2009).

15. U.S. DEP'T OF THE ARMY, FIELD MANUAL 3-0, OPERATIONS (Feb. 27, 2008) appendix A, para. A-1 [hereinafter FM 3-0].

16. *Id.*, at A-1–A-2.

17. For a comparative view of the principles of war and the way they have diverged among various armies in modern times, *see, e.g.*, Jan Angstrom & J.J. Widen, *Adopting a Recipe for Success: Modern Armed Forces and the Institutionalization of the Principles of War*, 31 COMP. STRATEGY 263 (2012). For an elaborated presentation of the main principles common to most militaries, *see* the discussion *infra*, text accompanying Chapter 2 notes 92–119.

18. *See generally*, Keiler, *supra* note 14.

19. *See, e.g.*, DIMA ADAMSKY, THE CULTURE OF MILITARY INNOVATION 106 (2010). Indeed, the effects-based operation doctrine, in general, and its application, in particular, are controversial (the U.S. army and navy seem to have been much less enthusiastic about adopting it than the air force). *See, e.g.*, James N. Mattis, *USJFCOM Commander's Guidance for Effects-based Operations*, 38 PARAMETERS 18 (2008); *cf.* Tomislav Z. Ruby, *Effects-Based Operations: More Important than Ever*, 38 PARAMETERS 26 (2008).

recently to subject itself to the self-imposed utilitarian effects-based restrictions of the counterinsurgency doctrine. This doctrine imposes unilateral professional constraints on counterinsurgency operations, aimed at minimizing civilian suffering and casualties: "In a COIN [counter-insurgency doctrine] environment, it is vital for commanders to adopt appropriate and measured levels of force and apply that force precisely so that it accomplishes the mission without causing unnecessary loss of life or suffering."[20] This "internal" self-imposed doctrine dictates greater constraints to American combatants than those "externally" required by the laws of armed conflict.[21] The doctrine "requires Soldiers and Marines to be ready both to fight and to build"[22] and, from a purely professional military perspective, points at the following paradoxes: "Sometimes, the more force is used, the less effective it is" or "[s]ome of the best weapons against counterinsurgents do not shoot."[23] The doctrine obliges soldiers and marines to accept greater risk to minimize harm to noncombatants: "This risk taking is an essential part of the Warrior Ethos."[24] Indeed, constraining brutality is in the self-interest of a professional trained military—it reflects its competence and discipline—and it is motivated by utilitarian concerns as well as moral and ethical ones.[25] After all, it was article 16 of the Lieber Code that stated a century and a half ago: "Military necessity does not admit of cruelty . . . [it] does not include any act of hostility which makes the return to peace unnecessarily difficult."[26]

From a legal perspective, however, restrictions stemming from moral or utilitarian professional considerations, which were not infused into the

---

20. U.S. Dep't of the Army, Field Manual 3–24, Counterinsurgency para. 1-142 (University of Chicago Press ed., 2007) [hereinafter FM 3-24].

21. *Cf.* Kenneth Watkin's argument that the restrictions on the use of force in COIN are legal ones, due to the "military advantage" gained by limiting civilian casualties. Kenneth Watkin, Fighting at the Legal Boundaries: Controlling the Use of Force in Contemporary Conflict 256–57 (2016).

22. FM 3-24, *supra* note 20, at para. 1-105.

23. *Id.*, para. 1-150 (headline) and para. 1-153 (headline); "Arguably, the decisive battle is for the people's minds; . . . Particularly after security has been achieved, dollars and ballots will have more important effects than bombs and bullets." *Id.*

24. *Id.*, para. 7-21.

25. *See supra* text accompanying the Introduction note 90.

26. U.S. War Dep't, General Order No. 100: Instructions for the Government of Armies of the United States in the Field, Apr. 24, 1863, http://avalon.law.yale.edu/19th_century/lieber.asp (last visited Aug. 16, 2017). [hereinafter Lieber Code].

prevailing system as specific legal norms (or custom), are almost irrelevant. Currently, any shot in the battlefield aimed against a combatant is generally lawful and could be legally justified as necessary. The mere fact that the target has "enough" formal military attributes usually justifies its targeting. In fact, it is currently lawful to shoot any combatant "freely" in the battlefield, unless specifically forbidden by law (for example, wounded soldiers or prisoners of war), and proportional civilian collateral damage stemming from the targeting process is acceptable too. The paradox, then, is clear. Although the military profession imposes its own internal constraints—requiring limited and precise shooting—the current legal requirement is less demanding. Targets legally approved by military lawyers might be considered irrelevant to, or ineffective for, the military campaign by the commanders in the field. Embarrassingly, economic considerations prevail over the legal ones in the taking and saving of lives.

This paradox is a direct consequence of the limits of the current law and, to a large extent, the impotency of the necessity principle. The following discussion will argue that although this principle is considered one of the pillars of the current construction of the law of armed conflict, its constraining effect is hollow and weak, substantially contributing to the instability of this regime.

1.2 The Prevailing Necessity Principle: A Hollow Rule and Its Effects

The necessity principle at the moment primarily pays lip service to the constraining function it was originally intended to fulfill, justifying, in fact, almost any belligerent activity. Historically, it did impose residual constraints upon the scope of lawful destruction during wartime. Burrus Carnahan illustrates these precedential constraints using President Abraham Lincoln's general order not to destroy "private property" in the latter stages of the Civil War and the fact that during most of the Korean War damaging the food supply by attacking irrigation dams in North Korea was not considered a military necessity.[27] Referring to this historic restrictive function, which "seems to have been forgotten," he then concludes that "military necessity is widely regarded today as an insidious

---

27. Burrus M. Carnahan, *Lincoln, Lieber and the Laws of War: The Origins and Limits of the Principle of Military Necessity*, 92 AM. J. INT'L L. 213, 229 (1998).

doctrine invoked to justify almost any outrage. As a result, the principle has not been allowed to play the creative role that it is capable of playing."[28] Indeed, when it comes to constraining brute military force, the necessity principle, as a legal rule, has almost no actual validity.

Currently, excessive force is restricted only by specific rules of the law, and the general principle seems to have lost its vitality and has not been applied independently. The International Committee of the Red Cross (ICRC) admits that "[i]n classic large-scale confrontations between well-equipped and organized armed forces or groups, the principles of military necessity and of humanity are unlikely to restrict the use of force against legitimate military targets beyond what is already required by specific provisions of IHL."[29] Eyal Benvenisti, too, concludes that "the traditional *in bello* proportionality analysis never required the attacker to explain the necessity of attaining the military objective; the necessity of such action was taken for granted."[30] The current impotency of the necessity principle might be explained by its perception by militaries as a nuisance, an additional "external" legal requirement, imposed upon soldiers. Militaries, like other bureaucratic organizations, are well trained to get rid of external annoyances.

Indeed, the current reality, in which the professional considerations and financial constraints experienced by an army dictate, as mentioned earlier, a higher threshold for "justified killing" than the legal one, is quite embarrassing and seems unacceptable. The current legal rules appear to turn a blind eye to the same reality in which soldiers are required by their own profession to open their eyes wide. Furthermore, this embarrassment is aggravated by the prevailing rule that requires a higher legal threshold (in terms of effectiveness) for targeting objects than combatants. Article 52(2) of Additional Protocol I strictly legalizes the targeting of military objects "which by their nature, location, purpose or use make an effective

---

28. *Id.* at 230.

29. International Committee of the Red Cross [ICRC], *Interpretive Guidance on the Notion of Direct Participation in Hostilities Under International Humanitarian Law* 80 (2009) [hereinafter, ICRC Guide] https://www.icrc.org/eng/assets/files/other/icrc-002-0990.pdf (last visited Apr. 24, 2016). The ICRC does note, however, that the principle's restraining function is still valid when a party to a conflict exercises effective territorial control in a non-international armed conflict and has a "duty to arrest" suspected belligerents unless circumstances do not allow it. *Id.* at 81.

30. Eyal Benvenisti, *Rethinking the Divide Between* Jus ad Bellum *and* Jus in Bello *in Warfare Against Nonstate Actors*, 34 YALE J. INT'L L. 541, 544 (2009).

contribution to military action and whose total or partial destruction, capture or neutralization, in the circumstances ruling at the time, offers a definite military advantage."[31] Although the "effective contribution to military action" is a precondition for lawful targeting of an object, soldiers' lives are cheaper. Even ineffective soldiers, the taking of whose lives does not offer a "definite military advantage," are currently considered, in practice, lawful targets.[32] The necessity of their being killed is taken for granted. No professional challenge, in terms of examining effectiveness, is required when it comes to killing them. Only the targeting of objects seems to pose such a challenge.

Substantiating the necessity requirement requires the use of tools taken from the military profession. Introducing professional military standards would strengthen this principle by infusing substantial constraining elements into it, as originally intended but currently lacking. The paradox that economic considerations are often much more restrictive of taking lives than the permissive legal considerations can be resolved by revisiting the necessity principle and imparting to this currently hollow concept a new vitality, based upon professional standards that are generally common to modern trained militaries (usually of liberal states). These inherent standards should serve as an important yardstick to be used when gauging the necessity of belligerent activities. Introducing it to the law of armed conflict would add another vital force, in the constraint of brute force and the reduction of war's hazards. Furthermore, revitalizing the necessity principle would affect the intrinsic balance of the prevailing legal norms and promote the judgment of law-abiding states' military activities.

1.3 The Effects of Transforming Professional Military Standards into Legal Norms

1.3.1 "If It Ain't Broke Don't Fix It": Why Transform Self-Imposed and Voluntarily Respected Professional Standards into Legal Norms?

The call for the transformation of self-imposed professional constraining standards into legal norms invites a preliminary question. If professional

31. API, *supra* note 10, art. 52(2).

32. *Cf.* the requirement *id.*, arts. 51(5)(b) and 57(2)(a)(iii) to assess military advantage under the "proportionality" assessment when collateral damage to civilians is being considered.

standards have their own internal effect of constraining the exercise of military force, why transform them into legal rules? If, as suggested, trained militaries tend to respect this internal professional restraint, there should be no need or room, prima facie, for external legal intervention. There seems to be no reason to turn autonomously working and effective rules into mandatory norms. Furthermore, such a transformation is liable to have a counter-effect: the efficient self-observed professional standard might come to be perceived by soldiers as yet another external and ineffective nuisance that ought to, and can, be bypassed.

The suggested legal transformation would have a dual effect upon the law of armed conflict that could not be attained by professional or ethical standards alone. The first effect, relating to war's casualties, would be to restrict the potential damage that might be caused both intentionally (to combatants and to military objectives) and unintentionally, collaterally (to noncombatants). It requires elevating the legal threshold for targeting by revisiting the necessity principle, introducing into it professional restraints against the use of excessive military force. The second relates to the potential injurers—the exercisers of military force—whose brutality could be restricted if professional standards were to be turned into legal norms. Indeed, there are relevant players in the battle zone who are either not obliged by the professional military standards or are unwilling to accept and respect them. The first group consists of the civilian political echelon, which currently is not directly obliged by professional military standards, and the second consists of militaries (or parts of them), which still believe in the advantages of exercising brutal force to achieve their aims and advantages. Before these two direct effects are introduced, a preliminary discussion is offered that relates to the institutional and substantive challenges of the suggested transformation.

1.3.2 The Institutional and Substantive Challenges

Advancing military professionalism to the forefront of the war-related legal discourse would have both institutional and substantive aspects. Institutionally, under the current legal approach, as reflected through the prism of judicial decisions and academic writers, it is the "outsiders"—the normative judicial players such as nongovernmental organizations (NGOs), judges, and advocates—who are the main watchdogs of the war arena: "If military necessity were to prevail completely, no limitation of any kind would have been imposed on the freedom of action of belligerent states: *à la guerre comme à la guerre.*"[33] Under this common approach, the responsibility of the "insiders"—the main players on the field, namely the soldiers and their commanders—has been minimized to their own criminal responsibility or their state's when such applies. Except for this important—yet, in many cases, residual—responsibility,[34] soldiers apparently cannot be relied upon to restrain their own activities, as far as the humanitarian issues are concerned. The checks and balances applying to wartime activities are apparently shaped in such a way that it is "their" (the soldiers') responsibility to kill and damage in war and it is "our" (the judicial player's or NGO's) duty to stop them, whenever appropriate. If in time of crisis all means may be used to achieve military goals, soldiers may be portrayed, under such a common approach, as a bunch of potential criminals: murderers, plunderers, or rapists. As anything can be expected in wartime, it is only the legal system that brings them back to the path of humanity by establishing a legal threshold of constraint.

A weaker, softer version of such a paternalistic approach could be deduced from the Supreme Court of Israel's ruling with regard to the ban on the use of torture in security interrogations, stating that a democracy must sometimes fight its non-law-abiding adversary "with one hand tied behind its back."[35] Under the common perception, with which the ruling seems to be consistent, imposing restrictions on the inherent brutality

---

33. Yoram Dinstein, The Conduct of Hostilities 16 (2004). *Cf.* his later argument: "Military commanders are often the first to understand that their duties can be discharged without causing pointless torment." *Id.*, at 17. The French proverb, loosely translated as "in war as in war," is often likened to the English phrase "all is fair in love and war." *See generally*, Luc Reydams, *A la guerre comme à la guerre: Patterns of Armed Conflict, Humanitarian Law Responses and New Challenges*, 88 (864) Int'l Rev. Red Cross 729 (2006).

34. Indeed, such an approach is well rooted in military culture. On the first page of his book, *On War*, von Clausewitz defines war as "an act of force to compel our enemy to do our will. Force, to counter opposing force, equips itself with the inventions of art and science. Attached to force are certain self-imposed, imperceptible limitations hardly worth mentioning, known as international law and custom, but they scarcely weaken it. Force—that is, physical force, for moral force has no existence save as expressed in the state and the law—is thus the means of war; to impose our will on the enemy is its object." Carl Von Clausewitz, On War 75 (Michael Eliot Howard & Peter Paret trans., indexed ed. 1984). Von Clausewitz's disdain for the ethical aspects and the effects of international law in wartime was inspired, inter alia, by Machiavelli's legacy, holding that national self-interests are "governed by considerations of raison d'etat, and are dominated by the direct and implied use of force." Azar Gat, The Origins of Military Thought: From the Enlightenment to Clausewitz 240 (1989).

35. HCJ 5100/94, *The Public Committee Against Torture v. The Government of Israel and Others* (1999), 53(4) PD 817, [39] (Isr.).

of military force requires an external legal force. The tied hand reflects brute military force's intrinsic lack of self-restraint—it is therefore lawful to exercise military force only partially, with the remaining free hand.

Common to such approaches is their paternalistic attitude toward the military profession and behavior. Indeed, one might be cautious in light of militaries' humanitarian record, which, in many cases, is very poor. The problematic thing, however, is the actual steps taken to address the danger, which are contrary to the prevailing moral and professional principles of responsibility and accountability from anyone who exercises force, of whatever kind. Any power holder is obliged, under well-rooted moral and professional rules, to constrain it. A truck driver is in charge of both the accelerator and the brake pedal, and this professional convention applies as well to any law enforcement officer. When it comes to belligerent activities, soldiers too should be morally and professionally accountable for the exercise and constraint of their force. The traditional legal approach does not seem to accept this convention (but for its criminal aspects). When it comes to military necessity, it assumes that no internal professional constraints—in fact, "no limitation of any kind"—are imposed upon soldiers.[36] This approach—which leaves insufficient room and, in some cases, none at all for military professionalism and the soldier's own ethics—has its consequences. It renounces an important brake on aggression and transgression in wartime. It places all (or most) of the burden upon external, legal brakes, ignoring the internal—moral and professional—checks.

That there is excessive brutality in many (or even most) military campaigns may be an established fact; it would be a mistake, however, to attribute it to the military's inherent requirements and virtues. From a military perspective, the source of this brutality is mainly external. It may derive from the ideological, psychological, religious, or cultural motives of soldiers (or a combination thereof); none of these, however, are inherent to the modern military profession. Certainly, though, these external sources of military brutality may be manipulated by some militaries by infusing them into their soldiers' spirit and actual behavior, but "it is incompetence, above all, that breeds brutality. . . . well-trained and well-disciplined armies

36. From this perspective, the duties of commanders, under API, *supra* note 10, arts. 86–87 (to report, prevent, and suppress breaches), are also perceived as an external legal brake.

are less brutal—and their officers and soldiers are less likely to think that brutality is necessary for victory."[37]

The assumption that militaries are brutal by their very nature is not limited to outside observers of the military establishment and apparatus. Indeed, there may be "old-fashioned militaries"—and there are soldiers probably in contemporary militaries—who even now believe in exercising excessive force and brutality as a professional imperative. In their beliefs and practices, they are still following the legacy of total war as advocated by Carl von Clausewitz and Napoleon. This total war perception has two dimensions. One advocates attacking civilian life and property,[38] whereas the other relates to the annihilation of the adversary's military. Indeed, there are currently brutal militaries that don't obey the distinction rule. They respect neither the outlawing of the intended targeting of civilians nor the request to minimize the collateral damage that can lawfully occur to them. Such unlawful militaries' activities are beyond the scope of this book's discussion, which presupposes abidance by the distinction rule. Contemporary militaries that aim at civilians, intentionally targeting them and their property, are using them as a means to win a war. The goal of their brutality is usually to stir up fear and panic in their adversary's civilian society, damaging both their morale and their physical war effort. Indeed, there are strong "internal" utilitarian and professional reasons not to endorse such a pattern, mainly due to its counter-effect, but at this stage of the discussion it is sufficient to focus upon the current illegality of such an attack. Under the prevailing legal rules, such brutal militaries are no longer acting in their military capacity, but as an organized terrorist group. They are engaging in terrorist activity. The fact that they are headed by governments, controlled by their commanders, wear military uniforms, and use military tools does not impart to their activities a professional military character. Therefore, the call in this chapter for the adoption of military

37. Michael Walzer, *Coda: Can the Good Guys Win?*, 24 EUR. J. INT'L L. 433, 442 (2013). *See also* Ohlin and May's analysis of Lieber's principle of necessity: "The principle of necessity . . . outlaws all actions *unrelated* to the war aim, such as killing inspired by pure hatred or vengeance alone. These actions have no role to play in the decisions of the professional soldier." JENS DAVID OHLIN & LARRY MAY, NECESSITY IN INTERNATIONAL LAW 98 (2016).

38. Attacking civilians is exemplified, for example, by Moltke's bombardment of Paris in 1870 and General William Sherman's "Atlanta campaign" and burning of the city during the American Civil War. *See infra* text accompanying Chapter 3 notes 40–50, and *see generally* MICHAEL HOWARD, THE FRANCO-PRUSSIAN WAR 352 (2d ed. 2001); GEOFFREY BEST, HUMANITY IN WARFARE: THE MODERN HISTORY OF THE INTERNATIONAL LAW OF ARMED CONFLICT 207–11 (1983).

professionalism as a legal tool relates only to the professional military capacity, aimed against military objects. Indeed, this capacity too might trigger excessive brutality, aimed lawfully at, and calling for, the utilization of (almost) all means against combatants and the destruction of "dual-use objects."[39] Such activity would be consistent with the military dimension of total war. It will be argued, however, that though it may be currently legal, such an all-out decisive war is not always perceived as professional or effective by the standards of well-trained militaries.

The intrinsic interest of a professionally trained military is to restrict these brutal forces—to voluntarily tie any brutal hands by way of self-imposed restrictions—and channel all of its force and energy into fulfilling its mission and objectives. The "tied hand" belongs to the incompetent, the unprofessional, or the psychopath; professional soldiers have both hands left free to fulfill their military mission. Indeed, a well-trained and disciplined military has, prima facie, only a residual need for an external force (that is, the judicial system) to appropriate this inherent task of internalizing professional standards.

The following discussion will concentrate on the positive effects of transforming professional constraining standards into legal norms, which could not be attained by professional—yet voluntarily enforced—standards alone. (Though the current discussion is restricted to the effects of the suggested transformation upon the law of armed conflict, it obviously might affect international criminal law as well.) The first direct effect relates to war's casualties, restricting the potential damage caused to both intentional and unintentional-collateral targets. The second direct effect, to be discussed later, relates to the exercisers of military force—the civilian leaders or the militaries (or parts of them) who still believe in the advantages of exercising brutal force to achieve their aims—whose potential brutality would be restricted if professional standards were to become legal norms.

1.3.3 The Suggested Effect upon Combatants: Soldiers' Lives Should Matter

Under the prevailing legal paradigm, all classes of soldiers (except medical personnel and chaplains) are considered to be lawful targets. Soldiers, as a collective, are considered legitimate targets so long as they are "in the war

---

39. *See infra* text accompanying note 81.

game."[40] The underlying rationale behind this classification is the notion that soldiers as a class (unless hors de combat) threaten their opponent's army, either actually or potentially. It is this assumption that in fact allows adversaries to circumvent the necessity principle with regard to combatants by designating all of them as necessary military targets. Indeed, "[i]n reliance on a status-based rule of distinction, soldiers need not engage in a costly and dangerous process of ascertaining the merits of each individual target."[41] Military professionalism and practice does, however, require an assessment of the "merits" of a target in terms of targeting priorities, based mainly upon types of units and their function.

The classification of all soldiers as a collective lawful targeted group has its own unjust cost. Most soldiers in any military are not actual combatants.[42] Yet all non-combat soldiers working in support roles are considered, prima facie, a lawful (necessary) target in the eyes of their adversaries, so long as they are still in service. In this matter, regarding the sub-classification of soldiers, the law of armed conflict has actually regressed. Historically, article 3 of the 1907 Hague Regulations gave legal effect to this well-known phenomenon of subclasses of soldiers by stating that "[t]he armed forces of the belligerent parties may consist of combatants and non-combatants." (Effectively, though, "both have a right to be treated as prisoners of war").[43] Additional Protocol I's current approach differs from this one, with the ICRC's commentary presenting the prevailing rule, preferring to ignore the actual relevancy of the soldiers' class to their military war effort: "In fact, in any army there are numerous important categories of soldiers whose foremost or normal task has little to do

---

40. API, *supra* note 10, art. 43(2).

41. Blum, *The Dispensable Lives of Soldiers, supra* note 5, at 120.

42. A recent McKinsey report placed the "tooth-to-tail" ratio (the number of combatant soldiers out of the total military force) in the U.S. military at 23 percent, the United Kingdom at 38 percent, China at 34 percent, France at 24 percent, Russia at 28 percent, and Germany at 28 percent. *See* McKinsey Incorporated, *Special Issue: Defense—Lessons from around the world: Benchmarking Performance in Defense*, 5 McKinsey on Government 3–4, specifically exhibit 3 (2010), www.mckinsey.com/~/media/McKinsey/dotcom/client_service/Public%20Sector/PDFS/McK%20on%20Govt/Defense/MoG_benchmarking_v9.ashx (last visited July 2, 2015).

43. Hague Convention (IV) Respecting the Laws and Customs of War and its Annex: Regulations Concerning the Laws and Customs of War on Land, Oct. 18, 1907, 187 C.T.S. 227, art. 3 [hereinafter 1907 Hague Regulations].

with firing weapons . . . All members of the armed forces are combatants, and only members of the armed forces are combatants."[44]

For the sake of the current discussion, however, this classification—which allows the killing of all of the adversary's soldiers as a group, without reference to the level of personal threat they represent—is taken as a given. What it calls for, though, is the introduction of a targeting-constraining test, based upon the effective operational contribution of units, to the *in bello* necessity. In order to effectively subdue an adversary, there is absolutely no need to kill all of its soldiers. Indeed, this notion is the legacy of the St. Petersburg Declaration of 1868: "That the only legitimate object which States should endeavour to accomplish during war is to weaken the military forces of the enemy; That for this purpose it is sufficient to disable the greatest possible number of men."[45] From this restrained perspective, the prevailing classification of combatants is challenged. The suggested necessity requirement would not suffice with the current *in bello* constraints upon bloodshed, which are limited mainly to the prohibition of intended—or "excessive" collateral—killing of civilians. (Neither would it rely upon the *ad bellum* proportionality requirement—aimed at determining what is considered proportionate in response to an "armed attack"—which might have affected the operational scope of a military, had it been agreed upon.[46]) Indeed, it would challenge the prevailing *in bello* distinction rule, classifying all soldiers as the "legitimized dead." Military force in general, targeting in particular, should be lawful only to the extent that it is effectively necessary for achieving a given military advantage. This means that the current carte blanche in regard to killing soldiers should be rejected. The killing of soldiers should not be allowed based simply upon

44. Jean de Preux, *Additional Protocol I Article 43—Occupants of Aircraft*, *in* COMMENTARY ON THE ADDITIONAL PROTOCOLS OF 8 JUNE 1977 TO THE GENEVA CONVENTIONS OF 12 AUGUST 1949, at 515, para. 1677 (Claude Pilloud et al. eds., 1987). Indeed, at the Conference of Government Experts, dealing with the draft of the Geneva Convention (III), it was discussed whether to adhere to the Hague Regulations by stating that the term "armed forces," those entitled to be treated as prisoners of war, covers both combatants and noncombatants: "It was finally considered that this statement was usually implicit in any general reference to armed forces, and moreover the matter had raised almost no difficulties during the Second World War." 3 JEAN S. PICTET, COMMENTARY ON THE GENEVA CONVENTIONS OF 12 AUGUST 1949, at 51 (1960).

45. Declaration Renouncing the Use, in Time of War, of Explosive Projectiles under 400 Grammes Weight, Saint Petersburg, 29 November–11 December 1868, www.icrc.org/IHL.nsf/FULL/130?OpenDocument (last visited Feb. 23, 2015) [hereinafter the St. Petersburg Declaration].

46. *See infra* the conflicting views regarding the scope of the requirement of proportionality in the exercise of self-defense, text accompanying Chapter 3 notes 110–112.

their indiscriminate classification as legitimate targets. Instead, it should be limited in accordance with the merits of a given conflict and the specific attributes of the military adversaries involved and their doctrines, which, in fact, define the specific function of their units. These are the prevailing professional considerations underlying the exercise of military power in general, targeting policy and priorities in particular, by a skilled military in a given campaign. The gap between the legal paradigm's assignment of a socialist equality to all soldiers and military professionalism, which does not accept this axiom on utilitarian grounds and requires further classification, should be bridged. The law of armed conflict cannot continue to turn a blind eye to the inequality of soldiers in reality.

Exercising the suggested criterion of operational effectiveness would be dependent upon the relevancy and effectiveness of given military units in a specific campaign. It is not the soldiers' specific personal role, level of training, or location that absolutely matters but, mainly, their unit's relevancy to the military operation. There might be cooks, "naked soldiers" taking a bath or swimming in a pool[47] or even "real fighters" who are ineffective or irrelevant in some campaign scenarios—for example, located in a distant border checkpoint that has no relevance to, or effect upon, the given campaign—whereas, in other cases, soldiers in similar roles, but in different units, may directly contribute to the success or failure of the campaign. The latter include the case of the chef of a combat battalion who prepares the "last meal" before a battle or that of the fighters (or military police) at a distant border crossing who are located there with their unit to allow and expedite the transfer of precious supplies, ammunition, and reinforcements directly to the front. The prevailing rule ignores the functional factor and prefers to adopt the entire class's entitlement to use weapons as the decisive element. In actual fighting, distinction is a crucial function in targeting, based mainly upon the military's priorities and the function of its adversary's units, which are much more important than soldiers' abstract entitlements. It is this unit-based functional criterion that I suggest be incorporated into the law of armed conflict by revisiting the distinction rule. Indeed, this is a division into subclasses or a bifurcated rule of distinction, based upon distinguishing units within the soldiers' class, which depends upon their importance and classification in a given

---

47. Michael Walzer, Just and Unjust Wars 138–43 (4th ed. 2006).

campaign's circumstances. Ineffective combatants' units should not be targeted; only effective ones should represent lawful targets.

The suggested unit-based distinction differs, to some extent, from Gabriella Blum's call for revising the distinction rule. She offers a reinterpretation of the principle of distinction, suggesting that the status-based classification be complemented by a test of threat. In her view, with which I totally agree, combatants who pose no real threat in their function should be spared from direct attack.[48] However, I cannot embrace her call for an individual-level inquiry based upon the assessment of the individual threat emanating from each particular combatant. She employs the term "threat" in this context "to denote something close to the 'guilt' or 'involvement' test that has been employed by governments in the war on terrorism."[49] The sub-classification of combatants suggested here differs from Blum's individual inquiry. The individual-level threat analysis of each combatant, however morally attractive, does not seem to be practical in wartime due to intelligence resource constraints.[50] Furthermore, the actual threat from an individual soldier derives, to a large extent, from the function of the military unit (subclass) he or she is affiliated with during a given campaign. In the usual case, it is not the soldier, per se, who creates the threat, but rather the function of the soldier's unit. Actual fighting differs from what is portrayed in the "Rambo" movies—in the usual case, it is not dependent upon one man's performance.

In a given military scenario, implementation of the suggested sub-classification of soldiers by the relevancy and operational effectiveness of their units (and their targeting necessity) may pose a dilemma. The difficulties are mainly due to a shortage of intelligence and problems with

---

48. Blum, *The Dispensable Lives of Soldiers, supra* note 5, at 120. The reinterpretation of the principle of distinction would be followed, on her recommendation, by a reinterpretation of the principle of military necessity, introducing a least-harmful means test, under which an alternative of capture or disabling of the enemy would be preferred to killing, whenever feasible. Ohlin and May propose a more moderate necessity principle limiting, when it is not necessary, the use of lethal force to accomplish military objectives: "[S]oldiers [should] be not only afforded the right not to suffer unnecessarily but also the right not to be killed unnecessarily." Ohlin & May, *supra* note 37, at 184.

49. Blum, *The Dispensable Lives of Soldiers, supra* note 5, at 155. Three dimensions of the suggested "threat analysis," derived from individual-level determination, are suggested by her: role (e.g., a military cook), time (a sleeping or bathing pilot), and geography (soldiers playing soccer in a civilian neighborhood). *Id.* at 155–60.

50. Indeed, the applicability of Blum's approach is more likely in asymmetric conflicts where many operations are of the law enforcement type.

its interpretation, although this is a regular phenomenon in the battlefield and does not change the utilitarian and morality-based, professional subdistinction principle. Indeed, "war is the realm of uncertainty," as suggested by von Clausewitz,[51] and the fog of war triggers inherent cases of doubt on the battlefield. In case of reasonable doubt, the traditional distinction rule should have a say. Although the desire to spare noncombatants' lives, a substantial pole of the current system, dictates that in cases of doubt noncombatants should be protected,[52] military necessity might nonetheless enable the targeting of "doubtful effective combatants." Indeed, this reflects the difference between the absolute ban on intended killing of noncombatants and the allowed but unnecessary killing of irrelevant, ineffective soldiers.

The suggested revised distinction rule, based upon the bifurcation into subclasses of military units pursuant to their military effectiveness, will be demonstrated by the case of the air bombardment on Highway 80 during the First Gulf War of the retreating columns of Iraqi soldiers from Kuwait to Basra, mainly on the night of February 26–27, 1991. The objectives of the First Gulf War, as outlined by American National Security Directive 54, dated January 15, 1991, were to force Iraq to withdraw from Kuwait, restore the Kuwaiti legitimate government, and promote security and stability in the Gulf.[53] Taking this strategic aim as well as the operational and tactical "military advantage" to be gained from the U.S. military campaign as given, was it necessary to bomb and kill these retreating soldiers? Under the suggested approach, the answer would be dependent on the extent to which these soldiers' units (in whole or in part) were relevant to the remaining Iraqi campaign and how effective they were after they withdrew. This was not an unresolvable problem. The coalition's intelligence knew the answers (at least, in substantial part) in real time; after all, this was one of its main tasks.

Indeed, in order to assess the necessity of targeting the retreating soldiers in the case of the "Highway of Death," the role played by, and the effectiveness of, those retreating soldiers would have to be evaluated. Such

51. Von Clausewitz, *supra* note 34, at 101.

52. API, *supra* note 10, art. 50(1).

53. *See* White House, National Security Directive 54 (Jan. 15, 1991) bush41library.tamu.edu/files/nsd/nsd54.pdf (last visited Feb. 23, 2015); *see also* President George H.W. Bush, Address to the Nation Announcing Allied Military Action in the Persian Gulf (Jan. 16, 1991), www.presidency.ucsb.edu/ws/?pid=19222 (last visited Feb. 23, 2015).

an assessment could be made based upon, inter alia, the Iraqi army's military doctrine, in general, and its troops' actual deployment during the Gulf War, in particular. Traditional Soviet military doctrine might serve as a reference for this inquiry (indeed, the degree to which the Iraqi military adhered to Soviet military doctrine is a matter of controversy[54] and therefore serves here merely as a reference). The Russian defense doctrine espoused several lines of defense set up to meet advancing enemy forces. The first line consisted of several relatively small units and obstacles, followed by a somewhat stronger line of defensive strongholds. Behind this line lay the bulk of the defender's forces, constituting the main defensive zone, followed by a rear defensive zone.[55] Testing this doctrine (as a reference) in the case of the Iraqi forces in the Gulf War would mean that the forward lines close to the border would have had to be manned by divisions of lower quality, which had been assigned some very limited military missions, mainly to provide real-time intelligence, weaken advancing enemy forces, and absorb the initial shock of the attack and channel their units to areas prioritized by the Iraqi high command. This might actually have been the case, as indicated by the fact that the Iraqi army chose to deploy along the border with Kuwait most of its weaker and less effective divisions, which had only a 57 percent manning rate.[56]

The necessity of targeting these forces retreating from the border on the "Highway of Death" is therefore dependent on their actual role once bypassed. If these soldiers were only meant to serve as shock absorbers and delay advancing forces, they were cannon fodder—the cheapest cards in Saddam's pocket—and he was keeping his most trained and qualified soldiers, the Republican Guards, somewhere else in the rear.[57] If that was

---

54. The dilemma is what lesson can be derived from the reliance of the Iraqi army on Soviet arms and supplies regarding its military doctrine. Thus, some experts claim that Iraqi military doctrine was comprised of a combination of British and Soviet doctrines supplemented by Iraqi additions. *See, e.g.*, Michael Eisenstadt & Kenneth M. Pollack, *Armies of Snow and Armies of Sand: The Impact of Soviet Military Doctrine on Arab Armies*, 55 Middle E. J. 549 (2001); Kenneth M. Pollack, Arabs At War: Military Effectivenesss 1948–1991, at 148–267 (2002).

55. Richard W. Harrison, The Russian Way of War: Operational Art 1904–1940, at 193 (2001) and *see infra* Chapter 2 note 81.

56. Anthony H. Cordesman & Richard R. Wagner, The Lessons of Modern War, Vol. IV: The Gulf War 115 (1996).

57. On Republican Guard deployment, *see id.* at 653. It should be noted, however, that the Republican Guards, Iraq's elite forces originally meant to protect the capital and president, had grown in size and were also deployed to Kuwait, albeit in separate locations, allowing

the case, once their job as shock absorbers was concluded, it was no longer necessary to target them from a military perspective, due to their future irrelevancy on the battlefield. However, if these soldiers were meant to retreat and reinforce the deeper lines of defense, then they were still an effective player in the battlefield and a viable and necessary target. An interesting—yet inconclusive—method to ascertain how the Allied forces saw these soldiers is by examining the ammunition used to target them. The use of precise and more expensive ammunition by Allied forces could indicate the importance of those forces in their eyes (of course, subject to the scattering and other attributes of the target and available ammunition). Indeed, this could be another example of the embarrassing phenomenon whereby tracking the economics of war leads to a much better moral result than that offered by the prevailing legal rules.

Morally speaking, and under the suggested reading of necessity, the killing of the retreating soldiers could be seen as doubtful (subject to the specific circumstances discussed earlier); yet under the prevailing rules, there seems to be no real doubt concerning its legality. The current rule is mechanical, based upon mere classification of combatants as targets: "There can be no question that the column was a legitimate target. It comprised enemy soldiers who had not surrendered."[58] However, the suggested rule, a qualitative-functional one, requires elevating the legal threshold for lawful killing by revisiting the necessity principle. It would mean confronting the Allied forces with the crucial question—the answer to which was probably well known to their intelligence—which is not related to the retreating soldiers' formal classification, but rather to their relevance: To what extent did their targeting serve the Allies' real military objectives?

1.3.4 The Suggested Effect upon Noncombatants: Reducing the Lawful Collateral Damage

Introducing professional military standards into the prevailing law of armed conflict would also substantially affect the scope of the lawful collateral damage caused to noncombatants. Currently, the intentional killing

them better access to loot and supplies from Kuwait compared with the regular corps. *Id.* at 115–24.

58. A.P.V. Rogers, Law on the Battlefield 31 (2d ed. 2004).

of civilians or targeting of their objects is totally forbidden. However, the general prohibition is fine-tuned to allow the consequential, unintended (collateral), and proportional targeting of civilians. Additional Protocol I prohibits "an attack which may be expected to cause incidental loss of civilian life . . . which would be excessive in relation to the concrete and direct military advantage anticipated."[59]

Under the suggested approach, with the focus on the military advantage side of the equation, no military statement would be taken at its face value. Any ostensible military advantage would be challenged and scrutinized in accordance with professional considerations and would thus be more limited in its scope. The legal threshold for risking innocent lives or civilian objects would be elevated because the military advantage would have to be justified by professional military standards and, therefore, based upon a cost-benefit analysis of alternative missions, objectives, and courses of action. Such a complementary rule, substantiating the "military advantage" part of the proportionality requirement, would dictate the less harmful military course of action for any given "military advantage." This change could be either explicit or implicit by way of interpreting the current proportionality equation. Indeed, it would provide tools to substantiate the norm, currently codified under article 57(2)(a)(ii) of Additional Protocol I, which requires the military planner to "take all feasible precautions in the choice of means and methods of attack with a view to avoiding, and in any event to minimizing, incidental loss of civilian life, injury to civilians and damage to civilian objects."[60]

Military planning is not a black box to be viewed solely in terms of its final products and results—for example, achieving a given military advantage—with no understanding or knowledge of its internal procedures and workings. In fact, the opposite is true. It is a professional system with its own manifest rules and procedures, most of which are in the public domain and well known, especially in Western democracies. To achieve a designated military aim or advantage, the military planning process requires the planner to develop and present a wide spectrum of

---

59. API, *supra* note 10, art. 51 para. 5(b).

60. *See also id.*, art. 57(3) (requiring that "the objective to be selected shall be that where the attack is expected to cause the least danger to civilians' lives"). *See also* David Luban's argument that military necessity requires taking civilians' interest into account ("necessity as proportionality"). David Luban, *Military Necessity and the Cultures of Military Law*, 26 Leiden J. Int'l L. 315, 343–45 (2013).

alternatives. Out of these preliminary alternative courses of action, only one is selected in a professional due process. For example, the wartime decision-making model used in the U.S. army consists of six steps,[61] including intelligence preparation and mission analysis,[62] the development of friendly courses of action[63] (COA),[64] the analysis of these COAs,[65] comparison of the relevant alternative courses and decisions,[66] the development of plans-orders,[67] and transition.[68] It requires the commander in the field to develop and present several relevant alternatives and choose the best course of action. The "operational estimate" is the British military's corresponding decision-making process.[69] Like the American manual, the British system requires the military planner to present several alternatives for a given mission.

The military planning process and the selection of a course of action out of the alternatives for achieving a designated military goal should be leveraged, by substantiating the prevailing norm requiring the minimizing of collateral damage to civilians. Once this noble objective is defined and compulsorily incorporated as an integral and important part of the planning process—requiring prioritization of the course of action expected to trigger the least collateral damage—it would be actually implemented and have better chances of being achieved. Indeed, here as before, in an environment that assumes "*à la guerre comme à la guerre*," there is no role or space for a constraining professional military humanitarian brake during

61. U.S. Naval War College, NWC 4111H, Workbook on Joint Operations Planning Process (Jan. 21, 2008), www.usnwc.edu/getattachment/Departments---Colleges/Joint-Military-Operations/NWC-4111H-21-Jan-08-Final.pdf.aspx (last visited Feb. 23, 2015).

62. *Id.* at 1-1.

63. *Id.* at 2-1.

64. "A COA is any concept of operation open to a commander that, if adopted, would result in the accomplishment of the mission. For each COA, the commander must envision the employment of his forces and assets *as a whole—normally two levels down*—taking into account externally imposed limitations." *Id.* at 2-1 (emphasis in the original).

65. *Id.* at 3-1.

66. *Id.* at 3-15–4-6.

67. *Id.* at 4-7–5-2.

68. *Id.* at 6-1.

69. U.K. Ministry of Defence, The Developments, Concepts and Doctrine Centre, Joint Doctrine Publication 5-00, Campaign Planning 2–32 (2d ed., change July 2, 2013), www.gov.uk/government/uploads/system/uploads/attachment_data/file/239345/20130827_JDP_5_00_Web_Secure.pdf (last visited Feb. 23, 2015).

wartime. So long as it remains the prevailing legal assumption that the legality of any "concrete and direct military advantage" to an army, to be achieved while fighting (especially in populated areas), should be taken at its face value, the result will be unnecessary excessive collateral damage to civilians. This assumption puts all (or most) of the constraining weight of the proportionality equation on the scale of human suffering, while (almost) ignoring the constraining force of military necessity, as reflected in the military advantage requirement.

However, its fallacy can be demonstrated at all levels of operations. At the tactical level, for example, a professionally trained soldier does not use his (or her) weapon unless he has a "concrete and direct" military target. He does not use military resources unless they are aimed at such an authorized target. It is the soldier's professionalism that should prevent him or her from targeting nonmilitary targets (though the possibility of mistakes, especially in urban areas, is always there). This professional requirement, if properly implemented, would reduce the unintended collateral damage. The transformation of this professional standard into a legal norm can dictate that a military—at all levels of operation—should adopt the least harmful course of action for any given military advantage.

The discussion thus far has dealt with the direct effect of the suggested transformation of professional standards into legal norms upon war's casualties, restricting the potential damage that might be caused both to combatants and to noncombatants. The following discussion will deal with the second, direct constraining effect, which relates to exercisers of military force.

1.3.5 Imposing Political Leaders' *in bello* Responsibility

Political leaders who command militaries, either directly (as "commander in chief")[70] or effectively (through the exercise of de facto authority over their state's military), are not currently obliged by their militaries' professional standards. Indeed, leaders are not usually connected to tactical and operational activities;[71] yet strategic decisions taken by leaders do affect, and are related to, such professional standards insofar as they directly

70. *See supra* Introduction note 88.

71. Indeed, some activities of leaders that might be perceived as tactical—for example, approval of targeted killings by drones or President Barack Obama's authorization of the Osama bin Laden raid—are, in fact, strategic, due to their strategic effects.

affect military operations. Turning these standards into legal norms would compel leaders to obey them. Currently, a convenient bifurcation exists for leaders: the *ad bellum* sphere is perceived to be their responsibility,[72] whereas the *in bello* sphere is perceived to be that of the soldiers. The suggested transformation would mean that leaders would be responsible for part of the latter, taking into account the direct effects of their strategic decisions upon their militaries' way of fighting.

An example of this scenario would be the collateral damage caused in the 1999 Kosovo campaign,[73] due to the direct causal link between its grand strategy and the scope of the operational collateral damage caused by it. In this campaign, NATO's leaders dictated a "zero military casualties" *in bello* paradigm to their militaries. They were motivated by a desire to limit their militaries' casualties by avoiding an attack using ground forces and, instead, conducting high-altitude bombings, thus evading Yugoslavian air defenses as well. The price of this strategy was probably inflated collateral damage. Yet the committee established to review the NATO bombing campaign followed the traditional paradigm, leaving the *in bello* sphere and

---

72. Indeed, though the *ad bellum* sphere is perceived to be the responsibility of leaders, the crime of aggression, in relation to leaders who cross the legal *ad bellum* Rubicon, has not yet come into force. Although article 5(2) of the Rome Statute of the International Criminal Court grants the International Criminal Court (ICC), inter alia, jurisdiction over "the crime of aggression," it suspends its actual operation until such time that a specific agreement on the definition of the crime and terms for its jurisdiction are agreed upon in accordance with the rules set forth for the amendment of the statute under articles 121 and 123 of the statute. United Nations Diplomatic Conference of Plenipotentiaries on the Establishment of an International Criminal Court, *Rome Statute of the International Criminal Court*, arts. 5(2), 121, 123, U.N. Doc. A/CONF.183/9 (July 17, 1998) [hereinafter ICC Statute]. Such an agreement was indeed reached during the 2010 ICC Review Conference in Kampala, setting two conditions to be met before the court is granted jurisdiction over the crime of aggression. The first is that the amendment be ratified by 30 state parties by January 1, 2017. That condition has been met. As of May 2017, 34 states have ratified the amendment defining the crime. *See* http://crimeofaggression.info/the-role-of-states/status-of-ratification-and-implementation (last visited Aug. 20, 2017). The second condition requires another review conference to be assembled after January 1, 2017 in which a decision by a two-thirds majority of the attending state parties is made to activate said jurisdiction; that conference has yet to be convened. *See* ICC Kampala Review Conference, *Resolution RC\Res. 6 on Crime of Aggression*, annex I, para. 3, concerning art. 15 bis (June 11, 2010) (at para. 3), http://crimeofaggression.info/documents/6/RC-Res6-ENG.pdf (last visited Nov.1, 2016).

73. A Human Rights Watch report assessing the damage to civilians in the aftermath of Operation Allied Force in Kosovo concluded that between 489 and 528 civilians were killed as a result of aerial bombings during the operation. *See* Human Rights Watch, *The Crisis in Kosovo* (2000), http://www.hrw.org/reports/2000/nato/Natbm200-01.htm#P153_32943 (last visited Apr. 24, 2016).

responsibility to the soldiers ("NATO air commanders").[74] However, the responsibility for the collateral damage caused in the Kosovo campaign lay primarily with the political leaders, who dictated a strategy directly affecting the tactics adopted. The responsibility lay not with the technicians, but rather with the master engineers. Had those leaders been subjected, as is suggested, to the inherent military professional standards, including those that constrain the use of force, an inquiry would have been conducted to determine whether these political leaders breached their legal obligations. (Such an enquiry would probably have reached the conclusion that the prevailing legal rules do not explicitly require soldiers to risk themselves, or their subordinates, in order to prevent or minimize collateral damage, although morally, they do have such a duty.)[75]

Indeed, although NATO air commanders should be responsible for their own operational and tactical decisions, accountability for the direct results of the "zero military casualties" *in bello* paradigm lies squarely upon the leaders' shoulders. They demonstrated a lack of willingness to risk their own soldiers' lives, knowing the probable effect this decision would have upon collateral damage caused to innocent civilians. The potential *in bello* effects of this choice as regards leaders are missing from the legal equation, which is currently beyond actual legal scrutiny. Under the suggested approach, however, this strategy—and the actual course of action taken—would have been examined with reference to the law of armed conflict in general, and to widely accepted military professional standards in particular.

Furthermore, turning professional military standards into legal norms would neutralize popular—but very problematic—political pressures exerted upon leaders, especially democratically elected ones, in times of war. An important, if not the most important, responsibility of elected leaders is to defend their citizens. For example, the 2010 American National Security Strategy states: "This Administration has no greater

74. ICC Office of the Prosecutor, *Final Report to the Prosecutor by the Committee Established to Review the NATO Bombing Campaign against the Federal Republic of Yugoslavia*, para. 56 (June 13, 2000) [hereinafter OTP Report], www.icty.org/x/file/About/OTP/otp_report_nato_bombing_en.pdf (last visited Apr. 24, 2016.

75. *See, e.g.*, Eyal Benevenisti, *Human Dignity in Combat: The Duty to Spare Enemy Civilians*, 39 Isr. L. Rev. 81 (2006); Walzer, *Coda*, *supra* note 37, at 437.

responsibility than the safety and security of the American people."[76] In situations of national emergency, political leaders come under huge pressure from their constituents and domestic political circles to fulfill this obligation in a short time and by all means. The temptation to please constituencies by exercising brute force is always there. This temptation is further encouraged by the frustration of both military and political leaders with the fact that the substantial modern targeting capabilities of militaries are not matched by the usually limited number of lawful targets.

Popular public opinion is capable of "legitimizing" the huge gap between capabilities and targets by reducing the legality threshold. Indeed, in national emergency circumstances, leaders face a substantial temptation to instruct their militaries to "find targets" by any means in order to exercise all (or most) of their actual military capabilities.[77] This combination of popular demands, politicians' temptations, and ambitions and the frustrations of militaries due to their inability to exercise their full capabilities might easily lead to excessive brutality. Introducing an *in bello* requirement of professionally limited targeting as a legal binding norm (or interpreting the prevailing rules in light of these professional standards) would offset those factors. It might prevent, or at least minimize, the effects of these external "noises," leaving the arena to military professionalism, including the inherent self-constraining standards of well-trained militaries.

1.3.6 Constraining Brutal Militaries and Vicious Soldiers

The second group of potential injurers that would be affected by the suggested transformation of professional military force-constraining standards into legal norms are those militaries (or parts of them) that are still unwilling to accept any force restrictions as professional standards. For example, those who still view inter-state wars as being between "peoples" rather than rival militaries cannot accept the current restrictions vis-à-vis civilians as being desirable to militaries rather than imposed upon them.

---

76. White House, National Security Strategy 4 (May 2010), http://nssarchive.us/NSSR/2010.pdf (last visited Aug. 16, 2017) [hereinafter White House 2010 National Security Strategy].

77. Furthermore, an existential threat might not only affect the political pressure but also have a legal affect upon the *in bello* rules, as admitted by the International Court of Justice regarding "an extreme circumstance of self-defence, in which the very survival of a State would be at stake." *See supra* Introduction note 85.

These "old school" soldiers are still obsessed with the Clausewitzian legacy of achieving victory by breaking the rival's will,[78] and brutality against the "enemy," including its civilians and objects, might often seem to satisfy this obsession.[79] However, the international law of armed conflict, which has developed since the Brussels Conference of 1874 and following the Hague Peace Conferences of 1899 and 1907, explicitly rejected the civilian dimension of total war as suggested by von Clausewitz. Between the contradictory definitions of the fighting adversaries—states or peoples—traditional law has explicitly chosen to limit the scope of war to the military in an attempt to limit the harm caused to civilians.[80]

Given the current illegality of exercising intentional force against noncombatants, those within military ranks who still believe that using excessive force against civilians is militarily desirable can still manipulate the rules to a limited extent, but mainly within a specific niche—when targeting dual-purpose objects. Whenever objects serve both civilian and military purposes—for example, power grids and bridges—overenthusiastic soldiers might inflate their military profile at the expense of their civilian functions in order to legitimize their targeting.[81] As described earlier, however, this school of military thinkers and practitioners unfortunately still possesses ample lawful maneuvering space when it comes to brutality against combatants, so long as they are still in the war game. Here the law of armed conflict remains silent in a way that allows brutality, and, in

78. "War is thus an act of force to compel our enemy to do our will." VON CLAUSEWITZ, *supra* note 34, at 75. Furthermore, "[t]o induce the principle of moderation into the theory of war itself would always lead to logical absurdity." *Id.* at 76.

79. Michael Howard points out, for example, that "[s]trategists before 1914 were in fact increasingly hypnotized by the Clausewitzian and Napoleonic idea of the decisive battle for the overthrow of the enemy." MICHAEL HOWARD, CLAUSEWITZ 63(1983).

80. "[T]his law ultimately upheld the 'Rousseauesque' [maxim that war was not a relationship between man and man but between state and state], not the 'Clausewitzian' conception [the need for wars to be a life or death struggle involving the whole of the population of the contending states]. Being based on the assumption that wars are clashes between states' armies, it distinguished between combatants and civilians and sought to shield the latter as much as possible from armed violence." CASSESE, INTERNATIONAL LAW, *supra* note 4, at 400.

81. As to the legal rule, *see* API, *supra* note 10, art. 52(2). *E.g.*, Normand and Jochnic have criticized the coalition's targeting of a substantial number of Iraqi power stations during the Gulf War (arguing that the military gains were negligible and disproportional relative to the amount of civilian suffering caused). Roger Normand & Chris A.F. Jochnik, *The Legitimization of Violence: A Critical Analysis of the Gulf War*, 35 HARV. INT'L L.J. 387, 403–05 (1994).

some cases, wickedness and even psychopathy, to flourish in the military environment.

Revisiting the necessity principle, as suggested, by introducing professional restraints against the use of excessive military force and transforming them into a legal standard and norms, would challenge contemporary "old school" militaries and soldiers to join the club of modern well-trained ones. The military culture supporting the exercise of brutality per se would have, to a large extent, to defer and consider the suggested standard and norms imported primarily from the cultures of contemporary well-trained militaries. (Historically, however, the moderate school of fighting originated thousands of years ago in Oriental cultures. Sun Tzu's moderate approach to war with its "emphasis on the use of force only as a last resort reflects Confucian idealism and the political culture that it spawned.")[82] Furthermore, even in the case of rigid militaries and iron-fisted soldiers, who are still obsessed with the exercise of brute force, the challenge to contemporary commanders is to choose the optimal course of action from the available alternatives. Merely knowing that the restricted-force option is an available one, professionally endorsed by leading militaries, may help persuade them to accept it as an imposed compulsory norm.

The discussion thus far has presented the effects of the suggested transformation of professional standards into legal ones. It currently invites a timing question: Why should strengthening the necessity principle, by infusing it with professional constraining standards, now work?

1.4 Why Now? Has the Time Come for Revised Military Necessity?

The traditional functional equation regarding the role of the law of armed conflict—to strike a balance between the demands of military necessity and concerns for humanity—is theoretically satisfying. The problem, however, lies with its current interpretation and implementation: the almost automatic validation of military necessity. A potential reply to this shortcoming—introducing new substance into the general principle of necessity and the norms derived from it, based upon professional standards—was offered in the previous discussion. But is there a real

---

82. Michael I. Handel, Masters of War: Classical Strategic Thought 136 (3d rev. ed. 2001); and *see infra* text accompanying Chapter 3 notes 57–58.

demand for such a reform? Taking the current hollowness of this principle as a given, the question is whether these dry bones can be brought to life again.[83] Indeed, the answer lies with the timing. Cultural, social, technological, and military changes that are now taking place have prepared the ground for the evolution of a revived necessity: a new legal principle made up of military professional standards that constrain the use of excessive military force.

Despite the focus placed by the law on the protection of civilians after World War II,[84] its mixed record since then in fulfilling this noble mission invites revised legal thinking. This need is further intensified due to the new urban battlefields. Current changes in the pattern of war—specifically, the prevailing asymmetric conflicts taking place, to a large extent, in heavily populated urban areas—pose a challenge to the humanitarian mission of the law of armed conflict. Furthermore, the changes of recent decades in both military and social Western-liberal thinking have substantially reduced the willingness to sacrifice lives and wealth to wars—the latter are perceived, often enough, as the new Moloch. These liberal ideologies are augmented by the development of military technology enabling modern militaries to obtain real-time intelligence and achieve precision in targeting. Cumulatively, all of these changes, which will be elaborated on in the following paragraphs, have created a new environment—one that may be ready to absorb constraining professional military standards as a mandatory legal norm.

When the horrors and disastrous results following the two World Wars became known, it triggered the assumption of a central role by the humanistic approach in the development of the prevailing rules of the law of armed conflict.[85] In actual effect, however, this approach has been less than successful. The problem stems partly from the limited scope of the legal rules in intra-state wars[86] and partly from poor compliance and lack of effective international enforcement. Empirically, the twentieth century

83. *Ezekiel* 37:1–14.

84. *See, e.g.*, Best, *supra* note 38.

85. *Id.* at 289–90.

86. *E.g.*, the Fourth Geneva Convention is applicable primarily to conflicts of an international character. Geneva Convention (IV) Relative to the Protection of Civilian Persons in Time of War, Aug. 12, 1949, 75 U.N.T.S. 287 (GCIV). The results of article 3 of the Convention applicable to non-international armed conflict have been minimal and uncertain at best.

is known for its poor record in protecting civilians.[87] Indeed, one of the reasons for this failure has been the change in the nature of war in the latter part of the twentieth century, particularly in regard to urban warfare.

As the humanistic approach to the laws of war advanced, parties to conflicts that were less committed to it began taking advantage of its rules, mainly by using urban areas as shelters in the context of burgeoning asymmetric warfare. The urban theater, once considered a death trap to nonstate fighters, whose adversaries could burn them in it together with its local citizens, now came to be perceived as a safe haven for them. It protects these fighters, while they assimilate into the civilian population, utilizing the prevailing principle of distinction.[88] The density of the urban arena and plurality of civilians in it have made it nearly impossible for the militaries of law-abiding states to avoid collateral damage when fighting in asymmetric wars. The weaker side may use this to its advantage and attack indiscriminately, while protecting its military assets in many cases by using civilians as human shields.[89] Indeed, this is a revolving trap: from a trap for nonstate fighters, the urban arena has turned into a "legal and moral trap" for the law-abiding state.

Add to this situation the change in social perceptions of heroism and killing in the modern period. The willingness of societies, primarily liberal ones, to sacrifice their own soldiers' lives and their acceptance of the need to kill the adversary's combatants, or especially "enemy civilians" (albeit collaterally), can no longer be taken for granted as before. This post-heroic era[90] is characterized by a lessening tolerance of casualties on both adversarial sides.[91] These social changes, new liberal norms, and public expectations, especially in Western democracies, have arrived together with relatively easy access by the different media to conflict zones, with all of the parties involved fighting for the public's "hearts and minds," both domestically and internationally. Furthermore, in counterinsurgency

---

87. Morrow, *supra* note 1.

88. AZAR GAT, VICTORIOUS AND VULNERABLE: WHY DEMOCRACY WON IN THE 20TH CENTURY AND HOW IT IS STILL IMPERILED 141–42 (2010).

89. Concerning the use of human shields, *see* Michael N. Schmitt, *Human Shields in International Humanitarian Law*, 47 COLUM. J. TRANSNAT'L L. 292, 292–94 (2008–2009). For an example of volunteers shielding potential military objectives in the Kosovo conflict, *see* ROGERS, *supra* note 58, at 21.

90. EDWARD N. LUTTWAK, STRATEGY: THE LOGIC OF WAR AND PEACE 68 (2001).

91. *Id.* at 72.

operations, added emphasis is placed on reducing the amount of force used in order to win the "hearts and minds" of the local population. How a war is perceived by public opinion and reflected in the media is becoming increasingly significant. The perceived narrative becomes crucial, in some cases even more than the actual deeds on the battlefield. Against this challenging background, new technologies have triggered developments in intelligence gathering and precise weaponry—the combination of both allows for much more surgical strikes than before.

The Industrial Revolution gave impetus to the development of the concept of total war and its industrialized mass killing,[92] which has been prominent in wars since the end of the eighteenth century. New intelligence-gathering capabilities and the precise weaponry reform have currently created new operational opportunities and challenging agendas for military strategists. The industrial approach to war has underlain the design and use of traditional weapons. The typical operational targeting process was quantitatively oriented, aimed at covering large areas with a huge amount of fire in order to hurt as many "enemies" as possible. Typically, the name of the game, from Napoleon's campaigns to Vietnam, was body count.[93] Whether it was World War I's artillery and machine gun slaughter in the trench warfare or World War II's "carpet bombing" or atomic bomb, the targeting aim was to achieve the desired mass killing. Today's weapons are much more accurate, with pinpoint targeting allowing for surgical strikes with relatively minimal collateral damage. For example, joint direct attack munitions and global positioning system navigation, which have been added to existing free-falling bombs, has allowed them to achieve an accuracy of 20 feet from 15 miles away, with great potential for decreasing collateral damage.[94] With this development, we may see operational targeting abandon its quantitative orientation in favor of a qualitative and selective orientation.

All of the aforementioned factors combined have created a window of opportunity for the suggested evolution: the introduction of

---

92. Indeed, the impact of the Industrial Revolution on military power developed gradually and, in some cases, very slowly. *See* John Frederick Charles Fuller, The Conduct of War, 1789–1961: A Study of the Impact of the French, Industrial and Russian Revolutions on War and Its Conduct 86–94 (1992).

93. The poor strategic thinking in Vietnam will be discussed *infra* text accompanying Chapter 3 notes 73–74.

94. Michael N. Schmitt, *Precision Attack and International Humanitarian Law*, 87(859) Int'l Rev. Red Cross 445, 449 (2005).

force-constraining legal norms and a revised necessity principle. Thus, the demand side for restricted use of force might currently meet the available supply, and a new equilibrium, internalizing the limitations of military power, should be created to actually balance the necessity and humanity principles. The potential for reform is there—all it requires is a conceptual and doctrinal reform to phrase it and the legal rules to establish it. Indeed, the combined effects of the changes in the nature of substantial parts of modern wars and in the social attitudes towards them, the development of the humanistic approach to the laws of war, and the introduction of new weapons and intelligence technology can all lead to new paradigms in military thinking. Von Clausewitz's bloody and brutal vision of total war, though common in the wars of the last two hundred years, can now be replaced, at least in part, with a far less brutal paradigm based upon the precise and measured use of force to accomplish a military mission. Indeed, this is nothing strange to military thinkers, nor is it new.

Two thousand years ago, Sun Tzu described this approach, saying that "those skilled in war subdue the enemy's army without battle."[95] A recent American example of a relatively moderate approach was offered by General Colin Powell, who argued against the complete destruction of the Iraqi army during the First Gulf War (1991), convincing President George H.W. Bush to end the ground war after one hundred hours.[96] The turning of the American doctrinal scale in favor of the moderate approach is not only reflected in traditional inter-state wars but was also actually demonstrated lately in its counterinsurgency doctrine.[97] Indeed, these new winds have opened a window of opportunity for a resubstantiation of the necessity principle based on professional norms.

1.5 Concluding Remarks

At the micro level, this chapter calls for the substantiation of the necessity principle and the prevailing legal norms with widely accepted professional military standards in a way that creates a new equilibrium between

---

95. Sun Tzu, The Art of War 79 (Samuel B. Griffith trans. foreword by B.H. Liddell Hart, 1963); and *see* the discussion *infra* text accompanying Chapter 3 notes 57–58.

96. *See, e.g.*, Eliot A. Cohen, Supreme Command: Soldiers, Statesmen and Leadership in Wartime 194–98 (2003).

97. *See supra* text accompanying notes 19–24.

humanity and military necessity; furthermore, it has demonstrated that the present may be the optimal time for such a reform. At the macro level, it has presented the two aims of this book's suggested paradigm: to reduce human suffering while creating an environment in which full abidance by the law becomes an attainable norm.

Though much effort has been devoted to convincing the reader that these professional constraining standards are currently well established in modern militaries (albeit, mainly in Western democracies), the main argument presented here is valid even if one thinks that the present writer has failed in this mission. For those who believe that the brutal Clausewitzian legacy is still vibrant in modern contemporary militaries, this chapter should be read as a call—an open invitation to a normative discussion (without the suggested basis of positive professional standards). The suggested discussion could lead to either explicit reform—codification of the professional necessity standard and the specific norms deriving from it—or an indirect one, through interpretation of the prevailing criteria and their being based on substantive, qualitative, professional requirements.

Humanity alone should not, and in fact cannot, substantially reduce war's hazards. The recognition and promotion of internal professional military constraints, meant to prevent an army from causing excessive damage to civilians or unnecessarily killing and inflicting suffering on its adversary's combatants, should be endorsed. The prevailing law seems to have internalized the importance of introducing professional military standards into the legal discourse. However, it currently accepts them in only a limited spectrum, though indeed in the very important niche of balancing the *in bello* proportionality equation. Thus, the legal assessment of an expected "military advantage" vis-à-vis collateral damage is carried out through the eyes of the reasonable commander. As the Committee Established to Review the NATO Bombing in Kosovo has stated, "[i]t is unlikely that a human rights lawyer and an experienced combat commander would assign the same relative values to military advantage and to injury to noncombatants. . . . It is suggested that the determination of relative values must be that of the 'reasonable military commander.' "[98]

98. OTP Report, *supra* note 74, at para. 50. *See also* HCJ 769/02, *The Public Committee Against Torture and Others v. The Government of Israel and Others* (2005), 62(1) PD 507, [57] ("The Court will ask itself if a reasonable military commander could have made the decision which was made.").

Indeed, the role assigned to the "reasonable military commander" in this delicate niche of proportionality assessment should be extended, with professional standards introduced into the legal *in bello* discourse as obligatory force-restricting standards and norms as well. The determination of military necessity is, to a large extent, the commanders' profession. It functions not as a justification for brutality but, rather, obliges them to exercise their forces competently, using their brains and professional skills when exercising force. Doing so will enable them to restrict unnecessary brutality while achieving their mission.

Based on both utilitarian and moral grounds, the time has come to revisit the necessity principle and challenge some prevailing norms, reflecting the current balance reached in light of the principles of humanity and military necessity. Such a reform's potential for success at present seems promising. The combined effect of the current changes in war's pattern and the law of armed conflict, and in the military and social liberal thinking of recent decades, as well as the new strategies available due to developments in new military technologies, has been to create a new war environment—of a kind that might be ready to absorb and even welcome the suggested reform. From this perspective, the "human rights lawyer" and the "reasonable military commander" should not find themselves in permanent confrontation, as the current axiom assumes, but rather should join forces in limiting war's hazards.

Although this chapter suggests a framework for substantiating the *in bello* necessity principle and the legal norms derived from it, it leaves open, to a large extent, their specific concretization. Questions related to the precise contour of the suggested norms and how they are to be promulgated—for either professional or nonprofessional military forces (and armed groups) to follow them—will require further elaboration. Here the diversity of militaries in their perception of professionalism and the variety in their actual practice—an issue to be elaborated in the next chapter—might serve as a source of inspiration (rather than a target of criticism). Indeed, different militaries share the main attributes of functioning and many of them adopt common war principles that affect their conduct of operations. Yet militaries still differ in their individual war doctrines, in some of their war principles and methods and fighting techniques. This practical diversity creates an elastic environment that allows for a normative discussion. It provides tools—indeed, grants a margin of appreciation—for setting the threshold of humanitarian-constraining norms within the necessity principle. Furthermore, issues related to the burden of proof—for example, whether (and to what extent) an apparent breach of professional standards might transfer the burden of proof to the wrongdoer—and to the scope of doubt should also be discussed. Moreover, the mere existence of established military standards and norms, as suggested earlier, might affect the prevailing custom—another legal dimension that ought to be dealt with. Indeed, the discussion in this chapter presents an open invitation to a wider analysis that internalizes the limitations of military power by revisiting the prevailing law of armed conflict's equilibrium between humanity and necessity principles.

The constraining potential of the necessity principle is what lies at the heart of this chapter. However, its enabling function cannot be ignored either. In this context, it should be remembered that wars are not humanitarian projects. They are destructive by their very nature, with military necessity serving as the justification for militaries' devastative actions. Yet it does not and should not justify excessive use of force. Not all is fair in war, but rather the opposite. Brutality in war is a product of incompetent and undisciplined militaries or a result of political, psychological and cultural pressures. True enough, the necessity principle justifies the mere use of lethal force to facilitate wielding the military sword. At the same time, however, it should also function as a shield, protecting combatants and noncombatants alike from excessive brutality. The constraining and enabling functions, as suggested in this chapter, are not mutually exclusive; on the contrary, the more successful a military is in containing unnecessary brutality, the more effective it is in achieving its mission. The scope of what is necessary, and which activities amount to excessive brutality, is primarily a professional matter to be scrutinized by professional standards. It affects both *ad bellum* (mainly leaders') decisions and *in bello* (mainly soldiers') operations. The military has a professional say in questions of given necessity, but it is not immune to external criticism or even punishment, if required, whenever such force is used unprofessionally. Here the main role of military lawyers, judges, NGOs, and public opinion is not to apply the brake to the military's destructive apparatus whenever appropriate—a task that is subject mainly to the professionals' responsibility and accountability—but rather to inspect its actual operation.

Whereas this chapter has presented the two aims of this book's suggested paradigm—to reduce human suffering, while reducing the gap between the law and the actual reality—the next chapter focuses mainly on the latter. It suggests the adoption of a professional military standard: the operational last resort for exercising self-defense, which should determine the *ad bellum* timing. If accepted, it would mainly narrow the gap between the law and states' actual practice and, to a lesser extent, serve the second aim of reducing humanitarian suffering.

2

Lawful War of Self-Defense

WHEN NOT TO BE A SITTING DUCK

Introduction

The UN Charter prohibits the unilateral exercise of military force in the international arena;[1] it does allow the use of force, however, for self-defense against an armed attack.[2] Self-defense, in general, does not require total passivity from the victim. An individual self-defendant in the domestic arena, for example, is allowed to defend herself actively from a forthcoming blow by raising her hand to halt it. The victim is not obliged by the Christian-pacifist doctrine of turning the other cheek[3]—responding to an aggressor without violence—nor is she restricted to an ex-post response, only after absorbing the blow. The lawfulness of a proactive self-defense against an "armed attack" in international law raises two questions. The first, quantitative in nature, relates to both the amount of force used by the aggressor, that is, the attack's level of aggression—the threshold that if crossed would allow the self-defendant to respond forcefully—and the constraints upon the amount of lawful counterforce used by the self-defendant.[4] This quantitative dimension has been debated, for example, by

---

1. U.N. Charter, art. 2(4).

2. *See supra* Introduction note 66.

3. The phrase originates from the Sermon on the Mount in the New Testament, in which Jesus says: "You have heard that it was said, 'An eye for an eye, and a tooth for a tooth.' But I tell you, do not resist an evil person. If someone strikes you on the right cheek, turn to him the other also." *Matthew* 5:38–39.

4. The focus here is on a lawful war of self-defense. Indeed, a victim state has a large spectrum of other nonmilitary counter-responses against the aggressor. *See* JAMES CRAWFORD,

the International Court of Justice, which has determined both the quantitative threshold of an aggressor's armed attack[5] that legitimizes a war of self-defense, and the requirements of necessity and proportionality that constrain the defendant's lawful self-defense.[6] The second question, which will be at the focus of this chapter, concerns the timing of the lawful proactive response. As article 51 of the Charter legitimizes the right of individual or collective self-defense "if an armed attack occurs against a Member," it is widely assumed that a lawful self-defense is contingent upon an attack that has already been carried out by the aggressor. This interpretation invites the question: When does the armed attack, legitimizing the self-defendant's military response, "occur"?[7]

Such framing of the legal question—within the contours of the UN Charter, which requires an armed attack—assumes that the defendant is not allowed to attack before the aggressor crosses the formal *ad bellum* Rubicon. It disallows a preventive war—aimed against an adversary's military capabilities in order to prevent it from attacking in the future[8]—but might consider the legality of a preemptive, anticipatory strike.[9] The latter

---

THE INTERNATIONAL LAW COMMISSION'S ARTICLES ON STATE RESPONSIBILITY: INTRODUCTION, TEXT AND COMMENTARY (2002). As to the legitimacy of a military response, but "short of war," *see supra* text accompanying Introduction notes 66–76.

5. Under the ICJ's ruling in the *Nicaragua* case, the court decided to limit the right to self-defense only against armed attacks of "significant scale." Military and Paramilitary Activities in and Against Nicaragua (Nicar. v. U.S.), Judgment, 1986 I.C.J. Rep. 14, ¶ 195 (June 27). "Insignificant" aggression against a defendant state does not, in the court's opinion, amount to an "armed attack." It should be noted, however, that the "scale and effects," or gravity of harm criteria, have not been universally accepted. *See, e.g.*, David Kretzmer, *The Inherent Right to Self-Defence and Proportionality in Jus Ad Bellum*, 24 EUR. J. INT'L L. 235, 243 (2013) (referring, inter alia, to the traditional view taken by the United States according to which an armed attack does not need to surpass some threshold of intensity).

6. *See, e.g.*, Legality of the Threat or Use of Nuclear Weapons, Advisory Opinion, 1996 I.C.J. Rep. 226, ¶41 (July 8). ("The submission of the exercise of the right of self-defense to the conditions of necessity and proportionality is a rule of customary international law.").

7. Another timing issue, which will not be dealt with here, relates to the required immediacy of the self-defendant's response—the last time at which it might be considered as such—following the execution of the aggressor's armed attack. *See, e.g.*, YORAM DINSTEIN, WAR, AGGRESSION AND SELF-DEFENCE 233–34 (5th ed. 2011).

8. Generally speaking, preventive war can have either a strategic goal (to prevent a shift in the balance of power) or an operative one (to prevent such a shift on the potential battleground, by keeping one's adversary militarily inferior). "Prevention provides a means of confronting factors that are likely to contribute to the development of a threat before it has had a chance to become imminent." LAWRENCE FREEDMAN, DETERRENCE 85 (2004).

9. "A pre-emptive war takes place at some point between the moment when an enemy decides to attack—or more precisely, is perceived to be about to attack—and the attack is

usually relates to a first strike when an attack does seem to be, from the defendant's perspective, imminent. The simple example of such imminence is when the aggressor's soldiers pull the triggers of their guns or missiles. Indeed, hitting them before their missiles reach their targets represents the opposite pole of the spectrum of imminence and the easiest case of justifying self-defense. The move on the scale, from this pole toward mere complete military preparation by the potential aggressor, hardens the justification for a proactive self-defense. This dilemma invites facing, and to some extent challenging, the apparent exclusivity over military-force initiatives at the beginning of a war that is granted currently, de facto, to aggressors (with the de jure exception of exercise of force authorized by a Security Council resolution[10]). It requires examining factual and theoretical issues. The legal meaning of an "armed attack" in general, of the actual starting point of such an attack in particular, needs to be defined. Practically, it must be determined when the aggressor's threat crystallizes into an armed attack, allowing the self-defendant to take the proactive initiative in its own self-defense and not requiring it to wait like a sitting duck.[11]

Out of the spectrum of potential military alternatives available to the self-defendant, the general question is: What leverage does the legal system grant it? Is it allowed to respond only at the "last minute" when it is left with only a very limited, residual, on-the-spot, tactical-military response to the aggressor; or is it allowed to exercise its self-defense earlier, when it still has some proactive operational alternatives in the military terrain vis-à-vis the aggressor? These operational alternatives are derived, of course, from the expected effect of the attack, and they are relative and contextually based: dependent on the subjective variables of the adversaries, the ability of the self-defendant to absorb the aggressor's strike (i.e., its geographic dimensions), the character of the threat (i.e., whether it is conventional or nonconventional), and its magnitude and scope.

---

actually launched." *Id.* at 86. Freedman further summarizes: "[p]revention is cold-blooded: it intends to deal with a problem before it becomes a crisis, while pre-emption is a more desperate strategy employed in the heat of crisis." *Id.*

10. The collective security rationale adopted in the Charter allows the Security Council to act unilaterally and proactively with military force.

11. *See, e.g.*, Myers S. McDougal, *The Soviet-Cuban Quarantine and Self-Defense*, 57 Am. J. Int'l L. 597, 601 (1963).

The chapter begins with a presentation of the ambiguity concerning the prevailing law of self-defense—which is lawful only against an "armed attack," including an imminent one (Part 2.1)—and the disharmony characterizing the actual practice of states (Part 2.2). This factual background invites a normative discussion regarding the timing of proactive self-defense. On the assumption that a potential self-defendant is not doomed to be totally passive when it faces an imminent threat, this chapter offers an innovative criterion to be used when vindicating the right of self-defense. The suggested criterion is the last reasonable point, according to the self-defendant's military circumstances and doctrine, at which it can successfully face the aggressor's threat and still operationally defend itself—including, when necessary, by taking the initiative in its own self-defense. In the application of this criterion, both variables of the imminent threat, magnitude and certainty, should be considered. If it is certain that an attack is underway, the self-defendant can lawfully intercept it. It is suggested, however, that if the imminence of the threat is only near certain, the threat to the defendant, vindicating its first strike, has to be existential. The suggested standard and its special attributes will be discussed in Part 2.3. The balance of advantages and shortcomings of the operational last resort criterion will be discussed in Part 2.4. Part 2.5 offers a few concluding remarks.

2.1 Self-Defense: The Prevailing Law

Under the prevailing rules, military force should be used only as a means of last resort. When a state faces an actual military threat amounting to an "armed attack," its belligerent response is justified only when it is necessary—that is, when no concrete alternatives exist—and provided that the force used is proportionate to the actual threat.[12] Under the common approach, where the military threat is not actual but hypothetical, or even when it is actual but does not cross the minimal threshold of severity—for example, the one established under the ICJ's *Nicaragua* decision[13]—the

12. *See, e.g.*, Legality of the Threat or Use of Nuclear Weapons, Advisory Opinion, *supra* note 6. As to the substance of these requirements, *see, e.g.*, Christine Gray, International Law and the Use of Force 148–55 (3d ed. 2008); Dinstein, War, Aggression and Self-Defence, *supra* note 7, at 231–33. For a detailed discussion of the problematic application of the *ad bellum* proportionality, *see infra* Chapter 3 text accompanying notes 106–112.

13. *See supra* note 5.

self-defense paradigm does not vindicate the use of military force by the actual or potential defendant. In response, the victim state has to exploit nonmilitary (i.e., economic) measures or channels—for example, through the Security Council—despite the accumulated threat against it.

A lawful self-defense does not derive from any speculative hypothesis regarding adversaries' wills and reactions. It requires actual and quantified aggression, not merely aggressive capabilities or intentions. "So long as you are sure of your diagnosis 'prevention is better than cure' is a good motto for foreign policy as it is for medicine. Unfortunately, diagnosis is no small test when considering political processes, which could develop in a number of ways, rather than incipient disease."[14] The uncertainty regarding one's enemy's intentions clearly disappears only when the potential threat of aggression crystallizes to the required threshold of an "occurring" armed attack. This invites the question: What, if any, are the attributes of this occurrence due to which an expected attack may be considered an occurring one, and that might justify an anticipatory strike by the self-defendant state?

The positive law surrounding an anticipatory strike is not fully clear, even in the "simple case" of conventional wars between states.[15] It is the subject of an intense legal and academic debate. There are legal opinions—relying mainly upon the reference in the UN Charter's article 51 to the "inherent" right of self-defense—arguing that the article preserves its earlier, pre-Charter characteristics under customary international law, allowing, inter alia, anticipatory self-defense[16] in cases where a state believes that another state is going to attack it.[17] The conflicting view argues, however, the opposite: that the meaning of the article is conclusive and clear, stating

---

14. FREEDMAN, DETERRENCE, *supra* note 8, at 106–07.

15. The legality of a first strike against different threats—whether sub-conventional (characterized mainly by terror) or mega-conventional (using weapons of mass destruction)—and the effect of their different attributes will be dealt with later, in our normative discussion. *See infra* text accompanying notes 151–163.

16. The expansionist view of self-defense has been advocated mainly by American and British jurists. *See, e.g.*, ANTONIO CASSESE, INTERNATIONAL LAW 358 (2d ed. 2005). *See also* McDougal, *supra* note 11; W. Michael Reisman & Andrea Armstrong, *The Past and Future of the Claim of Preemptive Self-Defense*, 100 AM. J. INT'L L. 525, 527–30 (2006); Anthony Clark Arend, *International Law and the Preemptive Use of Military Force*, 26 WASH. Q. 89, 92 (2003). For further examples of state practice with regard to anticipatory self-defense, *see infra* text accompanying notes 25–55.

17. *Cf.* Military and Paramilitary Activities in and Against Nicaragua, *supra* note 5 (dissenting opinion of Judge Schwebel), ¶ 200.

that the right of self-defense, between states,[18] arises strictly in cases where an armed attack has already occurred.[19] According to this conclusive interpretation, article 51 creates a lawful exception to the Charter's prohibiting rule, whereas the pre-Charter "inherent" right of self-defense served only as a political justification for a war, when the use of military force was not legally prohibited. But even if the exclusivity of the article regarding the legality of self-defense is adopted, that should not automatically exclude the legalization of an anticipatory strike, in certain circumstances. The condition of an occurring armed attack should not be read as imposing a mandatory passive strategy upon the victim state, requiring it to absorb the aggressive blow like a sitting duck.[20] The reactivity requirement seems neither necessary nor justified.

Dinstein, for example, advocates for the restrictive reading of article 51, banning any prevention-aimed strike, and argues that "[a]ny other interpretation of the Article would be counter-textual, counter-factual and counter-logical";[21] however, he does call for recognition of the anticipatory right when an attack is already underway:

> [T]he right to self-defence can be invoked in response to an armed attack as soon as it becomes evident to the victim State (on the basis of hard intelligence available at the time) that the attack is actually in the process of being mounted. There is no need to wait for the

---

18. As to the right of self-defense in response to terrorist attacks, *see infra* note 46.

19. *See, e.g.*, Gray's statement: "the majority of states reject anticipatory self-defense." GRAY, *supra* note 12, at 160. *See also* CASSESE, INTERNATIONAL LAW, *supra* note 16, at 361.

20. *See, e.g.*, ROSALYN HIGGINS, PROBLEMS AND PROCESS: INTERNATIONAL LAW AND HOW WE USE IT 242 (1995) (arguing that "in a nuclear age, common sense cannot require one to interpret an ambiguous provision in a text in a way that requires a state passively to accept its fate before it can defend itself"). Cassese, who advocates for the restrictive interpretation of article 51, legally banning an a priori, anticipatory self-defense strike, nonetheless offers a pragmatic "compromise" that might provide an excuse (or justification), at least partially, for such a strike in retrospect: "As for anticipatory self-defence, it is more judicious to consider such action as *legally prohibited*, while admittedly knowing that there may be cases where breaches of the prohibition may be justified on moral and political grounds and the community will eventually condone them or mete out lenient condemnation. This may in particular occur when the relevant State offers to the world community or to the UN convincing evidence of the impending attack, which it felt justified to pre-empt by use of force, and in addition shows that the anticipatory strike and the subsequent military actions have been proportionate to the threat, and limited to removal of such threat." CASSESE, INTERNATIONAL LAW, *supra* note 16, at 362.

21. DINSTEIN, WAR, AGGRESSION AND SELF-DEFENCE, *supra* note 7, at 196.

> bombs to fall—or, for that matter, for fire to open—if it is certain that the armed attack is under way (even in a preliminary manner). The victim State can lawfully (under Article 51) intercept the armed attack, with a view to blunting its edge.[22]

Dinstein further demonstrates his opinion by using the pre-Charter example of the 1941 Japanese attack on Pearl Harbor. The departure of the Japanese fleet toward its combat destination represents the crossing of the "legal Rubicon" of an armed attack, at the relevant time scale, and if any such thing were to occur today it would allow the Americans to intercept it, lawfully, by exercising their military force. The residual probability that the aggressive Japanese mission might still have been called off after its departure should have been ignored, under his view.[23] Indeed, under the common view, the "armed attack" requirement extends to include an imminent one as well, and in such a case the threatened attack is considered as actually occurring.[24]

This positive rule—albeit an ambiguous one, which gives rise to disharmony and conflicting views—invites us to face the strategic reality, the actual practice of states and its common justification.

2.2 *The Practice of States and Its Justification*

Introduction

It may sound counterintuitive but preemptive wars are a rare phenomenon (though endorsed by leading states, their actual occurrence, especially in conventional wars between states, is limited). Dan Reiter offers two reasons for this infrequency. The first concerns the political costs of such a preemptive attack. In World War I, for example, neither France nor

22. *Id.* at 200.

23. *Id.* at 203–04.

24. *See e.g.*, Reisman & Armstrong, *supra* note 16, at 532–33 (referring to the High-Level Panel's recommendation favoring a loosening of the strict "armed attack" requirement as long as the threatened attack is imminent); United Nations General Assembly [UNGA], *In Larger Freedom: Towards Development, Security and Human Rights for All*, ¶ 124, U.N. Doc. A/59/2005 (Mar. 21, 2005) (stating that "[i]mminent threats are fully covered by Article 51, which safeguards the inherent right of sovereign States to defend themselves against armed attack"); Kretzmer states that although "it is almost universally accepted that a state may not use force in order to prevent or deter future attacks, it is widely (but certainly not universally) acknowledged that it may do so to thwart an imminent attack." Kretzmer, *supra* note 5, at 248.

Germany wanted to strike first, as it was almost guaranteed that the victim of the strike would carry favor with Britain. Similarly, Israel, in the Six Day War, held back its preemptive attack until such time as it was certain it would be getting support for that move from its most important ally, the United States. The second reason concerns the "self-fulfilling prophecy" of the preemptive strike; the fear that it may spiral out of control prevents state leaders from subscribing to it.[25]

Historically, the United States and Britain with several other countries have consistently argued the case for anticipatory self-defense (even before 9/11). Their approach toward anticipatory self-defense can be traced back to the pre-Charter (1837) *Caroline* dispute between the United States and Britain.[26] Daniel Webster, the then-U.S. secretary of state, defined—in a way that has been accepted as representing customary international law[27]—the scope of the self-defense right and its limits. It arises only when there is a "necessity of self-defence . . . instant, overwhelming, leaving no choice of means and no moments for deliberation," and the military response by the victim state should be proportional ("nothing unreasonable or excessive").[28] The same line of policy by the United States regarding anticipatory self-defense continued well into the twentieth century to the post-Charter period, transforming the pre-Charter political justification for preemption into a legal one. For example, the U.S. government stated in 1946 that an armed attack—against which self-defense would be permissible—should be defined to include not merely the dropping of a bomb, but also "certain steps in themselves preliminary to such action."[29] That notion was supported by the UK and other states who contended in 1952 that a state threatened with an impending attack would be justified

---

25. Dan Reiter, *Exploding the Powder Keg Myth: Preemptive Wars Almost Never Happen*, 20 Int'l Security 5, 25–32 (1995).

26. In the *Caroline* case, British troops from British-controlled Canada attacked an American ship (the *Caroline*) docked on the American side of the Niagara River, claiming that the ship was used to support Canadian rebels. *See, e.g.*, Christopher Greenwood, *The* Caroline, *in* Max Planck Encyclopedia of Public International Law (Rudiger Wolfrum ed., 2009), opil.ouplaw.com/home/EPIL It should be noted, however, that, under the current definition, there was not then an armed conflict between the adversaries and the ongoing belligerency was, in fact, "short of war." Furthermore, the post-Charter prohibition on the unilateral use of military force was not valid then.

27. *See, e.g.*, Oscar Schachter, International Law in Theory and Practice 152 (1991) (quoting U.N. Doc. S/PV 2285-88(1981)).

28. *Id.*

29. Phillip C. Jessup, A Modern Law of Nations: An Introduction 166–67 (1948).

in attacking first in self-defense.[30] Later, for example, President Reagan claimed with regard to the U.S. air strike in Libya in 1986, which followed the bombing of a Berlin nightclub, that he was taking preemptive action, in this case justified under article 51.[31] Similarly, in the discussion in the Security Council on Israel's 1981 attack on the Iraqi nuclear reactor (at Osirak), the United States stated its belief in the customary nature of anticipatory self-defense.[32] This approach culminated with the U.S. and UK's favorable stand toward anticipatory self-defense after 9/11,[33] to be presented later.[34]

2.2.1 The Six Day War

A generic example of the legitimacy of an anticipatory strike is the Six Day War. In mid-May 1967, the Egyptian government began to transfer substantial parts of its military to the Sinai Peninsula, expelling the UN peacekeeping forces who had maintained a buffer zone in Sinai, between Israeli and Egyptian forces, since the 1956 war. On May 22, the Egyptian president Gamal Abdel Nasser announced the closure of an international waterway, the Straits of Tiran, to Israeli shipping (knowing that it would be considered a casus belli by the Israelis). In a public speech, delivered on May 29, Nasser declared that the Egyptian goal in case of a war would be the destruction of the State of Israel. On May 30, King Hussein of Jordan put the Jordanian military under Egyptian command in case of a

---

30. Derek William Bowett, Self Defense in International Law 189 (2d prtg. 2009).

31. President Ronald Reagan, *Address to the Nation on the United States Air Strike Against Libya*, 1 Pub. Papers 468, 469 (Apr. 14, 1986).

32. The United States refrained, however, from supporting Israel's claim in the case in point, noting that it had not exhausted all peaceful means to resolve the matter and therefore did not meet the requirements of anticipatory self-defense. *See, e.g.*, Cassese, International Law, *supra* note 16, at 358–60; and *see infra*, text accompanying notes 157–163.

33. *Cf.* Gray, *supra* note 12, at 160 and 209–16. With regard to the UK's currently favorable view of anticipatory self-defense against an imminent attack, *see, e.g.*, *Attorney General's Advice on the Iraq War: Resolution 1441*, 54 Int'l Comp. L.Q. 767, 768 (2005); Daniel Bethlehem, *Principles Relevant to the Scope of a State's Right as Self-Defense Against an Imminent or Actual Armed Attack by Nonstate Actors*, 106 Am. J. Int'l L. 770, (2012); Jeremy Wright, *The Modern Law of Self-Defence*, EJIL Talk (Jan. 11, 2017), https://www.ejiltalk.org/the-modern-law-of-self-defence/. The Australian government generally follows the UK's approach; *see* George Brandis, *The Right of Self-Defence Against Imminent Armed Attack In International Law*, EJIL Talk (May 25, 2017), https://www.ejiltalk.org/the-right-of-self-defence-against-imminent-armed-attack-in-international-law/.

34. *See infra* text accompanying notes 43–55.

war against Israel and joined the Egyptian-Syrian security treaty. Israel, while calling up its reservist units, started a diplomatic campaign aimed at the opening of the Straits and a demobilization of military forces on both sides. Inside Israel, the domestic effect of the Egyptian activities and rhetoric became intolerable. The Israel Defense Forces were based primarily upon reservists; the Israeli economy was substantially paralyzed and could not sustain the recruitment of its main labor force for a long period. The Israeli public, at least substantial parts of it, was in an existential panic.[35] Given this background to the Israeli preemptive strike on June 5, 1967, many commentators classify it as a justified self-defense:[36]

> The Israeli first strike is, I think, a clear case of legitimate anticipation. . . . The general formula must go something like this: states may use military force in the face of threats of war, whenever the failure to do so would seriously risk their territorial integrity or political independence. Under such circumstances it can fairly be said that they have been forced to fight and that they are the victims of aggression. Since there are no police upon whom they can call, the moment at which states are forced to fight probably comes sooner than it would for individuals in a settled domestic society.[37]

The justification for the anticipatory strike in the Six Day War seems to be even stronger than the case for legalizing a hypothetical American preemptive strike against the Japanese fleet sailing toward Pearl Harbor (but before the Japanese armed attack actually started). Egypt had created an existential threat to Israel (whereas Japan in Pearl Harbor did not initiate any such threat toward the United States), and this was exacerbated by the unlawful acts it committed, mainly the closure of the Straits of Tiran. Indeed, in retrospect, one could argue that the Egyptian president, Nasser,

---

35. This historical background is based upon MICHAEL WALZER, JUST AND UNJUST WARS 82–85 (4th ed. 2006) (*see* there an elaborate presentation of this background).

36. *See, e.g.*, FREEDMAN, DETERRENCE, *supra* note 8, at 90 ("The UN Security Council did not condemn this."). On the general perception by Western states of the Israeli action as legitimate and the lack of condemnation by the UN General Assembly and UN Security Council of Israel's conduct during the war, *see* ANTONIO CASSESE, THE CURRENT LEGAL REGULATION OF THE USE OF FORCE 443 (1986).

37. WALZER, JUST AND UNJUST WARS, *supra* note 35, at 85.

did not mean to exercise his threats and attack Israel.[38] But the legitimacy of the preemption should be examined ex ante, from the self-defendant's reasonable perspective. At the beginning of June 1967, an imminent all-out Egyptian attack, which might have posed an existential threat to Israel, was perceived as a natural and probable consequence of all of Nasser's preceding activities.[39] This precedent, as Franck concludes, "does not amount to an open-ended endorsement of a general right to anticipatory self-defense, but it does recognize that, in demonstrable circumstances of extreme necessity, anticipatory self-defense may be a legitimate exercise of a state's right to ensure its survival."[40] Not surprisingly, Israel, however, did not justify its attack on the grounds of anticipatory self-defense; rather, it argued that the actions of the Arab states in general, the blocking of the Straits of Tiran in particular, aggregated to an "actual" armed attack justifying a lawful self-defense, within the framework of article 51.[41]

2.2.2 Prevention in the Guise of an Anticipatory Strike: The American Lessons

The notion of eliminating the enemy's capabilities before they can be used is not new to the United States' strategic thinking. In its previous form, at the beginning of the Cold War, the focus was not upon terrorist threats but on nonconventional threats by states. One assumption at the time was

---

38. *See, e.g.*, Freedman, noting that it may be "as historians now judge, that they [the Arab states] had never expected to be taken that seriously . . ." FREEDMAN, DETERRENCE, *supra* note 8, at 90.

39. The notion that one may be responsible and judged for acts that one has yet to commit, but are probable consequences of another unlawful activity that one has commenced upon, is not strange to moral and legal thinking; further, it applies even if the acts were committed by a related third party. For example, this is the case in a criminal legal system, when participants in an offense are liable for additional offenses committed by their partners in the course of an unlawful activity, provided that the additional offense is a probable, foreseeable consequence of their original criminal collaboration. *See, e.g.*, WAYNE LAFAVE & AUSTIN W. SCOTT, JR., CRIMINAL LAW 590 (2d ed. 1986).

40. THOMAS M. FRANCK, RECOURSE TO FORCE: STATE ACTION AGAINST THREATS AND ARMED ATTACKS 105 (2002).

41. Yet, as Franck concludes: "[a]lthough Israel also based its justification on actual self-defense against such aggressive acts as the closure of the Strait of Tiran, its words and actions clearly asserted a right to anticipatory self-defense against an imminent armed attack." *Id.* at 103. Gray too notes that Israel's self-defense justification was consistent with common states' practice of avoiding the use of the disputed doctrine of anticipatory self-defense and relying upon the undisputed self-defense right of article 51, whenever possible. GRAY, *supra* note 12, at 161–65.

that the only way to win a nuclear war was by eliminating the adversary's nuclear capabilities before it had a chance to use them. Putting aside the moral and legal problems relating to the initiation of such a war with its inevitably catastrophic consequences, this strategy could not—and indeed, did not—hold in practice. Even if such an attack, say by the United States, had the potential of being very "successful" in the sense that it would have destroyed most of Russia's nuclear arsenal, it would have been a pyrrhic victory. If even a very small part of that arsenal was not damaged, Russia would have had the chance to retaliate. In a reality where both superpowers internalized this notion, it is not surprising that both the United States and Russia had "first strike" and "second strike" (hidden, immune from the first attack) capabilities. In fact, this phenomenon neutralized the very notion of such a preventive nuclear strike,[42] and the deterrence strategy—oriented toward containment of conflicts—was preferred, during the Cold War, over the preemptive one.[43]

The events of 9/11 gave new life to the proactive and preemptive—one might even say aggressive—strategy. First, a wider interpretation of the right of self-defense seemed called for in terms of the identity of the adversaries, granting it to states fighting against terrorist groups (non-state actors) and not, as formerly argued by many, limiting the right to fighting between states. Second, a wider interpretation of the substantial essence and scope of this right seemed called for, as well. The first dimension received its legal backing in Security Council Resolution 1368,[44] "*[r]ecognizing* the inherent right of individual or collective self-defence" against the "terrorist acts" of 9/11.[45]

> [B]efore 9/11 it was clear that the right to use force in self-defence against terrorist attacks was controversial. But the almost universal support of states for a US right of self-defence in response to 9/11 may be seen as raising the question whether there has been

42. *See generally* THOMAS C. SCHELLING, ARMS AND INFLUENCE 244–48 (1966) (noting how shielding nuclear weapons in a way that allows second-strike capabilities dissuaded both sides of the Cold War from "jumping the gun") and FREEDMAN, DETERRENCE, *supra* note 8, at 87–88.

43. *See generally* PATRICK M. MORGAN, DETERRENCE NOW 1–26 (2003). The strategic and legal aspects of deterrence will be elaborated on in Chapter 4.

44. S.C. Res. 1368 (Sep. 12, 2001). *See also* S.C. Res. 1373 (Sep. 28, 2001).

45. S.C. Res 1368, *supra* note 44.

> a significant change in the law. For some this is just a continuation of the existing wide right of self-defence; for others it is a new right based on a re-interpretation of Article 51 of the UN Charter, justified by the fiction of instant custom or, more realistically, by universal acceptance by states of a new legal rule; for others the acceptance is merely political and did not serve to create a wider right of self-defence.[46]

The substance of this newly (re)established right of self-defense aimed against terrorist acts makes it necessary to examine the way this right is being (and ought to be) exercised and its timing. It invites the question: To what extent, if any, do the unique attributes of the modern, usually asymmetric, threat affect it?

At the center of our current discussion will be the formally accepted 2002 National Security Strategy for the United States of America,[47] adopting the preemptive strategy against hostile states and terrorist groups. Facing a reality in which radical terrorists and rogue states are the primary threats to U.S. security and deterrence has no (or lesser) relevance, the strategy pointed out that the development and acquisition of weapons of mass destruction by terrorists and rogue states will require the United States to identify and destroy any terrorist threat before it reaches the country's shores. In Chapter 5, it focused upon the strategic challenges facing the United States from both "rogue states and terrorists" and their effects:

> Given the goals of rogue states and terrorists, the United States can no longer solely rely on a reactive posture as we have in the past. The inability to deter a potential attacker, the immediacy of today's threats, and the magnitude of potential harm that could be caused by our adversaries' choice of weapons, do not permit that option. We cannot let our enemies strike first.

---

46. Gray, *supra* note 12, at 198. Indeed, even after 9/11, the legality of self-defense by a state fighting against a nonstate actor is not accepted by all. Concerning the limitation of the right to self-defense only against armed attacks by military forces of states, *see* Legal Consequences of the Construction of a Wall, Advisory Opinion, 2004 I.C.J. 136, ¶ 139 (July 9); for minority views, *see, e.g.*, Legal Consequences of the Construction of a Wall, Advisory Opinion, 2004 I.C.J. 207, ¶¶ 14–19 (separate opinion of Judge Higgins).

47. *See* White House, National Security Strategy (Sept. 2002) [hereinafter 2002 National Security Strategy] http://georgewbush-whitehouse.archives.gov/nsc/nss/2002/index.html (last visited May 5, 2016).

> In the Cold War, especially following the Cuban missile crisis, we faced a generally status quo, risk-averse adversary. Deterrence was an effective defense. But deterrence based only upon the threat of retaliation is less likely to work against leaders of rogue states more willing to take risks, gambling with the lives of their people, and the wealth of their nations.
>
> In the Cold War, weapons of mass destruction were considered weapons of last resort whose use risked the destruction of those who used them. Today, our enemies see weapons of mass destruction as weapons of choice . . .
>
> Traditional concepts of deterrence will not work against a terrorist enemy whose avowed tactics are wanton destruction and the targeting of innocents; whose so-called soldiers seek martyrdom in death and whose most potent protection is statelessness. The overlap between states that sponsor terror and those that pursue WMD compels us to action.[48]

In the face of these strategic challenges, the transformation in the nature and attributes of the United States' enemies, and the asymmetry between the United States and its adversaries, the 2002 National Security Strategy of the United States promoted and justified an anticipatory strike as an integral part of exercising its right of self-defense. In fact, it calls for widening its scope:

> The United States has long maintained the option of pre-emptive actions to counter a sufficient threat to our national security. The greater the threat, the greater is the risk of inaction and the more compelling the case for taking anticipatory action to defend ourselves, even if uncertainty remains as to the time and place of the enemy's attack. To forestall or prevent such hostile acts by our adversaries, the United States will, if necessary, act preemptively.[49]

Although the explicit rhetoric of this strategy—which was followed later in 2006 by a new version of the National Security Strategy[50]—favors

48. *Id.*, ch. V.

49. *Id.*

50. The 2006 version of the National Security Strategy states: "The place of pre-emption in our national security strategy remains the same" (Chapter 5 section C4). It further

preemptive action, its implicit message is oriented toward prevention. The drafters of the 2002 National Security Strategy were fully aware of the distinction between a preemptive strike and preventive war; yet they extended the concept of imminent threat, which is embedded in the preemption rationale, to a new extreme of elasticity, stating that

> For centuries, international law recognized that nations need not suffer an attack before they can lawfully take action to defend themselves against forces that present an imminent danger of attack. Legal scholars and international jurists often conditioned the legitimacy of preemption on the existence of an imminent threat—most often a visible mobilization of armies, navies, and air forces preparing to attack. We must adapt the concept of imminent threat to the capabilities and objectives of today's adversaries.[51]

It was not the explicit adaption of the concept of imminent threat to today's reality and adversaries that formally distorted the legality of the Second Gulf War. This war's legality was rationalized, in a very controversial way, by previous UN Security Council resolutions.[52] Practically, however, the application of this strategy to this war might serve as an example of an artificial extension of the "imminent threat" concept. The Gulf War's aim seemed to be, inter alia, to eliminate a future Iraqi threat.[53] Saddam

---

reaffirmed all of the relevant section of the 2002 strategy on the use of force. It differed, however, with regard to the nature of the threat in the war on terror. It focused upon "Islamic extremists" and states who support them such as Iran and Syria (rather than Iraq and North Korea), dubbed "sponsors of terror" (Chapter 3 Section B). *See* WHITE HOUSE, NATIONAL SECURITY STRATEGY (Mar. 2006) [hereinafter 2006 NATIONAL SECURITY STRATEGY] http://georgewbush-whitehouse.archives.gov/nsc/nss/2006/ (last visited May 5, 2016).

51. 2002 NATIONAL SECURITY STRATEGY, *supra* note 47, at Section V.

52. The U.S. reasoning for going to war in Iraq was based in part on UNSC Res 1441 finding Iraq in material breach of its obligations regarding inspection of its compliance with disarmament. President George W. Bush specifically mentioned the resolution in his speech giving Saddam Hussein a 48-hour ultimatum before commencing the war on Iraq. *See* President George W. Bush, *Address to the Nation on Iraq 2003*, 39 WEEKLY COMP. PRES. DOC. 338 (Mar. 17, 2003). Critics such as Thomas Franck claim that UNSC Res 1441 did not automatically authorize the use of force in the event of Iraq's failure to comply with the resolution, but rather left it to the Security Council's discretion. *See, e.g.*, Thomas M. Franck, *What Happens Now? The United Nations After Iraq*, 97 AM. J. INT'L L. 607, 610–12 (2003).

53. For a review of the position that the 2003 war in Iraq was meant in essence to eliminate a future threat rather than an existing one, *see, e.g.*, Joseph Cirincione et al., *WMD in Iraq: Evidence and Implications* (Carnegie Endowment for Int'l Peace 2004), http://carnegieendowment.org/files/iraq3fulltext.pdf; Vaughn P. Shannon & Jonathan W. Keller,

Hussein's regime did not pose a real threat, nor was there potentially an imminent Iraqi attack on the United States at the time the war was declared, for Saddam was weak enough then, and unable to retaliate.[54] From this perspective, this war was probably an unlawful preventive war disguised, as a lawful one.

The gap between the legal rhetoric and actual practice, as reflected, for example, in the Bush strategy, its radical change under President Obama's administration,[55] and the ambiguity surrounding the prevailing rules, invites a normative discussion regarding the scope of proactive self-defense and its main challenges. In developing such a discussion I shall turn, in the next Part, to a concrete suggestion calling for the adoption of an operational standard while framing the contours of a lawful first strike.

2.3 *Lawful Self-Defense against an "Occurring" Armed Attack: A Suggested Operational Standard*

2.3.1 Normative Introduction: A Self-Defendant Is Not Doomed to Be a Sitting Duck

In order to clarify the ambiguity surrounding the normative discussion, it might be useful to map the anticipatory scale: the various potential attributes of an attack (including an imminent one) that might be perceived as occurring. At one end of the scale is when a full-scale armed attack

---

Leadership Style and International Norm Violation: The Case of the Iraq War, 3 Foreign Policy Analysis 79, 89 (2007).

54. Freedman, Deterrence, *supra* note 8, at 102. ("it was unclear whether Iraq was being chosen because it was the most serious threat or because it was the most accessible." *Id.* at 101).

55. The 2010 National Security Strategy reflects a different approach calling for "credibly underwriting US defense commitments with tailored approaches to deterrence." This Strategy states:

> While the use of force is sometimes necessary, we will exhaust other options before war whenever we can, and carefully weigh the costs and risks of action against the costs and risks of inaction. When force is necessary, we will continue to do so in a way that reflects our values and strengthens our legitimacy, and we will seek broad international support, working with such institutions as NATO and the UN Security Council.
>
> The United States must reserve the right to act unilaterally if necessary to defend our nation and our interests, yet we will also seek to adhere to standards that govern the use of force. Doing so strengthens those who act in line with international standards, while isolating and weakening those who do not. White House, National Security Strategy 22 (May 2010), http://nssarchive.us/NSSR/2010.pdf (last visited Aug. 20, 2017).

has already occurred and the legality of self-defense against such aggression is beyond moral or legal question. At the other end of the spectrum lies hypothetical speculation, based upon gossip and rumor, regarding the adversary's intentions. When an adversary has not actually acted in an aggressive manner, the presumption of an attack—solely due to its declared intentions, which have not been followed by any concrete, actually threatening activity—is unwarranted. Aggressive declarations by state leaders or high-ranking officials should carry some weight and might even justify some countermeasures by the victim state; however, they should not be perceived as an armed attack and cannot justify a preventive war. Speculations—even reasonable ones—about one's enemy's intentions do not justify, per se, seeing it as a crossing of the *ad bellum* Rubicon.[56] Thus, a war that is aimed against an enemy's mere intentions is neither just[57] nor lawful. By the same token, a preventive war aimed against a potential adversary's mere capabilities (not accompanied by very concrete hostile intentions)—and rationalized as being to maintain the balance of power among potential adversaries (and thus, also the "international order")—is not justified either. Morally speaking, "[w]e don't want to fight until we are threatened, because only then can we rightly fight."[58]

Legally, it seems that only a combination of actual activities carried out by an adversary, on a very substantial aggressive scale, followed by manifest belligerent intentions, might be considered to have passed the imminence threshold, triggering a lawful self-defense. The move on the anticipatory scale from the speculative-hypothetical pole toward the absolute one should be very substantial and concrete, and fine-tuned to the magnitude of the threat and its certainty, in order to vindicate such a strike. If it is certain that an armed attack is underway—for example, the Japanese attack on Pearl Harbor—the self-defendant can lawfully intercept it;[59] the *ad bellum* threshold has been crossed due to the attack,

---

56. For example, the U.S. Army's standing rules of engagement distinguish between "hostile act" and "hostile intent"; the latter should be a "demonstrated" one in order to justify the exercise of the "inherent right of self-defense." *See Inherent Right of Self-Defense, in* Int'l & Operational Law Dep't, The Judge Advocate General's School, U.S. Army, JA 422, Operational Law Handbook 75–76 (2008) [hereinafter JA422].

57. *See* the moral discussion regarding preventive war in Walzer, Just and Unjust Wars, *supra* note 35, at 76–80.

58. Walzer, Just and Unjust Wars, *supra* note 35, at 80.

59. *See supra* note 23.

:ing a self-defendant's response. It is suggested, however, that if the threat is not absolutely certain, it is the combination of the magnitude of the risk to the self-defendant and its probability that should determine the legal self-defense threshold. Thus, if the imminence of the threat is only near certain,[60] it needs to be an existential (or at least very substantial) threat to the defendant to vindicate its first strike: for example, the Six Day War. The higher the magnitude of the threat the lesser the level of (near) certainty required. After all, legalizing the taking of the unilateral belligerent initiative—in the name of self-defense—is a matter of life and death to both adversaries and should be scrutinized accordingly. Indeed, the existentiality of the threat might affect not only the *in bello* rules—as admitted by the International Court of Justice, regarding the threat or use of nuclear weapons[61]—but, as suggested, the *ad bellum* timing, as well.

The prevailing concept of imminent threat[62] in general, the assessment of two of its variables (the magnitude of the threat and its certainty) in particular, seems to be too vague and requires elaboration.[63] To lessen this ambiguity, this chapter suggests a strategic-military professional standard to substantiate the contours of the lawful timing of a potential self-defendant's response. The suggested criterion is the last reasonable point in time, according to the self-defendant's military circumstances and doctrine, at which it can successfully face the aggressor's threat and still operationally defend itself, including, when necessary, by taking the initiative in its own

60. Should it be analogous to the "beyond a reasonable doubt" standard of criminal law? *See, e.g.*, Kristen E. Eichensehr, *Targeting Tehran: Assessing the Lawfulness of Preemptive Strikes Against Nuclear Facilities*, 11 UCLA J. INT'L L. & FOREIGN AFFAIRS 59, 66 (2006).

61. *See supra* Introduction note 85.

62. *See supra* notes 24, 33, 51. Although the common legal wisdom points at the imminent threat (whatever precisely that means), Michael Walzer challenges it by focusing upon the weight of the threat rather than on the proximity of the attack, pointing at the sufficient threat: "The line between legitimate and illegitimate first strikes is not going to be drawn at the point of imminent attack but at the point of sufficient threat. That phrase is necessarily vague. I mean it to cover three things: a manifest intent to injure, a degree of active preparation that makes that intent a positive danger, and a general situation in which waiting, or doing anything other than fighting, greatly magnifies the risk." WALZER, JUST AND UNJUST WARS, *supra* note 35, at 81.

63. *See, e.g.*, DINSTEIN, WAR, AGGRESSION AND SELF-DEFENCE, *supra* note 7, at 205–06 (arguing, inter alia, that "imminence may mean different things to different people." *Id.* at 205); *see also* Bethlehem, *supra* note 33, at 774 (arguing, inter alia, that "while 'imminence' continues to be a key element of the law relevant to anticipatory self-defense in response to a threat of attack, the concept needs to be further refined and developed to take into account the new circumstances and threats from nonstate actors that states face today").

self-defense.[64] (In many cases, although it is the self-defendant's civilian leaders who take the final *ad bellum* decision related to exercising their military forces, it is argued that they should be guided by this suggested professional-military standard.)

In fact, what is suggested here is a revised reading of article 51, striking a new balance from two perspectives: first, a macro-balance between the international desire, as reflected in the UN Charter, to maintain international peace and security by preserving the status quo and the self-defendant's existential interests; and second, a micro-balance, from the self-defendant's viewpoint, between the imminent threat of an armed attack against it and its ability to exercise its inherent right to defend itself.

The following discussion will present the suggested professional standard, allowing, whenever necessary, proactive military activities within the defensive sphere. As a preliminary matter, however, introducing the suggested criterion of a self-defendant's operational last resort requires convincing the reader that military professionalism does exist and that it should have a legal effect. The following sections will address the issue of military professionalism and the legal standards, related to belligerencies, which can be distilled from it. The risks its adoption involves—mainly manipulation, abuse, and escalation—will be dealt with later in this chapter.

2.3.2 Military Professionalism: Learning Its Objectives and Subjective Variants

In an earlier discussion in Chapter 1, the duality of military professionalism was highlighted, in that it allows the use of lethal force but at the same time constrains it. The focus in this Part will be upon its functioning. Militaries—especially well-trained and disciplined ones—adhere to their doctrine, operational principles, fighting techniques, and values, in their strategic planning and military operations. Professional standards reflect the way militaries think, function, and fight. The scope of these standards and their wide universality will be presented. Admittedly, however, there are no absolute military norms universally accepted by all. Militaries'

64. Michael Schmitt suggests a similar (though probably less restrictive) standard vindicating a preemptive strike: "the *last possible window of opportunity* in the face of an attack that was almost certainly going to occur." Michael N. Schmitt, *Preemptive Strategies in International Law*, 24 MICH. J. INT'L L. 513, 535 (2003).

doctrines and rules, though they share a lot in common, do vary, reflecting the adversaries' different cultures and other relevant circumstances. The main equivalences and variances and their effect will be presented here.

Let us start with the preliminary question: Do combatants have a profession, or is it just a trade, occupation, vocation, or job? The answer could be framed in absolute terms: either everyone in the military is a professional or no one is. In the middle of the spectrum, there are those who believe that only the officer corps is professional. Leo Tolstoy in *War and Peace* presents the most extreme view in denying military professionalism. One of his heroes, the disappointed Prince Bolkonsky, who was trained as a professional soldier, declares: "there was not and could not be a science of war . . . What theory or science is possible where the conditions and circumstances are unknown and cannot be determined, and especially where the strength of the active forces cannot be ascertained?"[65] Indeed, the prince's presentation of the facts corresponds with Clausewitz's dictum, "war is the realm of uncertainty,"[66] and to some extent reflects the reality of war. His conclusion, however, is unconvincing. Militaries' performances are not random and incidental. Rather, they are contingent upon their officers' and soldiers' professional skills. Though the "fog" of war[67] is a crucial factor in understanding military reality, its surprising potential and inherent ambiguity require that this phenomenon be faced and managed professionally.

Indeed, military command is usually perceived as a profession that has its own characteristics. Samuel Huntington, while setting out a theory of civil-military relations, begins his theory with the classification of officership as a profession that is in charge of the "management of violence."[68] Like the professions of medicine or law, officership requires expertise in its field, a sense of responsibility toward the society, and corporateness, reflected by commitment to members of its group.[69] According to Huntington, the peculiar skill of a military officer—the management of

---

65. Leo Tolstoy, War and Peace 774 (1968).

66. *See supra* Chapter 1 note 51.

67. *See supra* Introduction note 87.

68. Samuel P. Huntington, The Soldier and the State: The Theory and Politics of Civil-Military Relations 11–18 (20th prtg. 2003). Huntington distinguishes officers from enlisted soldiers, specialists in the application of violence but not in its management. *Id.* at 17–18. *Cf.* Ann E. Rondeau, *Identity in the Profession of Arms*, (2011) 62(3) Joint Forces Q. 10, 12 (2011).

69. Huntington *Id.* at 8–10.

violence—"is universal in the sense that its essence is not affected by changes in time or location. Just as the qualifications of a good surgeon are the same in Zurich as they are in New York, the same standards of professional military competence apply in Russia as in America and in the nineteenth century as in the twentieth."[70] Indeed, such a broad perception of officer professionalism is disputed; it might be argued that it bears no resemblance to medicine or law, in either the (universal) skills required or their definite goals.[71]

Whatever one's view regarding the professional status of the officers' guild, our focus is not on their prestige or the classification of their titles but on their professional competence: the professional function of militaries and the skills required by their combatants. Military operations, at all ranks, require knowledge, competence, and skills. Soldiers are required to operate these skills in problematic circumstances in a domain of knowledge, and to operate in light of a set of principles and norms underlying their operation.[72] Though the frustration of Tolstoy's Prince Bolkonsky reflects the difficulties in exercising these skills on the battlefield, it does not refute the notion that there are standards and norms that can be regarded as underlying the profession of arms at all ranks. Although in practice there is no absolute coherency between different militaries, many of their principles are universally shared, and the differences should not prevent the profession of arms from being considered as such, just as it does not prevent lawyers from being considered professionals regardless

70. *Id.* at 13.

71. As opposed to these professions whose ultimate goals are straightforward (i.e., for doctors to cure their patients or alleviate their pain and for lawyers to achieve the best possible results for their clients), the soldiers' ultimate purposes are usually ambiguous, politically oriented, and uncertain. *See, e.g.*, Eliot A. Cohen, Supreme Command: Soldiers, Statesmen and Leadership in Wartime 257–59 (2003). Indeed, whereas doctors specialize in the science of healing, and lawyers in the science of regulating society, soldiers specialize in the application of lethal force. Kevin M. Bond, *Are We Professionals?* 58(3) Joint Forces Q. 62, 63 (2010). However, a doctor's misapplication of his skill may result in a patient's death, a lawyer's misapplication of her skill may result in her client being punished, but a soldier's misapplication of his knowledge may result in the nation's loss. *See generally* Thomas P. Galvin, *A New Way of Understanding (Military) Professionalism*, 62(3) Joint Forces Q. 25 (2011). In addition, the occupational path of soldiers, in contrast to doctors or lawyers, has different attributes that might prevent them from being considered professionals. The low threshold is reflected by the relatively short career and high turnover rate of officers, their lack of a professional association, and a relatively low level of autonomous judgment.

72. Galvin *Id.*

of the legal regime and the country they operate in.[73] At the higher level of the military profession, strategic planning and military command require special training and skills, and they have their own professional standards and rules. In the modern era military strategy developed into "a general body of knowledge from which leaders could draw. The strategist came to be a distinctive professional . . . "[74] Similarly, military command requires professionalism,[75] and enlisted soldiers require vocational training and acquire combatants' skills. Soldiers at all levels have their own military standards and rules, as well as tools and mechanisms for exercising them.

Militaries' doctrines—namely, the fundamental set of principles that guides military forces as they pursue their objectives—are their professional North Star. The military doctrine of any army is its anchor, usually deeply rooted in its culture and based upon many years of prewar training and operational planning. Indeed, militaries' doctrines do vary, reflecting their different cultures[76] and other relevant circumstances (e.g., strategic and economic). As NATO defines it, military doctrine is "fundamental principles by which military forces guide their actions in support of objectives."[77] Though it is considered authoritative, it nonetheless "requires judgment in application."[78] As it deals with the higher level of military directive and force application, the Soviets explicitly divided the term into two aspects: social-political, dictated by the civilian leadership, and military-technical, dictated by the general staff. In their view a doctrine is a "state's officially accepted system of scientifically founded views on the nature of modern wars and the use of the armed forces in them."[79]

---

73. *Cf.* the universal skill argument of Huntington, *supra* note 70.

74. Lawrence Freedman, Strategy 72 (2013).

75. *See* the discussion above and *see, e.g.*, Martin Van Creveld, Command in War (1985).

76. For a general discussion of the effect of cultural attributes upon strategic behavior and the way they shape military doctrines, *see, e.g.*, Dima Adamsky, The Culture of Military Innovation (2010).

77. Allied Administrative Publication (AAP)-06, NATO Glossary of Terms and Definitions 2-D-9 (2013). Similarly, the U.S. definition reads: "Fundamental principles by which the military forces or elements thereof guide their actions in support of national objectives." Joint Chiefs of Staff, Joint Pub. 1-02, Department of Defense Dictionary of Military and Associated Terms 71 (Nov. 8, 2010, as amended through June 15, 2015) [hereinafter Joint Pub. 1-02].

78. *Id.*

79. *The Soviet Dictionary of Basic Military Terms*, as quoted in William E. Odom, *Soviet Military Doctrine*, 67 Foreign Affairs 114, 117 (1988).

A military doctrine is firmly implanted among a military's rank and file, long before any belligerence has taken place. It reflects the reliance a military places in its soldiers and the relative value it ascribes to their lives. For example, the Soviet defense doctrine, discussed earlier in the context of the Gulf War,[80] was improvident, in that it was based upon several lines of defense set up to meet advancing enemy forces.[81] Soviet offensive doctrine worked in much the same wasteful way, being comprised of two echelons[82] on top of the reserve forces.[83] Ultimately, it is the culture of a given society, besides its geostrategic considerations, that largely dictates its military doctrine and strategy.[84] The patterns of war, the way militaries fight and their doctrines are controlled primarily through the cultural domain. Even military tactics "are usually the product of social and economic factors rather than of purely military ones."[85] This reality explains why a military doctrine cannot be transformed overnight; a doctrinal transformation may take years. War practices can generally change when there is a shift in the culture of the relevant society.[86] For example, Michael Handel traces the source of Sun Tzu's moderate approach to Confucius's idea of attaining ends without violence.[87] Even Clausewitz, the military theorist, agreed that important factors in evaluating changes in war's pattern are social and

---

80. *See supra* Chapter 1 note 55.

81. In fact, this pattern of fighting was not an original one: "The [Roman] legion was formed in three separate lines, with the veteran troops waiting calmly in the rear. Detached in this way, they were able to counter any adverse development in the front rather than be engulfed in it themselves." Azar Gat, The Development of Military Thought: The Nineteenth Century 33 (1992).

82. The first echelon was meant to penetrate or defeat the enemy's forward defenses, and then continue its attack. The second echelon was tasked with exploiting the success of the first echelon while taking care of enemy forces bypassed by the first echelon. It also had the task of reinforcing first-echelon forces. U.S. Dep't of Army, Field Manual 100-2-1, The Soviet Army Operations and Tactics 2–10 (July 16, 1984) http://fas.org/irp/doddir/army/fm100-2-1.pdf (last visited Dec. 2, 2015) [hereinafter FM 100-2-1].

83. The rear reserve forces worked in a way similar to the second echelon but without pre-assigned tasks, employed wherever they could be used effectively in light of the offensive mission. *Id.* at 2–11.

84. *See supra* note 76.

85. Van Creveld, *supra* note 75, at 19.

86. *See, e.g.*, Moltke's view that war could only be limited through a general cultural change in the moral sensibilities of societies at large. Geoffrey Best, Humanity in Warfare: The Modern History of the International Law of Armed Conflict 145 (1983).

87. *See supra* text accompanying Chapter 1 note 82.

cultural and, as such, subject to change: "Very few of the new manifestations in war can be ascribed to new inventions or new departures in ideas. They result mainly from the transformation of society and new social conditions."[88] Other dimensions affecting military doctrines and strategies are geographic and economic. For example, American strategy has long leaned toward the use of overwhelming force, a choice influenced by the country's sheer size, wealth, and production capabilities: "The strategy of attrition and annihilating the enemy with firepower was the best way to transform the [American] nation's material superiority into battlefield effectiveness. The translation of enormous resources into firepower, technology, and logistical ability and a consequent inclination for direct attack date back to the military experience of the American Civil War."[89]

The variances and nuances between militaries are usually well known: as regards Western states' militaries, their basic military doctrines are usually intentionally public domain (e.g., through army field manuals), whereas the doctrinal texts of dictatorships become known due to intelligence gathering and academic research.[90] Furthermore, the application of the various military doctrines is carried out by militaries, while they train and exercise, with substantial transparency. Indeed, during the Cold War, both the Soviet defense doctrine and offensive doctrine[91] were well known around the world. Similarly, the military doctrine of its main adversary, NATO, was known too and published, for example in its militaries' manuals.

In light of their versatile doctrinal approaches, militaries have developed their own operational principles, as well. Those principles of war

---

88. Carl Von Clausewitz, On War 515 (Michael Eliot Howard & Peter Paret trans., indexed ed. 1984).

89. Adamsky, *supra* note 76, at 78–79. This choice of mass force by the Americans was also noted by Eliot Cohen: "World War II both shaped and revealed American strategic culture as no other war with the exception of the Civil War. Two dominant characteristics stand out: the preference for massing a vast array of men and machines and the predilection for direct and violent assault." Eliot A Cohen, *The Strategy of Innocence? The US, 1920–1945, in* The Making of Strategy: Rulers, States and War 428, 464 (Williamson Murray, MacGregor Knox & Alvin Bernstein eds., 1994). Russell R. Weighley, The American Way of War: A History of United States Military Strategy and Policy (1973).

90. *See, e.g.*, Adamsky, *supra* note 76, at 68.

91. For the Soviet defensive doctrine, *see, e.g.*, Richard W. Harrison, The Russian Way of War: Operational Art 1904–1940 193 (2001). For the offensive, *see, e.g.*, FM 100-2-1, *supra* note 82.

"represent the most important nonphysical factors that affect the conduct of operations at the strategic, operational and tactical levels."[92] Indeed, there are several main principles common to many militaries that appear in each army in one form or another.[93] For example, the principle of *objective*—requiring a clearly defined and attainable objective[94]—appears literally in the United States' principles of war,[95] and it is called "Selection and Maintenance of the Aim" in the British version.[96] The USSR's version of the principles of military art did not name the principle per se, but called to "select the principal army objective to be seized and the best routes for attacking it."[97] In a similar fashion, the principle of *concentration of force*—requiring that forces be concentrated in the most effective way in light of their mission[98]—appears directly in the UK's principles of war,[99] and is referred to in the U.S. Army as the *principle of mass*,[100] requiring the concentration of "the effects of combat power in the decisive place and time."[101] And although the USSR's principles of military art did not call the principle of *concentration of force* by its name, they did call for "the decisive concentration of combat power at the correct time," uniting it with the principle of objective.[102] Another example of the commonality of war principles is the principle of *maneuver*, requiring a fighting force

---

92. U.S. Dep't of the Army, Field Manual 3-0, Operations A-1 (Feb. 27, 2008) [hereinafter FM 3-0]. The USSR called its own version the principles of military art, or the principles of operational art and tactics. FM 100-2-1, *supra* note 82, at 2-2.

93. For a comparative view of the principles of war and the way they have diverged among various armies in modern times, *see, e.g.*, Jan Angstrom & J.J. Widen, *Adopting a Recipe for Success: Modern Armed Forces and the Institutionalization of the Principles of War*, 31 Comp. Strategy 263 (2012). *See also* the discussion *supra*, concerning the demand for effectiveness and efficiency from trained militaries, text accompanying Chapter 1 notes 15–18.

94. *Id.* at 267–70.

95. FM 3-0, *supra* note 92, at A-1.

96. U.K. Ministry of Defence, Army Doctrine Publication, Operations 2A-2 (Nov. 2010), https://www.gov.uk/government/uploads/system/uploads/attachment_data/file/33695/ADPOperationsDec10.pdf (last visited Aug. 24, 2016) [hereinafter U.K. Operations Manual].

97. FM 100-2-1, *supra* note 82, at 2-2.

98. Angstrom & Widen, *supra* note 93, at 271.

99. U.K. Operations Manual, *supra* note 96, at 2A-4, and *see infra* Chapter 3 note 109.

100. FM 3-0, *supra* note 92, at A-2.

101. *Id.*

102. FM 100-2-1, *supra* note 82.

to be flexible on its feet so as to quickly adapt its maneuver to the battlefield's changing circumstances.[103] It appears in name and meaning in the U.S. principles of war,[104] and is called *flexibility* in the UK version.[105] The USSR version, for its part, required Soviet forces to be "fully prepared to accomplish the mission regardless of the conditions under which war begins or must be conducted,"[106] in essence requiring them to be prepared for any eventuality. Additional common principles include surprise,[107] initiative,[108] and security of operations.[109] Another universal principle is that of *economy of force*, which means that due to the limited resources at the fighting force's disposal, only that much force should be allocated to a military task as is required and necessary to achieve it.[110] The Soviet version called upon commanders to make "full use of all available military assets and capabilities to achieve victory,"[111] while adapting the end to the means.[112]

Despite their broad common denominator, militaries do differ in some of their principles. For example, the principle of *sustainability*—requiring commanders to make sure their forces are ready both physically and mentally at every stage throughout the campaign, from preparation, through the operation itself, to redeployment and recuperation—appears in the UK's principles

---

103. Angstrom & Widen, *supra* note 93, at 271.

104. FM 3-0, *supra* note 92, at A-2.

105. U.K. OPERATIONS MANUAL, *supra* note 96, at 2A-5.

106. FM 100-2-1, *supra* note 82, at 2-2.

107. FM 3-0, *supra* note 92, at A-3; U.K. OPERATIONS MANUAL, *supra* note 96, at 2A-3; FM 100-2-1, *supra* note 82.

108. Dubbed "offensive" in the United States, FM 3-0, *supra* note 92, at A-1; dubbed "offensive action" in the UK, U.K. OPERATIONS MANUAL, *supra* note 96, at 2A-3; FM 100-2-1, *supra* note 82, at 2–3.

109. FM 3-0, *supra* note 92, at A-3; U.K. OPERATIONS MANUAL, *supra* note 96, at 2A-3; FM 100-2-1, *supra* note 82, at 2–4.

110. Angstrom & Widen, *supra* note 93, at 271; FM 3-0, *supra* note 92, at A-2; U.K. OPERATIONS MANUAL, *supra* note 96, at 2A-4. *See supra* text accompanying Chapter 1 notes 14, 16.

111. FM 100-2-1, *supra* note 82, at 2-2. It should be noted that the translations of Soviet principles of operational art vary from one source to the next. For this reason this chapter makes use of the U.S. Army's version of the principles. The Army's study points out that the original principle of *economy of force* disappeared during the 1970s as a response to the nuclear age. *Id.*

112. Jonathan F. Keiler, *The End of Proportionality*, 39 PARAMETERS 53, 58–59 (2009).

of war[113] and in the USSR's[114] (where it is dubbed "preservation of combat effectiveness of friendly forces"), but does not appear in the United States' basic nine principles.[115] On the other hand, the United States is the only one to include simplicity of plans in its principles of war,[116] whereas *troop morale* is only included in the UK's principles of war,[117] but not in the United States' or USSR's. Similarly, the UK is also the only one of the three superpowers compared here that does not include *unity of command* in one form or another in its principles.[118] Indeed, the differences between militaries' cultures are, to a large extent, reflected in their war principles. Not surprisingly, then, the 1955 Chinese military doctrine included a principle of political mobilization, whereas West Germany's military doctrine of 1962 included legitimacy.[119]

The discussion to this point has shown that although armies differ in their individual methods, they usually still share the main professional pillars such as doctrine and war principles. Underpinning these pillars is another common feature: fighting techniques, which are usually categorized in accordance with war theaters. The U.S. Army, for example, has field manuals for urban terrain,[120] counterinsurgency,[121] mountain operations,[122] and other technique manuals based on the type of weaponry used.[123] In addition to the aforementioned hierarchical pillars of military professionalism in the form of doctrine, principles of war, and

---

113. U.K. Operations Manual, *supra* note 96, at 2A-5.

114. FM 100-2-1, *supra* note 82, at 2–3.

115. A similar principle, *perseverance*, appears in the expanded version of the principles, which adds a set of three joint operational principles (perseverance, legitimacy, and restraint), calling the unified body *the principles of joint operations*. FM 3-0, *supra* note 92, at A-3.

116. *Id.* at A-3.

117. U.K. Operations Manual, *supra* note 96, at 2A-2.

118. FM 3-0, *supra* note 92, at A-3 (US); FM 100-2-1, *supra* note 82, at 2-2.

119. Angstrom & Widen, *supra* note 93, at 269.

120. U.S. Dep't of Army, Field Manual 3-06, Urban Operations (Oct. 26, 2006).

121. U.S. Dep't of Army, Field Manual 3-24, Insurgencies and Countering Insurgencies (June 2, 2014).

122. U.S. Dep't of Army, Field Manual 3-97.6, Mountain Operations (Nov. 28, 2000).

123. *See* comprehensive list at: http://www.globalsecurity.org/military/library/policy/army/fm/ (last visited Dec. 2, 2015). Similar manuals exist with the British Army as well. *See, e.g.*, British Army, British Army Field Manuals and Doctrine Publications (Liddell Hart Centre for Military Archives 2008).

techniques, another professional commonality is military planning and decision-making. As presented earlier, military planning is a very well structured process.[124] Furthermore, due to its hierarchical structure, militaries' command and control is designated at each level and unit, where authority is exercised by a "properly designated commander over assigned and attached forces in the accomplishment of the mission."[125] Indeed, militaries' performances are not unintentional or incidental, nor are their results a matter of chance. Rather, to a very large extent they reflect each military's level of professionalism. Indeed, exercising self-defense is, above all, a professional matter that, as will be argued below, should have legal effect.

2.3.3 Operational Last Resort: A Professional Standard

When it comes to the imminence of a potential attacker's threat, a self-defendant, acting in a bona fide manner and professionally in light of its own circumstances, has a reasonable sphere in which it can defend itself against an existential threat. From its perspective, this is the last point in time at which it can still execute an effective self-defense and be proactive if necessary, and not be doomed to being a passive sitting duck. Indeed, this is the essence of the inherent right of self-defense. Elihu Root, then U.S. secretary of war, stated in 1914 that it is the "right of every sovereign state to protect itself by preventing a condition of affairs in which it will be too late to protect itself."[126] The defendant state does not have to turn

124. *See supra* text accompanying Chapter 1 notes 60–69.

125. Joint Pub. 1-02, *supra* note 77, at 40. An earlier version of the dictionary elaborates on this concept by noting that "Command and control functions are performed through an arrangement of personnel, equipment, communications, facilities, and procedures employed by a commander in planning, directing, coordinating, and controlling forces and operations in the accomplishment of the mission." Joint Chiefs of Staff, Joint Pub. 1-02, Department of Defense Dictionary of Military and Associated Terms 53 (Nov. 8, 2010, as amended through Aug. 15, 2012). Other features of the profession of arms, common to many states (in whole or in part), include recognition of the profession as such, existence of a judicial body prohibiting or allowing practice of the profession (such as military courts), entry level requirements to enter the profession and remain part of it (training), a system of rewards (promotion) and punishment (demotion, prison), and controls over the application of knowledge. *See* Galvin, *supra* note 71, at 27–28.

126. Quoted by Freedman, Deterrence, *supra* note 8, at 90. Freedman further observes that "The key shift here was the argument that the test should not be one of immediacy, waiting until absolutely the last moment even if this turns out to be too late, but of necessity, acting at the point where an attack can still be forestalled." *Id.* at 94.

a blind eye, nor any of its cheeks, to its adversary's aggressive activities. There comes a time in which the state of affairs entitles—indeed, in many cases obliges—a reasonable party to protect itself proactively.

The criterion of reasonableness (and the reasonable sphere) is no stranger to the international law relating to war. For example, according to the Committee Established to Review the NATO Bombing in Kosovo, the legal assessment of the *in bello* proportionality, requiring that an expected "military advantage" be balanced vis-à-vis collateral damage,[127] is performed through the eyes of the reasonable commander.[128] Indeed, the role assigned to the reasonable military commander in proportionality assessment should be extended to the "reasonable military strategist"—the military commander or civilian leader who takes the final *ad bellum* decision related to the exercise of military force—with professional reasonable standards introduced into the *ad bellum* self-defense discourse, too. It has already been suggested by Yoram Dinstein, concerning the related issue of proportionality, that "It is perhaps best to look at the demand for proportionality in the province of self-defence as a standard of reasonableness in the response to force by counter-force."[129] The challenge, of course, is to locate and characterize professionally the reasonable, contextually based, "last possible point in time" for an operational (and possibly, proactive) act of self-defense: one that both is moral and ought to be lawful.[130] Although the operational last resort standard is primarily a matter to be scrutinized using professional-strategic criteria, the military does not have a monopoly over it. It is not immune to external assessment and critique, whenever an anticipatory strike is carried out unprofessionally.

---

127. *See supra* Chapter 1 note 59.

128. *See* ICC Office of the Prosecutor, *Final Report to the Prosecutor by the Committee Established to Review the NATO Bombing Campaign Against the Federal Republic of Yugoslavia*, para. 50 (June 13, 2000) [hereinafter OTP Report], www.icty.org/x/file/About/OTP/otp_report_nato_bombing_en.pdf (last visited Apr. 24, 2016) and *see supra* Chapter 1 note 98.

129. Dinstein, War, Aggression and Self-Defence, *supra* note 7, at 232–33.

130. The U.S. Army's standing rules of engagement seem to define *Imminent Use of Force* through this prism: "The determination of whether the use of force against US forces is imminent will be based on an assessment of all facts and circumstances known to US forces at the time and may be made at any level. Imminent does not necessarily mean immediate or instantaneous." JA422, *supra* note 56, at 76.

Recently, in the Tallinn Manual a majority of international experts similarly concluded that either a cyber or kinetic anticipatory self-defense may be taken at the "last feasible window of opportunity." The Manual elaborates: "[t]his window may present itself immediately before the attack in question, or, in some cases long before it occurs. The critical question is not the temporal proximity of the anticipatory defensive action to the prospective attack, but whether a failure to act at that moment would reasonably be expected to result in the State being unable to defend itself effectively when the attack actually starts."[131]

Indeed, the last-resort criterion should be interpreted not as the last possible tactical reaction—such as raising one's hand to stop a blow—but rather operationally, from a wider military perspective. This is, after all, a case of self-defense by a state, not by an individual. The operational level is the middle level of action between the strategic and tactical levels;[132] it includes each separate tactical maneuver capable of affecting any other and the theater as a whole.[133] It is the operational art of war that triggers "a higher combination that is more than the sum of its tactical parts."[134] It is therefore important for a state to look at self-defense at the operational rather than the tactical level, coordinating the various tactical maneuvers, be they defensive or offensive, for that goal.[135] The justified prohibition on the unilateral use of military force in a preventive war, aimed against one's adversary's capabilities, prevents it from taking the strategic initiative; it should not be interpreted, however, as prohibiting last-resort operational acts necessary in its own self-defense.

What might be perceived as a confusing discussion, blurring the lines between reactive (defensive) and proactive (offensive) measures, is absolutely clear from a military perspective. The dichotomy between the offensive and defensive does not exist at the operational and tactical levels: "[E]ven in the defense, seizing and retaining the initiative requires

131. TALLINN MANUAL 2.0 ON THE INTERNATIONAL LAW APPLICABLE TO CYBER WARFARE 351 (Michael N. Schmitt ed., 2016); and *see supra* note 64.

132. On the division of a military's activity into three levels—strategic, operational, and tactical—*see infra* text accompanying Chapter 3 notes 20–27.

133. EDWARD N. LUTTWAK, STRATEGY: THE LOGIC OF WAR AND PEACE 113 (2d prtg. 2003).

134. *Id.* at 112.

135. Edward N. Luttwak, *The Operational Level of War*, 5 INT'L SECURITY 61, 61 (1980).

executing offensive operations."[136] The U.S. Army defines "mobile defense," for example, as "a defensive task that concentrates on the destruction or defeat of the enemy through a decisive attack by a striking force."[137] Similarly, during the Cold War, NATO forces adopted a defensive strategy, aimed against the Warsaw Pact militaries' potential offensive against Western Europe; yet within this defense they also planned proactive military measures—that is, counterattacks against the expected attacking Communist forces.[138] Indeed, the notion that offense and defense are absolutely dichotomous concepts is not accepted by military thinking, but rather, as Clausewitz noted, "defense in war can only be relative . . . a defensive campaign can be fought with offensive battles, and in defensive battle, we can employ our divisions offensively."[139] In reality, there are military scenarios that validate the cliché: "The best defense is a good offense." Legally, too, this phenomenon is reflected in API art. 49(1), which states: " 'Attacks' means acts of violence against the adversary, whether in offence or in defence."

To bridge the apparent separation between self-defense and proactivity and introduce professional standards to substantiate the contours of the lawful timing of a potential self-defendant's proactive response, we must first, in the coming discussion, look at the special attributes of this operational last resort available to the self-defendant.

---

136. FM 3-0, *supra* note 92, at 3-8.

137. U.S. Dep't of Army, Field Manual 3-90-1, Offense and Defense, Vol. 1 ¶ 6-6 (Mar. 22, 2013).

138. NATO's strategy at the time, known as "Forward Defense," was meant to engage Warsaw Pact forces along the front line before their attack could make any headway and wear them down in a war of attrition. John J. Mearsheimer, *Maneuver, Mobile Defense and the NATO Central Front*, 6 Int'l Security 104, 105 (1981/1982). The strategy itself included a "threat of escalation" component, meaning that in case of a Warsaw Pact attack, NATO forces could turn to the offensive and escalate the situation so as to convince the Pact that the risks to it as a result of the attack would be too great. *See* North Atlantic Military Committee, *Final Decision on MC 14/3: A Report by the Military Committee to the Defence Planning Committee on Overall Strategic Concept for the Defense of the North Atlantic Treaty Organization Area* para. 22 (Jan. 16, 1968), http://www.nato.int/docu/stratdoc/eng/a680116a.pdf (last visited May 5, 2016).

139. Von Clausewitz, *supra* note 88, at 357.

3.4 Military Necessity of the Self-Defendant in Case of an Imminent Threat: The Special Attributes of the Operational Last Resort

The ability of states to face aggressive armed attacks varies. Thus, their "last chance" to respond effectively, and proactively if so required, is dependent, inter alia, upon their expected risk from the aggression. The magnitude of a given aggressor's threat is based upon the self-defendant's specific and unique circumstances. In conventional warfare, for example, if the self-defendant does not have a territorial buffer zone that can mitigate the offensive blow, it faces a much greater risk from an attack than a state that has one. The risk to the former might become an existential threat to it. The Russian territory, as was demonstrated in World War II[140] as well as in the Napoleonic War,[141] was wide enough to absorb such an aggressive blow; West Germany (during the Cold War) and South Korea, due to their geographic circumstances, could not afford to do so.[142] "Most states understood [regarding the 1967 Israeli anticipatory strike in the Six Day War] that a very small, densely populated state cannot be expected to await a very probable, potentially decisive attack before availing itself of the right to self-defense."[143] When evaluating the magnitude of a threat to a victim state from an attack, not only the geographic dimensions of the conflict should be taken into consideration, but also the balance of power between the adversaries in all dimensions (military, economic, social,

---

140. For Hitler's forces, after having swiftly advanced on the Netherlands, Belgium, and France, the depth of the Russian territory proved too much, their advance being stopped at its deepest point, still some 60 miles from Moscow. *See, e.g.*, LUTTWAK, STRATEGY: THE LOGIC OF WAR AND PEACE, *supra* note 133, at 21–23.

141. Though Napoleon managed to reach Moscow, it did him little good, proving the usefulness of strategic depth. The Russians left the city barren in accordance with "scorched earth" tactics and retreated hundreds of kilometers to Kaluga. Because he had to pursue them in order to obtain food, Napoleon's supplies and forces became thin and exhausted until he was finally stopped by the Russians. *See* CARTER MALKASIAN, A HISTORY OF THE MODERN WARS OF ATTRITION 17–19 (2002).

142. As Luttwak points out, in the case of West Germany during the Cold War, the German frontier suffered from three major disadvantages: it was unshielded by major geographic obstacles, lacked strategic depth, and contained large cities very close to the threatened border. The narrow strategic depth in South Korea during the Korean War also meant that by the end of January 1951, the Chinese military managed to reach deep into South Korea, some 40 miles beyond Seoul. *See* LUTTWAK, STRATEGY: THE LOGIC OF WAR AND PEACE, *supra* note 133, at 139–42.

143. FRANCK, RECOURSE TO FORCE, *supra* note 40, at 107.

and cultural) and their international standing and allies (including collective self-defense agreements, if any); that too determines the expected risk and not only its absolute volume. The risk is relative to the adversaries' attributes. Indeed, a well-equipped modern military—one with high technology—can usually take more risks and accept more constraints than an inferior one. An elephant, too, can usually survive an all-out attack by a mosquito.

The endurance capacity of a victim state depends upon a combination of both physical and mental considerations. For example, Andrew Roberts, analyzing Japan's short-term success in its surprise attacks following Pearl Harbor—in which "her forces were able to sweep through Asia, capturing one sixth of the surface of the planet in only six months"[144]—compares it to Germany's immediate achievements, during World War II, in its invasion of Russia. In both cases he points to the counter-factors, which, at the end of the military campaign, offset the initial gains of the aggressor: "[I]n Russia the weather, size of population and spirit of the ordinary Red Army soldier; in the Far East superior Allied technology and military production—could operate to reverse the early successes."[145] These examples demonstrate that the last reasonable sphere, which should determine the legitimacy of the victim state taking the initiative and striking first, is not and cannot be fixed universally, but rather depends upon both adversaries' relevant circumstances in their wider sense. Yet, despite this variance, the special attributes of the operational last resort of any given state, under its different military circumstances, are mainly known in advance, and the reasonableness of its military's defensive actions can be objectively judged by professional observers.

The acceptance by the international community of the Israeli first strike in the Six Day War can serve as an example of recognition of the specific and unique attributes determining the operational last resort in this case.[146] Another example, this time purely hypothetical but more internationally oriented, will be presented here regarding NATO's legitimacy, during the Cold War, to strike first, as a matter of last resort, in case Warsaw

---

144. Andrew Roberts, The Storm of War: A New History of the Second World War 200 (2009).

145. *Id.*

146. *See supra* notes 35–41 and accompanying text.

Pact forces posed an existential, imminent (conventional) threat against any of its member states.

This hypothetical is based upon both international adversaries' specific attributes and military doctrines and is grounded mainly on the scenario presented by Sir Gen. John Hackett in 1978 during the Cold War, forecasting what World War III would have looked like had it started in 1985.[147] This imaginary war would have been triggered by the Warsaw Pact's desire to take advantage of its conventional forces' quantitative superiority to subdue NATO forces and take over substantial parts of Europe, before NATO could make up for it by way of quality. The Russian planners estimated that NATO would not turn to the nuclear option if the Pact were to stop its invasion after reaching a pre-declared line encompassing Western Germany, the Netherlands, and Austria. According to the scenario, the majority of NATO's regular forces would have been stationed along its central front—stretching from Flensburg, Western Germany, in the north, along the border between the two Germanys, and down to Linz, Austria, in the south—and deployed in a forward formation along the borders. The substantial part of NATO forces would have been concentrated in the front due to lack of strategic depth, with large cities very close to the border.[148] The alliance estimated, however, that it would have 14 days' strategic early warning—during which the Warsaw Pact would deploy its numerically superior forces[149] along the central front—allowing it to call up its reserves and arrange its in-depth defense. In this expected state of affairs, NATO's planners estimated that its forwardly-deployed regular forces would be required to hold the line for only two days before the arrival of reinforcements (16 days after their call-up). It was this basic assumption of 14 days' warning that the Warsaw Pact's surprise attack was aimed at. The main attack targeted the central front's northern sector—exploiting NATO's

---

147. John Winthrop Hackett et al., The Third World War August 1985 (1978). It should be noted that one of the major criticisms leveled against this book (in its revised version called *The Third World War: The Untold Story*, 1982) was that it overestimated NATO forces' abilities, including facing such a hypothetical scenario. *See, e.g.*, Christopher Lehmann-Haupt, *Books of the Times*, N.Y. Times, Sept. 22, 1982, http://www.nytimes.com/1982/09/22/books/books-of-the-times-167230.html (last visited May 5, 2016).

148. As to the three major disadvantages of the German frontier for its defenders, *see supra* note 142.

149. In total, in this scenario NATO's forces along the central front included 36 divisions compared to the Warsaw Pact's 93. For a fully detailed chart, *see* Hackett, *supra* note 147, at 356.

lack of substantial strategic depth and reserve power—followed by a decoy invasion staged against the southern sector. The success of such an attack would have been mainly dependent on its surprise; the ability of the Pact to concentrate substantial forces under the guise of summer exercises, resulting in that once the invasion started, NATO's regular forces alone would have had to maintain their positions for 10 days, rather than the planned two, before their reinforcements' arrival—an expectation both adversaries knew was probably unrealistic.

In light of the above circumstances and all the other attributes of the war arena, an anticipatory strike by NATO on the Warsaw Pact's main forces would seem to have been its last operational resort to exercise successfully its collective self-defense obligation[150] against the imminent existential threat. It was a reasonable way to bridge the timing gap between the expected invasion and its anticipated doctrinal progress and the arrival of NATO's reinforcements, and to prevent the fall of Germany's major cities.

The above discussion demonstrated some of the considerations—relating mainly to the magnitude of the threat—affecting the self-defendant's operational last resort in a conventional war between states. Of course, the considerations might differ when the potential threat is either sub-conventional or mega-conventional. Yet when it comes to self-defense in these latter types of wars, the imminence of the attack requirement, as well as the last resort operational standard, should remain valid, though, of course, affected by these threats' special circumstances.

The differences in nonconventional wars in both variables of the imminent threat (magnitude and certainty) and the self-defendant's ability to respond effectively might be due to either the information (intelligence) gap or to the specific operational and strategic challenges that characterize them. The latter, however, differ from the former in the sense that they are not relative—dependent upon the effective allocation of resources and skills by the self-defendant—but mainly absolute, deriving inherently from the nature of these threats.

The difficulties in collecting intelligence regarding the adversary's intentions, capabilities, and actual belligerent preparations in these types of wars—for example, in the case of a terrorist group or a potential nuclear aggressor—are real; yet a self-defendant facing this challenge should respond to it, at least in part, by taking professional steps aimed at

150. *See* The North Atlantic Treaty, art. 5, Apr. 4, 1949, 34 U.N.T.S. 243.

ing its intelligence capabilities and skills, and not only by looking ...gal concessions. Intelligence, from all available sources, is the main vehicle for minimizing the uncertainty regarding an adversary's intentions and activities, and for evaluating the magnitude of the threat deriving from them. Its insufficiency is an operational challenge to the self-defendant, to be solved, in many cases, by improving its professional practices of collecting and analyzing military data—not by gambling on the capabilities, intentions, and activities of its enemy. As in any other professional decision, especially those that are a matter of life and death—for example, a surgeon considering whether to operate on a cancer patient—gambling and intuition are no substitute for hard evidence. Indeed, a self-defendant's obligation to substantiate the information regarding the threat it faces—if it is an imminent one—should not be absolute but rather relative, depending on its cost and its expected effect on the self-defendant's decision to attack first. The difficulty in obtaining this information, however, doesn't grant the self-defendant an automatic exemption from this effort.

In retrospect, the argument that Saddam Hussein was developing and possessed weapons of mass destruction (WMDs), justifying the Second Gulf War—which to a large extent seems to have been a preventive and a very controversial war, per se[151]—can serve as an example of such unprofessional gambling.[152] Instead of pushing directly toward the war at the beginning of the 2000s, the United States should have concentrated its efforts, including by threatening to use its military force, toward restoration of the UN inspection regime, an apparatus that probably would have supplied it with reliable data regarding Iraq's capabilities. Had a rational decision been taken, based upon such intelligence, the fiasco that led to U.S. intelligence's belief that Saddam Hussein was in possession of WMDs might have been prevented. Indeed, the level of certainty required in order to recognize an imminent threat should be high, and based upon reliable data; reasonable probability of an adversary's intention will not

151. *See supra* text accompanying notes 52–54.

152. The claim that Saddam Hussein was in possession of WMDs before the 2003 war in Iraq was made, for example, by President Bush in his statement to the nation regarding Operation Iraqi Freedom on March 22, 2003. President George W. Bush, *Radio Address*, 39 Weekly Comp. Pres. Doc. 353 (Mar. 22, 2003). The Senate later issued a committee report addressing the mistaken assumptions that led to the 2003 Iraq war. *See* S. Rep. No. 108-301 (2003) http://www.gpo.gov/fdsys/search/pagedetails.action?browsePath=108/SRPT/%5b300%3b399%5d&granuleId=CRPT-108srpt301&packageId=CRPT-108srpt301 (last visited May 5, 2016).

suffice. Lack of intelligence and hard evidence in cases of nonconventional belligerency should spur the potential self-defendant's intelligence agencies to work harder and collect the required data. The burden and responsibility of presenting and proving the facts of the threat, its magnitude and urgency, is theirs.[153]

The strategic and operational difficulties in facing, and if necessary fighting, nonconventional threats differ from the intelligence-gathering challenges, in the sense that they are inherent, not dependent upon the capabilities, performance, and skills of the self-defendant. The relatively short time required to execute a nuclear attack or an armed attack by a terrorist group (compared to the time it takes to execute a conventional attack), or the attack's potential for immediate devastating effects (e.g., as regards the nuclear threat), is not dependent upon the self-defendant's investment, skills, and efforts. Even the most efficient military with the best intelligence has to take these attributes as a given.[154] Similarly, the lack of rationality (in its traditional sense) in the case of an "undeterred terrorist"—such as, for example, those who are not afraid and willing to die due to their religious belief—is a relevant factor in deciding the lawful timing of a potential self-defendant's proactive response. Due to the lack of an effective deterrence, the self-defendant usually cannot contain such a threat, and it cannot expect the irrational player to act proportionally either. The lack of these conventional barriers, in the case of nonconventional transgressors, affects both the magnitude and certainty of the imminent threat.[155] Indeed, as Christopher Greenwood stated, the horrific threat

---

153. As to the effect of mistaken but reasonable beliefs, *see* the discussion in George P. Fletcher & Jens David Ohlin, Defending Humanity: When Force is Justified and Why 170–74 (2008).

154. This phenomenon should trigger legal effects, as well. Indeed, "[a]t San Francisco, however, it is beyond dispute that the negotiators deliberately closed the door on any claim of 'anticipatory self-defence,' a posture soon to become logically indefensible by the advent of a new age of nuclear warheads and long-range rocketry." Franck, Recourse to Force, *supra* note 40, at 50. Commentators focused on the political, metalegal argumentation in this context. "[I]n an era of missiles and nuclear weapons . . . it would be a naive and self-defeating State that should await the attack by another country, in the full knowledge that it is certain to take place and likely to involve the use of very destructive weapons." Cassese, International Law, *supra* note 16, at 358. *See also* Kretzmer, *supra* note 5, at 248 n.70.

155. Indeed, it increases the expected value of the threat. In finance literature, expected return is defined as an estimate of the return on an investment. It is calculated by averaging possible returns weighted by their probabilities. Thus, if an investment has a 10 percent chance of a 100 percent return and a 90 percent chance of a 50 percent return, then the expected return is 55 percent: (0.1x100 [10] + 0.9x50 [45] = 55).

posed by a nuclear weapon is in a different league than the threats posed by cross-border raids conducted by one's adversary's infantry. "Where the threat is an attack by weapons of mass destruction, the risk imposed upon a State by waiting until that attack actually takes place compounded by the impossibility for that State to afford its population any effective protection once the attack has been launched, mean that such an attack can reasonably be treated as imminent in circumstances where an attack by conventional means would not be so regarded."[156]

The unique attributes of nonconventional threats should be internalized and affect the lawful timing of a potential self-defendant's proactive response. The correlation between the existentiality of the threat and its immanency in an "extreme circumstance of self-defence, in which the very survival of a State would be at stake,"[157] should influence the lawful timing of a self-defendant's response. However, although the magnitude of a nuclear threat affects its imminence threshold, this does not nullify the requirement for that threshold to have been reached. A potential self-defendant cannot attack prematurely its adversary's nuclear facilities without a high level of certainty related to its existential threat. Israel's 1981 strike, which destroyed the Iraqi nuclear reactor (under construction), was condemned in UN Security Council Resolution 487,[158] on the ground that there was no imminent threat to Israel. As noted by the Council, Iraq was in full compliance with the safeguards required by the International Atomic Energy Agency,[159] leading the Council to condemn "the military attack by Israel [as being] in clear violation of the Charter of the United Nations and the norms of international conduct."[160] The Israeli argument that if the attack had been delayed any further, it would have been too

156. Christopher Greenwood, *International Law and the Pre-emptive Use of Force: Afghanistan, Al-Qaida, and Iraq*, (2003) 4 San Diego Int'l L.J. 7, 16 (2003). Cf. Yaniv Roznai, *Let the "Caroline" Sink! Assessing the Legality of a Possible Israeli Attack on Iranian Nuclear Facilities and Why the Traditional Self-Defense Formula Is Incompatible with the Nuclear Age*, 18 Cal. Int'l L.J. 18, 32 (2010) (arguing that the imminent threat standard does "not distinguish between threats deriving from guns, cannons and tanks, or nuclear missiles albeit their inherent differences").

157. *See supra* Introduction note 85.

158. S.C. Res. 487 (June 19, 1981).

159. *Id.*, at the preamble.

160. *Id.* para. 1. *Cf.* Dinstein, War, Aggression and Self-Defence, *supra* note 7, at 199, arguing that the strike might have been legalized on the ground of the prolonged existing state of war between Iraq and Israel.

dangerous to bomb an activated, "hot" reactor due to the collateral damage that might have been caused to Iraqi civilians, was rejected. The explanation that Israel had to prevent an existential threat to it before the window of opportunity closed was not accepted. The threat was not considered imminent and the attack was perceived as a preventive one. From the perspective of a decade later, did history present another irony? As Franck comments,

> No conclusive, or even highly probabilistic, evidence was produced by Israel to support its claim of extreme necessity . . . Sometimes views of the probity of evidentiary proof change with the passage of time and as more evidence comes to light. By the time Iraq invaded Kuwait in 1990, the UN's harsh judgment of Israel's anticipatory strike was being reappraised, especially as it became apparent that Baghdad, possessing a sophisticated medium-range ballistic delivery system, indeed had developed an extensive array of nuclear, biological, and chemical weapons and that its *animus* evidently was not peaceful. Had Israel not struck in 1981, the reversal of Iraq's invasion of Kuwait a decade later might well have been impossible.[161]

The unanimous condemnation of Israel—though its strike might have been justified on the ground that "[a] single attack could be effective now but not later; afterwards, only a full-scale war could have prevented the Iraqi acquisition of nuclear weapons"[162]—demonstrates the prevailing, uncompromising demand for hard evidence relating to both the magnitude and certainty of the threat: a demand that Israel failed to meet. The imminent threat requirement has prevailed, even though over time this assessment might have changed, as Franck concludes.[163]

---

161. Franck, Recourse to Force, *supra* note 40, at 106–07.

162. Michael Walzer, Arguing about War 147 (2004).

163. Limiting our discussion to the common perception of the prevailing law—the requirement of an imminent "armed attack"—exempts us from dealing with the difficult situations in which the threat's magnitude is high (i.e., nuclear) and relatively certain but not so imminent—indeed, an Osirak-type scenario in which a grave threat is not so certain but the window of opportunity to prevent it is closing. Thus, if the rationale for imposing the immense requirement upon a potential self-defendant is "wait to the last minute," here the notion of last opportunity confounds the issue.

3.5 The Operational Last-Resort Standard Is Consistent with the UN Charter

The legal prohibition on the unilateral use of military force is normatively desirable when the exercise of force is politically motivated and aimed at intentionally changing international peace and order by force. Prohibiting the unilateral use of military force in a preventive war, aimed against one's adversary's capabilities, is consistent with the Charter's vision of maintaining international peace and security,[164] but an absolute prohibition of operational acts of last resort, essential for a state's own self-defense, is not. Maintaining international peace and security requires promoting necessary and proportional self-defense measures[165] against armed attacks. The suggested balance between the (near) certainty of the threat of an armed attack and the ability of the self-defendant to exercise its inherent right to self-defense validates article 51. Thus, when from a professional operational perspective a first strike against an existential threat is a matter of last resort for a self-defendant, as required by its own military necessity, it should be legal. An effective defense requires, when appropriate, proactive measures. A first strike might be considered as such. Indeed, it has its own disadvantages as well, and the following discussion will try to present a short balance of the advantages and shortcomings of the operational last-resort standard.

2.4 *Challenges to the Operational Last Resort Standard: A Normative Balance*

The suggested standard, vindicating a first strike by a self-defendant when appropriate, has its disadvantages, as well. Like any legal norm, it is universal and applicable to all states, including rogue ones; in some cases, it might be abused; in others it might escalate conflicts rather than promote peace and security. In the following discussion I present these potential disadvantages of the proposed operational last-resort standard; however, in light of its substantial benefits, I conclude in favor of its introduction, whenever justified.

Legitimizing a first strike might provide a pretext for potential aggressors by way of granting them a lawful façade for their transgression. The

164. *See* U.N. Charter, at the preamble.

165. *See supra* note 6.

attractiveness of a proactive self-defense doctrine as a legal shield for "real" defenders might be appealing to potential aggressors as a sword, justifying their aggression. Adopting the last resort standard in general, and in particular its consideration of the self-defendant's attributes, might be leveraged opportunistically by adversaries.

Furthermore, even when adversaries act in a bona fide manner, a lawful first-strike rule, which by definition applies to both sides, might escalate a conflict rather than contain it. Adopting the requirement of imminence of an armed attack might escalate a conflict when two adversaries are involved in military preparations for the sake of their own self-defense and one mistakenly believes or suspects that the other's acts are aggressive in nature and pulls the trigger first. Instead of sparking a race to the top in promoting peace and international security, the suggested standard might drive adversaries to the bottom, provoking them to attack first. This race to the bottom argument is reflected by what might be perceived as an "aggressive doctrine paradox": the acceptance of "aggressive" military doctrines as given may come at the expense of more moderate ones, since between two adversaries with competing circumstances, the suggested standard might grant the privilege of the first lawful strike to the one that had adopted the more aggressive doctrine. Indeed, for these two reasons the conservative wisdom prohibiting an anticipatory strike might well be embraced; for after all, such a strike is based on subjective and arbitrary appraisals by individual states, may easily be abused[166] or manipulated, and might trigger a counter-effect of escalation.

The main argument supporting the suggested standard has already been presented. The right of a self-defendant to defend itself is a substantial one and its fulfillment deserves professional leverage and margin. The sitting duck approach has been rejected both morally and legally. Furthermore, this rejection has a practical dimension, as well. The actual practice by states will not support total passivity on the part of a self-defendant facing an existential threat. The suggested contours of a proactive right of self-defense will make it possible to bridge the gap between the actual expected practice of states and the legal rhetoric.[167]

---

166. *See, e.g.*, Cassese, International Law, *supra* note 16, at 361.

167. An alternative, maintaining the prohibition on a first strike yet recognizing the reality that might justify a first strike by a self-defendant, is drawn from the criminal law rules of excuses and justifications. *See supra* note 20.

As mentioned earlier, the suggested standard seems to be consistent with the UN Charter's aim of maintaining international peace and security, and it would deter potential aggressors. Deterrence—a strategy that is aimed at influencing the adversary's decision and containing conflict[168]—requires effective tools to discourage potential aggressors by increasing their spectrum of risks. It is incompatible with a mandatory requirement of passiveness on the part of victim states. That an aggressor should enjoy the privilege of exclusivity regarding the military initiative at the crucial stages of a war's opening is unacceptable. As the defendant cannot be expected to be stronger everywhere and at all times in its defense, a military strike by an aggressor might give the attacker substantial tactical and operational advantages. If the self-defendant is legally obliged to adopt a sit-and-wait strategy—and first receive the operational blow from the aggressor's armed attack, whenever and wherever it is convenient to the latter—it creates a counter-effect in terms of the desired deterrence. Mandatory passiveness by the defender might decrease the aggressor's expected risk from its own aggression, encouraging it in essence to pursue its armed attack. Thus, within the prevailing paradigm of self-defense, a self-defendant has to have proactive—deterring—tools in its arsenal against potential aggressors. Even under the restrictive approach to the reading of Article 51, according to which the right of self-defense only arises if an armed attack actually occurs, the timing of the attack's "occurrence" should be construed widely, allowing the victim state to respond proactively, as its own last resort.

Indeed, the suggested standard of operational last resort is not a precise one; it might be perceived as too vague, especially due to having specific attributes taken from the different military circumstances of adversaries. Yet the tension between concrete legal rules and much more "open" standards is valid regarding any legal standard.[169] Furthermore, the suggested approach is based, to a large extent, upon objective criteria relevant to the adversaries, usually well known, of strategic circumstances and military professional standards. It allows a proactive self-defense only against threats that leave the self-defendant no choice, according to its military circumstances, but, as a last resort, to strike first. From this perspective, it restricts the scope of ambiguity in the realm of self-defense, while allowing

---

168. *See generally* FREEDMAN, DETERRENCE, *supra* note 8; and *see* the coming discussion in Chapter 4.

169. For the distinction between rules and standards, *see supra* Introduction note 93.

the defendant only last-resort operational activities that are proportionate to the threat. Further, the suggested standard does not legitimize the various military doctrines ex ante, nor does it prefer one over the others; it just takes them as a given and offers them as an ex-post prism through which to examine the legality of a first strike whenever it might be perceived professionally as an operational last resort.[170] A military enjoys no exclusivity in either the application of the suggested criterion or its assessment. The fact that it has a professional say in questions of given necessity of an anticipatory strike doesn't immunize it from external criticism whenever military force is used unprofessionally.

Like any other legal right, self-defense, per se—which is the mother of the suggested right of first strike—is subject to abuse and manipulation, as well. These risks are inflated in an international arena characterized by the absence of effective central enforcement and a central judicial system. As Christopher Greenwood argues, reality shows that "no State involved in a conflict will ever concede that it is the aggressor . . . "[171] History presents examples of extremely cynical manipulation of article 51, such as the USSR's intervention in Hungary in 1956.[172] Yet, although the right of self-defense has been the subject of continuing abuse, "it is never seriously suggested that international law should not include the right of a State to defend itself."[173] Indeed, when it comes to an anticipatory strike, the potential for abuse and opportunistic misuse is even greater since more uncertain variables are involved than in the case of "regular" self-defense against an armed attack that has already occurred. However, merely the potential manipulation of a right should not be reason to reject it. The more challenging moral and legal discussion comes mainly when the bona fide

170. Though we are dealing here with *ad bellum* professionalism, the argument that the suggested standard promotes aggressive and brutal doctrines might have an *in bello* analogy, as well. The excessive brutality in many military campaigns was dealt with above (Chapter 1). In sum, the inherent interest of a trained military is to constrain and contain these unnecessary—indeed, unprofessional—forces in both its *ad bellum* decisions and *in bello* practices.

171. Christopher Greenwood, *Command and the Laws of Armed Conflict* 2 (Strategic and Combat Studies Institute, Occasional Paper No. 4, 1993).

172. The justification for this invasion—ousting the newly established liberal regime—was advanced by the Warsaw Pact, claiming to be acting in self-defense "against an indirect aggression conducted by the West through stealth, propaganda and ideological subversion." Franck, Recourse to Force, *supra* note 40, at 70.

173. *See* Christopher Greenwood, *International Law and the NATO Intervention in Kosovo*, 49 Int'l Comp. L.Q. 926, 931 (2000).

rationale for the anticipatory strike, from a law-abiding self-defendant's perspective, is defensive in nature. Though the law is universal, applicable to law-abiding states as well as to "professional transgressors," the focus of the legal discourse should be on the former states that need to defend themselves legally, and not on the latter that simply do not care.

The answer to the challenges of potential abuse and manipulation should be based mainly on military professionalism and transparency requirements. The burden of proof lies with the self-defender who is actually the first to exercise military force. It has to convince both the public (domestic and international) and the international community (and, if necessary, its organs) that it was professionally-militarily justified to attack, in light of its last-resort defensive alternatives, according to all of its own relevant circumstances. Transparency (even ex post) of the relevant circumstances and considerations of the first strike decision-making process—either carried out intentionally as is common in liberal democracies, or involuntarily through the domestic and international media, or due to international demand—would make it possible to minimize the risk of abuse of the rhetoric of self-defense as a pretext for aggression. To a slightly lesser extent, these two requirements—professionalism and transparency—may also reduce the risk of escalation, the race to pull the trigger first; yet when it comes to bona fide mistaken beliefs regarding one's adversary's real intentions, transparency in real time, when applicable, will be more effective in preventing miscalculations than ex-post transparency.[174] Though the risk of escalation is real, history has shown that leaders will often engage in "self-denying prophecy," trying to alleviate the opponent's fear of a surprise attack and reduce this risk.[175]

Furthermore, any potential misuse would have to contend with the current post-heroic era,[176] which is characterized by a lessening tolerance, especially in Western democracies (but not limited to them), toward "wars of choice" and their costs, especially in human lives, on both sides. These social changes, new liberal norms, and public expectations, though not

---

174. Such real-time transparency can be achieved, for example, by way of a hotline—a direct communications link—between two adversaries, thus preventing misunderstandings. The most famous of those hotlines is the one between Washington and Moscow set up during the Cold War, where both parties agreed to inform each other of accidents and unauthorized use of nuclear weapons. *See, e.g.*, JAMES MAYALL & CORNELIA NAVARI, THE END OF THE POST-WAR ERA 135–37 (1980).

175. *See* Reiter, *supra* note 25, at 28–32.

176. *See supra* text accompanying Chapter 1 notes 90–91.

prevailing to the same extent in all states, together with the relatively easy access by the different media to conflict zones, might impede any unprofessional, reckless, or opportunistic misuse of a first strike as a pretext for aggression.

2.5 *Concluding Remarks*

Our discussion has been limited to the common perception of the prevailing law of self-defense—requiring an actual "armed attack," yet including an imminent one as well. Metaphorically, we dealt with the width of the formal *ad bellum* Rubicon that whenever crossed by an aggressor entitles the self-defendant to respond, if necessary proactively. Limiting the discussion to the interpretation of what is perceived as the positive rule excludes dealing with wider alternatives: neither those calling for extensions through a different interpretation of the positive rule (relying, mainly, on customary law and the "inherent right" of self-defense) nor those requiring a normative change. We have not dealt closely, for example, with legitimizing exceptions to the rule—in an "extreme circumstance of self-defense, in which the very survival of a State would be at stake,"[177] where the realization of the threat is relatively certain, but not so imminent[178]—nor elaborated upon potential ex-post excuses and justifications for such actions.[179]

Within this scope, this chapter has called for substantiating the legality of the anticipatory strike by evaluating all of the self-defendant's relevant strategic circumstances, both domestic and international, and by introducing operational military standards as criteria. While adopting the conservative approach and limiting the scope of lawful self-defense only against an occurring armed attack (including an imminent one), it offers an innovative interpretation related to the balance required by article 51 from two perspectives: first, a macro-balance between the international desire to maintain international peace and security and the self-defendant's existential interests; and second, a micro-balance, from the self-defendant's

---

177. *See supra* Introduction note 85.

178. In retrospect, democracies in the 1930s should have preferred preventive actions, including a preventive war, against Nazi Germany. *See, e.g.*, Allan M. Dershowitz, Preemption: A Knife That Cuts Both Ways 158–173 (2006) (arguing, inter alia, that "no option, not even full-scale preventive war, should be taken off the table if the dangers are grave enough, if the certainty is high enough, and if other options are unrealistic enough." *Id.* at 173).

179. *See supra* note 20.

t, between the imminent threat of an armed attack against it and its inherent right to defend itself. On both moral and practical grounds, the argument that self-defense allows the self-defendant only reactive measures is rejected. But what are the time limits of a potential self-defendant's proactivity? What are the contours of the occurring attack (including an imminent one), which justify the self-defendant's military response?

The suggested source for drawing the answers to these questions is the strategic analysis of all the relevant circumstances of the potential belligerency. In light of the vagueness and ambiguity of the prevailing law and the substantial gap between legal rhetoric and actual state practice—indeed, in many cases, declared policy and practice—this chapter has suggested adopting an operational standard to frame the contours of lawful self-defense, defining it as the last reasonable point in time, according to the self-defendant's relevant military circumstances and military doctrine, in which it can successfully face the aggressor's accumulated armed activities and still operationally defend itself, including, when necessary, by taking the initiative and striking first. Though this standard is neither precise nor absolutely clear-cut, its components are generally well known and can be examined objectively in both real time and ex post by outside professional observers. Indeed, the suggested standard has its own disadvantages and might be subject to mistakes, abuse, and manipulation. The balance of its advantages and shortcomings seems, however, to support its application. A self-defendant deserves a fair chance and arena to exercise its self-defense. Granting it, as a last resort, the operationally-reasonable freedom to defend itself—including, if necessary, by proactive measures—would promote the UN Charter's aim of preserving international peace and security and might have a positive deterring effect upon potential aggressors.

In the context of this book, this chapter has explored the potential application of military professionalism—reflecting the way militaries think, function, and fight[180]—in determining the lawful timing of the *ad bellum* self-defense, focusing mainly on narrowing the gap between the law and states' practice (and declarations of practice). Indeed, a law that is abided by, per se, would probably, though indirectly, also serve the second aim of reducing humanitarian suffering. Furthermore, the suggested professional standard, determining the operational last resort of exercising

180. Military professionalism was presented in Chapter 1, too, but with a different focus. There it was mentioned in the context of revitalizing the *in bello* military necessity, with the focus on its duality, in both allowing and constraining the use of lethal force.

self-defense, might directly affect this noble aim, as well. Though the focus of this chapter has been on the timing of the necessary last-resort self-defense and not on its quantification, the *in bello* proportionality and necessary requirements[181] followed by the development of new technology, allowing both accurate intelligence and precise targeting, might minimize the humanitarian suffering caused by a self-defendant's first strike. Legalizing minimal (only necessary) proactivity, in due cases, might offer a self-defendant a means to minimize the humanitarian suffering caused by its self-defense in general, the collateral damage caused by it to its adversary's noncombatants in particular. Even though the self-defendant was pulled unwillingly into the fight, due to the proactivity leverage it might still select, to some extent, the attributes of its first strike and confine it to the belligerent arena, as compared to a totally reactive self-defense scenario in which all relevant dimensions of the belligerency's opening (i.e., time, place, pattern, magnitude, and focus) are selected by the aggressor. Although this chapter, then, corresponds only in part with the suggested paradigm, the coming discussion in the next chapter does so entirely. It calls for thinking strategically in order to reduce war's hazards. As wars are fought strategically, it calls for leveraging this phenomenon legally, by controlling the selected strategy and moderating its devastating effects.

---

181. *See* the *in bello* proportionality equation, *supra* Chapter 1 note 59, and *see* the discussion in Chapter 1 above, calling for a revision of the *in bello* necessity rule.

3

Military Strategy

THE BLIND SPOT OF INTERNATIONAL HUMANITARIAN LAW*

Introduction—Thinking Strategically to Reduce War's Hazards

It is the strategic level of war—not the operational or tactical[1]—that most affects war's conduct. A war strategy determines the aims and, to a large extent, the scope and consequences of a war, and substantially shapes its targeting policy.[2] Yet the prevailing law of armed conflict[3] does not deal directly with the selection by a belligerent of a military strategy in general and the determination of a war's aims in particular. This disregard has a price. A natural assumption from this silence is that the law takes a wide spectrum of types of war between states as legitimate, including the worst-case strategic scenario. It accepts, albeit by default, the Clausewitzian all-out war strategy—aimed at the decisive and total destruction of the

---

* This chapter is based mainly on, Yishai Beer, *The Blind Spot of International Humanitarian Law*, 8 HARV. NAT'L SECURITY J. 333–78 (2017).

1. *See supra* Introduction note 86.

2. Targeting has been defined as "[t]he process of selecting and prioritizing targets and matching the appropriate response to them, considering operational requirements and capabilities." CHIEFS OF STAFF, JOINT PUB. 1-02, DEPARTMENT OF DEFENSE DICTIONARY OF MILITARY AND ASSOCIATED TERMS 238 (Nov. 8, 2010, as amended through June 15, 2015) [hereinafter JOINT PUB. 1-02]. As for the targeting process, *see, e.g.*, Kenneth Watkin, *Targeting in Air Warfare*, 44 ISR. Y.B. HUM. RTS 1, 17–19 (2014).

3. As mentioned above, NGOs and most academic writers prefer the alternative name IHL (International Humanitarian Law) over the law of armed conflict. *See supra*, Introduction note 1.

adversary's military and the extinction of its will to fight[4]—as an acceptable prototype. This implicit acceptance of the total war prototype triggers a counter-effect: it damages the law's goal of humanizing war's arena, a vision specifically established following the trauma of the two World Wars.[5] The effect of this distortion of the law of armed conflict will be demonstrated in this chapter by examining the targeting rules, where the restrictive attributes of military strategy, which could play a significant role in limiting targeting, seem to have been forgotten. The earlier sin of turning a blind eye to military strategy, especially its restrictive attributes, has its own consequences for the prevailing law of targeting. This distortion and its endorsed correction is the subject of this chapter.

The targeting rules are derived, inter alia, from a fundamental rule of the law of armed conflict: the distinction rule, which requires that noncombatants be kept out of harm's way in war and that their property should be spared.[6] Only combatants and military objects represent lawful targets ("military objectives").[7] Military objectives are limited to "those objects which by their nature, location, purpose or use make an effective contribution to military action and whose total or partial destruction, capture or neutralization, in the circumstances ruling at the time, offers a definite military advantage."[8] Nonetheless, despite the definite selection in favor of civilian immunity, civilians might be hurt, both in body and in property, in a lawful war. Although the intended targeting of civilians is absolutely prohibited, their consequential unintended (yet foreseen)

---

4. Carl Von Clausewitz, On War 90 (Michael Eliot Howard & Peter Paret trans., indexed ed. 1984).

5. Mainly by the four 1949 Geneva Conventions and their 1977 Additional Protocols. The Conventions are aimed at strengthening the basic rights of prisoners of war, protecting the wounded and the sick, and promoting the protection of civilians during wartime and in war zones. The 1949 Geneva Conventions updated the terms of the first Geneva treaties (1906, 1929)—concerned with combatants—and added the fourth treaty "for the Protection of Civilian Persons in Time of War." *See* Geneva Convention (IV) relative to the Protection of Civilian Persons in Time of War, Aug. 12, 1949, 75 U.N.T.S. 287 (GCIV); Protocol Additional to the Geneva Conventions of 12 August 1949, and relating to the Protection of Victims of International Armed Conflicts (Protocol I), June 8, 1977, 1125 U.N.T.S. 3 (API); Protocol Additional to the Geneva Conventions of 12 August 1949, and relating to the Protection of Victims of Non-International Armed Conflict (Protocol II), June 8, 1977, 1125 U.N.T.S. 609 (APII).

6. *See, e.g.*, API, *supra* note 5, at Part IV ("Civilian Population").

7. *Id.* at art. 52(2).

8. *Id.*

harming might be legal if consistent with the proportionality criterion, applicable in times of war. The proportionality requirement prohibits the initiation of a military attack, in which the harm caused to civilians might be "excessive" (disproportional) relative to the attack's "concrete and direct military advantage anticipated."[9] Furthermore, though civilian property is not considered a lawful target, the intended targeting of dual-purpose objects—objects that serve both civilian and military purposes such as, for example, power grids and bridges—might be legal. These objects may be targeted if they are classified as "military objectives," subject to the proportionality rule.[10] Thus, the adversaries' pursuit of "military advantage" is restricted by two—contextually based—legal barriers. The first barrier limits "military objects" (which pass the attributes threshold[11]) to only those whose "total or partial destruction, capture or neutralization" offers a "definite military advantage."[12] The second barrier—aimed at minimizing the damage caused to civilians when a military objective is targeted—prohibits damage caused collaterally to noncombatants if it is not proportional (excessive) relative to the attack's "concrete and direct military advantage anticipated."[13]

From which military perspective—tactical, operational, or strategic—should these two legal barriers be examined? Regarding both the definition of military objects and the proportionality equation, two different schools have developed. One is tactically oriented and restricts lawful targets to concrete military objectives. The other school is much broader and strategically concerned; in its targets list it includes, inter alia, infrastructure and state resources supporting the war effort. I will argue that both schools are mistaken on both theoretical and practical grounds. They do not attain the optimal equilibrium between the two perceived poles of the law of armed conflict: necessity and humanity.[14] They neither promote

---

9. *Id.* at art. 51(5) (b).

10. *Id.* at arts. 52(1)–(2). The application of this legality is, however, controversial. For example, *see supra* Chapter 1 note 81.

11. "[T]hose objects which by their nature, location, purpose or use make an effective contribution to military action." API, *supra* note 5, at art. 52(2).

12. *Id.*

13. *Id.* at art. 51(5) (b).

14. For a call to revisit the prevailing paradigm and challenge the current dichotomy between the two pillars—assumed to be polar opposites—of the law of armed conflict, necessity and humanity, *see supra* Chapter 1.

the best interests of military necessity nor encourage, as might have been expected, the humanizing of war's arena.

Wars are fought strategically. The aims of a war and its scope are, above all, the product of an elective strategy. The tactically oriented school's inclination to turn a blind eye to this reality is doomed to fail on realpolitik grounds, and its disregard of preferences at the strategic level works against its agenda of minimizing civilian suffering. On the other hand, the strategic school of targeting, though consistent with reality, has been applied in only a partial and manipulative way. This school uses strategy only as an enabler, to widen the scope of a war and its lawful targets list, but ignores its constraining attributes. Many if not most contemporary wars are not total wars, but rather are limited in their aims. Limited wars are constrained by their own definition as such. Requiring adherence in targeting to strict and definite war aims, as strategically selected by a belligerent, might substantially affect the scope of lawful targets, especially in limited wars. Were the law to require states—for example, one fighting lawfully in self-defense[15]—to publicly define their strategic war aims, it would dictate to their militaries a coherent targeting practice, consistent with the selected strategy. In every limited war, such a coherent targeting requirement would usually impose effective, substantial restrictions upon the scope of lawful targets. Strategy in war is not generic but contextually based. However, the contemporary legal environment—which accepts the Clausewitzian total war as a lawful generic default prototype—naturally creates a wide scope for a generic "targets bank" (including, for example, a belligerent state's infrastructure, which might relatively easily be considered a military object, due to its dual purpose). In order to contend with the reality of limited wars, it is necessary to untie the apparent Gordian knot between any selected strategy (and its war aims) and the generic (usually excessively wide) lawful targets list. Every war is unique in its aims, and its specifically selected strategy determines, and might have the potential to limit, its targets list.

The suggested approach requires adding a new dimension to the nexus, demanded by treaty law, between a potential object and the military action. The current causality nexus requires that the military objects, characterized "by their nature, location, purpose or use," should have "an effective contribution to military action" and that a definite military

15. U.N. Charter art. 2(4) prohibits the proactive use of military force in international relations, recognizing just two exceptions; *see supra* text accompanying Introduction notes 59–60.

advantage should be gained upon their destruction.[16] These requirements will here be termed the "horizontal nexus"—a connection between the potential objective and the actual military action. In addition, this chapter advocates introducing a legal requirement of a "vertical nexus," a connection between the strategic aim of the war and its actual application, as reflected in the desired operational and tactical military advantages. The latter should always be within the scope of the former, and any lawful military target should reasonably be located within this contour. The vertical nexus—based upon a revised reading of the necessity principle—requires a concrete connection between all levels of war and the selected military objects. It should define—and in most cases, reduce—the potential lawful targets bank in a given war, from its opening and at every stage of it.

In assessing the vertical nexus, the strategic military selection is taken as a given (as long as it is lawful), but its application is scrutinized. Under the suggested approach, the law of armed conflict would require militaries to operate coherently by adhering to their own professional standards. Thus, where a strategy of limited war has been selected, there is usually no professional military request for a decisive victory, and this should have a moderating effect upon the scope of the war and its lawful targets. In a limited war, for example, targeting the adversary's entire dual-purpose infrastructure—even if it might be legally permissible—seems to be strategically unwise. Strategy, for legal purposes, should not be perceived as a wild horse, only enabling a wide range of intended or collateral harms, but rather should be leveraged as a constraining tool. Legally, connecting strategy and actual targeting practice, as suggested, can be perceived as a call to introduce the prevailing *in bello* necessity principle into the *ad bellum* sphere.[17]

This chapter proceeds as follows: Part 3.1 presents the importance of military strategy in affecting militaries' operations and tactics. Part 3.2 demonstrates the pendulum movement of the pattern of wars and the current shift from the total war to the limited war prototype—a strategic change that reflects, to a large extent, the internalization (mainly by Western liberal democracies) of the limitations of force. The change in the contemporary strategic environment has not been fully backed by

16. API, *supra* note 5, at art. 52(2).

17. The *ad bellum* rules determine whether the use of military force is legal. The law of armed conflict determines the prevailing *in bello* rules. As for the potential linking of the *ad bellum* principle of proportionality to the *in bello* conduct, *see infra* text accompanying notes 106–112.

the prevailing law, which by default remains loyal to the total war legacy. Part 3.3 focuses upon this blind spot—the turning of a blind eye to the more crucial issue of war's aims and strategic dimensions—and its effects. In the face of this contemporary strategic and legal reality, Part 3.4 turns to the prevailing, and normatively desirable, targeting rules. It presents the two mistaken dichotomist schools and suggests that lawful targeting be scrutinized through the strategic prism, while limiting the spectrum of military objectives by requiring coherency in targeting to definite war aims. Whereas the current discussion is focused on the horizontal axis, between the object and the military action, Part 3.5 introduces the suggested vertical nexus: connecting strategy to lawful targeting. Finally, Part 3.6 offers concluding remarks relating to the suggested evolution of the law of armed conflict and its future potential.

3.1 Strategy Determines War's Patterns and Scope

A military campaign is conducted in light of a strategy, or what Liddell Hart calls its grand strategy. The higher level of strategy "coordinates and directs all the resources of a nation, or band of nations, towards the attainment of the political object of the war."[18] Whereas the grand strategy deals with "policy"—which is decided, in liberal democracies, by the civilian leadership—the military strategy deals with on-the-ground military activities, related to a concrete armed conflict and aimed at the fulfillment of governmental policy. At the level of military strategy, the political objectives of a state are transformed into military ones,[19] which in turn are exercised in the campaign theater, with the aim of meeting those policy goals. It is this military strategy that affects militaries' operations and tactics.

Military activity is usually classified into three hierarchic levels: strategic, operational, and tactical. Under common definitions, the strategic level of war "determines national or multinational (alliance or coalition)

---

18. B.H. Liddell Hart, Strategy 322 (2d ed. 1991). *Cf.* the British Army Doctrine definition of "National Strategy" that "sets out a path, using the diplomatic, economic and military instruments of power, to achieve the national interests." U.K. Ministry of Defence, Army Doctrine Publication, Operations 3–17 (Nov. 2010). https://www.gov.uk/government/uploads/system/uploads/attachment_data/file/33695/ADPOperationsDec10.pdf (last visited Aug. 24, 2016) [hereinafter U.K. Operations Manual].

19. "The military contribution to strategy is the application of military resources to achieve national strategic objectives . . . " *Id.* at 3–18.

strategic security objectives and guidance, then develops and uses national resources to achieve those objectives."[20] The operational level is the "level of war at which campaigns and major operations are planned, conducted, and sustained to achieve strategic objectives within theaters or other operational areas."[21] And the tactical level is the "level of war at which battles and engagements are planned and executed to achieve military objectives assigned to tactical units or task forces."[22]

The classification of the operational as an independent level is relatively new. The classical distinction of military activity level was between strategy and tactics only.[23] Its introduction in the twentieth century came in response to the demand to bridge the gap between the strategic and tactical levels through the introduction of a middle level of action.[24] It includes each separate tactical maneuver capable of affecting any other and the theater as a whole.[25] It is the operational art of war that triggers "a higher combination that is more than the sum of its tactical parts."[26]

The differentiation among different military levels is well rooted in the hierarchical construction of militaries.

> The underlying principle was that at each level the objectives would be passed down from the higher. At the level of grand strategy, a conflict was anticipated, alliances forged, economies geared, people braced, resources allocated, and military roles defined. At the level of strategy, the political objectives were turned into military goals; priorities and specific objectives were agreed upon and allocations of men and equipment made accordingly. At the level of grand tactics or operations, judgments were made as to the most appropriate form of warfare to achieve the goals of that particular campaign in

---

20. Joint Pub. 1-02, *supra* note 2, at 229.

21. *Id.* at 178.

22. *Id.* at 236; and *see also* the definitions at Joint Chiefs of Staff, Joint Pub. 3-0, Joint Operations I-13 through I-14 (Aug. 11, 2011) http://www.fas.org/irp/doddir/dod/jp3_0.pdf (last visited Nov. 19, 2015) [hereinafter Joint Pub. 3-0].

23. Clausewitz, for example, distinguished strategy, which involves "the use of engagements for the object of the war," from tactics, which involve "the use of armed forces in the engagement." Von Clausewitz, On War, *supra* note 4, at 128.

24. *See* the definitions in Joint Pub. 3-0, *supra* note 22, at I-13 through I-14.

25. Edward N. Luttwak, Strategy: The Logic of War and Peace 113 (2d prtg. 2003).

26. *Id.* at 112.

> the light of the prevailing conditions. At the level of tactics, military units attempted to push forward the goals of the campaign in the specific circumstances in which they found themselves.[27]

This model of hierarchical command structures can be challenged, especially when other disciplines (i.e., business practice) are motivated by the desire to flatter hierarchies. Furthermore, in limited wars the lines between these different levels are blurred and the distinction may disappear. For example, this could occur when every "simple" soldier, usually connected through the hierarchy to the tactical level, might become a "strategic corporal," with a substantial effect upon the outcome of an entire military campaign.[28] Yet the strategic, operational, and tactical levels of war constitute fundamental aspects of applying and understanding modern warfare and its scope. (Not surprisingly, the hierarchical command structures are consistent with militaries' cultures.) Indeed, "it is the interaction between the various levels of war that affects the scope of the conflict, impacts on what targets are struck . . . to degrade an enemy's ability to conduct military operations."[29] It is this interaction that determines, at all stages of a military campaign, the desired military advantages to be gained, at all levels of war, from a given course of action[30] selected by a military. Indeed, the military advantages are different at each level—since the respective prisms used by the higher strategic command and the foot soldier to evaluate risks and opportunities on the battlefield are not the same. Yet it is the synchronization process that looks at a potential target within the context of the entire military campaign and therefore shapes the contours of the relevant potential targets bank for that specific campaign. The legality of exercising each target in this bank, by way of actual targeting, depends, inter alia, upon which of the conflicting schools, with their divergent normative

---

27. Lawrence Freedman, Strategy: A History 206 (2013).

28. *Id.* at 206–07.

29. Kenneth Watkin, *Military Advantage: A Matter of "Value," Strategy and Tactics*, 17 Y.B. Int'l Humanitarian L. 277, 320 (2014).

30. To achieve a designated military aim or advantage, the military planning process requires the planner to develop and present a wide spectrum of alternatives. *See* the COA's discussion *supra* text accompanying Chapter 1 notes 61–69.

lens—either tactically or strategically oriented—ought to be used when it comes to interpreting the military advantage to be gained.[31]

3.2 The Strategic Change: The Rise and Decline of Total War

3.2.1 A Pendulum Movement: The Evolution of "Total War"

Historical observation of the pattern of war over the years reveals a pendulum movement: from limited wars with limited, sometimes very modest, objectives to the evolution of total wars, then back to limited wars. The modern all-out prototype of war is the combined military legacy of Napoleon and Clausewitz. In the following historical discussion, I will show that Napoleon's bloody practice and Clausewitz's theory do not hold a monopoly on military thinking and practice, neither in the past nor in the present. Currently, in fact, the total war prototype is the exception rather than the rule. Yet this state of affairs has not prevented the modern law of armed conflict from legitimizing that prototype, albeit by default.

The pattern of wars, especially their scope and duration, has changed dramatically over the years. The pendulum movement of this pattern derives from the dynamic political, economic, technological, social, and cultural context of war. For example, "in the Middle Ages, the political, economic, and social context of war had in various ways inhibited the raising and risking of large numbers of men for and in battle, to make the phenomenon of large-scale battle relatively rare."[32] Toward the end of the eighteenth century, Napoleon's "Grand Army" introduced the prosecution of war through grand-scale battles: "Napoleon's system of warfare was based on decisive battles. Not for him were either bloodless maneuvers . . . or protracted struggles of attrition . . . he aimed at first pushing his opponent into a corner from which there was no escape, then battering him to pieces."[33] This pattern of war was echoed by Clausewitz. As Azar Gat points out, "Clausewitz's conceptions were clearly a particular

---

31. For example, in the *Gotovina* case reference was made to both operational and tactical level targets having been identified for artillery engagement, Prosecutor v. Gotovina et al., Case No. IT-06-90-T, Judgment, Vol. I, ¶ 1189 (Int'l Crim. Trib. for the Former Yugoslavia, Apr. 15, 2011), http://www.icty.org/x/cases/gotovina/tjug/en/110415_judgement_vol1.pdf.

32. Russell F. Weigley, The Age of Battles xii (1991).

33. Martin Van Creveld, Command in War 90 (1985).

reflection of Napoleonic warfare as perceived in its peak years."[34] Clausewitz asserts: "Battle is the bloodiest solution. While it should not simply be considered as mutual murder . . . it is always true that the character of battle, like its name, is slaughter [*Schlacht*], and its price is blood."[35] These words, which sound as if they might have been taken from Bram Stoker's 1897 novel *Dracula*,[36] reflect Clausewitz's focus on total war, the type of engagement involving masses of combatants. His vision of a direct and crushing operation from a central position has been conceived as the focal point of war, rather than any other less bloody alternative such as enveloping maneuvers: "Thus it is evident that destruction of enemy forces is always the superior, more effective means, with which others cannot compete."[37]

The Clausewitzian vision of battle has two dimensions: military and civilian. An all-out war usually pertains to both the military and the people of both adversaries. It means not only a total war between mass armies (namely, both adversaries' combatants),[38] but also total war between the civilian populations of the rival states.[39] Two examples from the second half of the nineteenth century well demonstrate the classical conception of total war, especially with regard to its civilian dimension: Moltke's bombardment of Paris in 1870 and General William Sherman's "Atlanta campaign" during the American Civil War.[40]

Field-Marshal Helmuth von Moltke, Prussian Chief of the General Staff (1857–1888),[41] endorsed the total war vision. In his view, war was to be fought in an all-out manner by attacking "all the resources of the enemy government, his finances, his railroads, his supplies and even his

34. Azar Gat, The Origins of Military Thought: From the Enlightenment to Clausewitz 206 (1989).

35. Von Clausewitz, On War, *supra* note 4, at 259.

36. Bram Stoker, Dracula (Penguin Books, 1994) (1897).

37. Von Clausewitz, On War *supra* note 4, at 97.

38. "The greatest successes are obtained where all engagements coalesce into one total war." *Id.* at 258.

39. *Id.* at 590–93 and *see supra* Chapter 1 note 80.

40. The Atlanta campaign refers to a series of battles held in 1864 between Union Gen. William T. Sherman and Confederate Gens. Joseph E. Johnston and John Bell Hood, who later replaced Johnston. *See, e.g.*, James M. McPherson, Battle Cry of Freedom 683 (2003).

41. The nickname "elder" differentiates Helmuth von Moltke from his nephew of the same name who was a field marshal with the German army at the start of World War I. On Moltke the elder, *see, e.g.*, Arden Bucholz, Helmuth Von Moltke: A Modern Biography (2007).

prestige."[42] He justified the intentional targeting of civilians in the context of war as a legitimate leverage for achieving its aim.[43] His decision to bombard Paris in 1870 was undertaken "not . . . to destroy Paris, but to exert a final pressure on the inhabitants."[44]

General Sherman reached Atlanta in 1864,[45] with two military objectives: to damage the war-related industries in the South and fight the large Confederate army around the Atlanta area.[46] When the Southern army got out of his way and invaded Tennessee, a decision was made by Sherman and Ulysses Grant, the commander of the Union military forces, not to pursue it but to drive through Confederate territory. Rather than aim directly at the Southern army, they chose to damage the local Southern economy and the property of its civilian population.[47] This strategy change, and the new focus on the civilian dimension of the war, was approved by President Lincoln.[48] The Union leaders "were driven to this by a common realization that the war had become (in the ordinary sense of the words) a people's war and that it could only be brought to conclusion by fighting it

---

42. Geoffrey Best, Humanity in Warfare: The Modern History of the International Law of Armed Conflict 145 (1983). In 1890 the field marshal wrote in support of this notion: "The time of the cabinet wars is over, we will have only a people's war." Helmuth KB Graf von Moltke, *The Russo-Turkish Campaign in Europe 1828–1829*, published in (1891–1893) 7 Gesammelte Schriften und Denkwürdigkeiten 139. *Quoted in* Michael D. Krause, *Moltke and the Origins of the Operational Level of War*, *in* Historical Perspectives of the Operational Art 113, 144 (Michael D. Krause & R. Cody Phillips eds., 2005). On Clausewitz's influence on Moltke, *see, e.g.*, Gerhard Ritter, The Sword and Sceptre: The Problem of Militarism in Germany, Vol. I: The Prussian Tradition 1740–890, at 187–263 (1973).

43. James J. Reid, *Total War, the Annihilation Ethic, and the Armenian Genocide, 1870–1918*, *in* The Armenian Genocide: History, Politics, Ethics 21, 21, 30 (Richard G. Hovannisian ed., 1992).

44. *Id.* at 30 [footnotes omitted]. Indeed, there is strong evidence indicating that on utilitarian grounds Moltke was not supportive of the bombardment, even though he made plans for it and carried it out. *See* Michael Howard, The Franco-Prussian War 352 (2d ed. 2001).

45. McPherson, Battle Cry of Freedom, *supra* note 40, at 653.

46. *Id.* at 751.

47. As Sherman himself noted, his march through Confederate territory resulted in $100 million worth of damage to property, of which $80 million were "simple waste and destruction." Sherman's report of January 1, 1865, *quoted in* Mark Grimsley, The Hard Hand of War 1861–1865, at 200 (1995).

48. Best, Humanity in Warfare, *supra* note 42, at 208. *See also* art. 21 of the Lieber Code, which states: "The citizen or native of a hostile country is thus an enemy, as one of the constituents of the hostile state or nation, and as such is subjected to the hardships of the war." U.S. War Dep't, General Order No. 100: Instructions for the Government of Armies of the United States in the Field, Apr. 24, 1863, http://avalon.law.yale.edu/19th_century/lieber.asp (last visited Aug. 16, 2017). [hereinafter Lieber Code].

in (to use the Clausewitzian concept) an absolute style."[49] Following this strategy, Sherman demanded the evacuation of all of Atlanta's inhabitants and then ordered the city burned.[50]

Both these generals of the same generation, Moltke and Sherman, exhibited similar views and practices on both sides of the Atlantic, identifying the adversary as a "people," including the entire civilian population. From their perspective, the civilian suffering was a stated goal of the total war, not just its natural consequence. Furthermore, their military logistical necessities always prevailed over the adversary's civilian interest. The only way in which the mass armies of the late eighteenth century (and to a lesser extent those of the nineteenth) could supply themselves was by exploiting local resources. Their logistical support was obtained at the expense of the local civilian population. "An army marches on its stomach, said—or is reported to have said—Napoleon. He could better have said, armies march on civilian stomachs, for that is what really happened."[51]

The Clausewitzian conception of total war, as well as the effects deriving from it, was not the only one available. By contrast, the following discussion will present alternative perceptions regarding the desired models of war.

3.2.2 Napoleon's Practice and Clausewitz's Theory Do Not Hold a Monopoly on Military Thinking and Practice

Before the era of the French Revolution, wars were usually fought along an entirely different pattern than Napoleon's bloody version. From the middle of the seventeenth century to the end of the eighteenth century, civilians were not usually considered to be relevant players on the battlefield, at least not directly.[52] Furthermore, the wars fought by professionals were usually

---

49. BEST, HUMANITY IN WARFARE, *supra* note 42, at 208.

50. In his famous letter to the mayor and councilors of Atlanta on September 12, 1864, General Sherman wrote in reply to their request to revoke his order: "You cannot qualify war in harsher terms than I will. War is cruelty, and you cannot refine it; and those who brought war into our country deserve all the curses and maledictions a people can pour out . . ." *Id.* at 209. As for Sherman's demand that all of Atlanta's inhabitants be evacuated, *see, e.g.*, MARC WORTMAN, THE BONFIRE: THE SIEGE AND BURNING OF ATLANTA 326–27 (2010).

51. BEST, HUMANITY IN WARFARE, *supra* note 42, at 89.

52. *See, e.g.*, ANTONIO CASSESE, INTERNATIONAL LAW 400 (2d ed. 2005) ("For a number of historical reasons between 1648 and 1789, wars tended to take the shape of contests between professionals, conducted as a sort of game and without any direct involvement of the civilian population." *Id.*).

characterized by their limited scope. In some cases, they were contained in their physical dimensions—for example, restricted to a single daylong pitched battle[53]—and in others they had limited objectives, such as seizing border provinces or securing overseas colonies. These relatively modest objectives were the result of the strategic military thinking of the time, which emphasized form and caution and the sociopolitical composition of the armies as dynastic and hierarchical rather than national.[54] The moderate nature of eighteenth-century warfare was summed up by Alexander Hamilton: "The history of war, in that quarter of the globe [Europe], is no longer a history of nations subdued and empires overturned; but of towns taken and retaken—of battles that decide nothing—of retreats more beneficial than victories—of much effort and little acquisition."[55] It may therefore be concluded that "more humane rules were able to flourish in the period of limited wars from 1648 to 1792 but that they then came under pressure in the drift towards continental warfare, the concept of the nation in arms and the increasing destructiveness of weapons from 1792 to 1914."[56]

In fact, a leading theorist who endorsed this type of limited "light" war preceded Clausewitz by more than two thousand years. The Chinese strategist Sun Tzu emphasized the notion that the use of military force is justified only as a last resort, noting: "Those skilled in war subdue the enemy's army without battle. They capture his cities without assaulting them and overthrow his state without protracted operations. . . . Your aim must be to take all under Heaven intact." In contrast to the bloody version of war as represented by Napoleon's model and endorsed by the Clausewitzian approach, Sun Tzu preached the opposite: "For to win one hundred victories in one hundred battles is not the acme of skill. To subdue the enemy without fighting is the acme of skill."[57] Clausewitz, who probably never

---

53. *See, e.g.*, the description of a typical pitched battle, by James Q. Whitman, The Verdict of Battle: The Law of Victory and the Making of Modern War 12–14 (2012).

54. Larry H. Addington, The Patterns of War Since the Eighteenth Century 7 (2d ed. 1994).

55. The Federalist No. 8 (Alexander Hamilton), "The Effects of Internal War in Producing Standing Armies, and Other Institutions Unfriendly to Liberty," *in* Alexander Hamilton, John Jay and James Madison, The Federalist and Other Constitutional Papers [NO. 8] 43, 43–44 (E.H. Scott ed., 1898).

56. A.P.V. Rogers, Law on the Battlefield 1 (2d ed. 2004).

57. Sun Tzu, The Art of War 79, 77 respectively (Samuel B. Griffith trans., foreword by B.H. Liddell Hart, 1963).

read Sun Tzu,[58] ridicules this type of "bloodless war" approach, noting that "[r]ecent history has scattered such nonsense to the winds."[59]

Furthermore, not all twentieth-century strategists and theorists accepted Clausewitz's bloody vision, nor did they all agree on its application. For example, Fuller and Liddell Hart, both of them military historians and theorists, contested it. Fuller's analysis of World War I criticized the underlying assumption and perception of "the General Staffs of Europe," on the eve of the war, "that policy is best enforced by destruction." He argued that militaries and their commanders were "hypnotized" by total wars involving "unlimited slaughter," which was the explanation for their futile activities and bloody operations in that war.[60] Furthermore, Fuller based his criticism not only on professional military grounds, but on economic justifications as well. He followed Keynes in arguing that the war also had a counter-effect, from a utilitarian-economic perspective.[61] "[T]actically, it was based on a gigantic misconception of the true purpose of war, which is to enforce the policy of a nation *at the least cost to itself and enemy* and, consequently, to the world, for so intricately are the resources of civilized states interwoven that to destroy any one country is simultaneously to wound all other nations."[62]

Liddell Hart also argued in favor of a vision that limited war's aims while simultaneously reducing its heavy price. He thus defined the purpose of strategy as "the reduction of fighting to the slenderest possible proportions." He further argued against those "who are obsessed with the Clausewitzian saying that 'blood is the price of victory.' . . . For even if a decisive battle be the goal, the aim of strategy must be to bring about this battle under the most advantageous circumstances."[63] Liddell Hart's theory stemmed largely from his recognition of the fallacy of the "grand

---

58. Handel states this lack of knowledge of Clausewitz as a fact. *See* MICHAEL I. HANDEL, MASTERS OF WAR: CLASSICAL STRATEGIC THOUGHT 152 (3d rev. ed. 2001).

59. VON CLAUSEWITZ, *supra* note 4, at 259 ("Laurels were to be reserved for those generals who know how to conduct a war without bloodshed." *Id.*).

60. JOHN FREDERICK CHARLES FULLER, THE REFORMATION OF WAR 75 (1923). Indeed, Michael Howard points out that "Strategists before 1914 were in fact increasingly hypnotized by the Clausewitzian and Napoleonic idea of the decisive battle for the overthrow of the enemy . . . " MICHAEL HOWARD, CLAUSEWITZ 63 (1983).

61. *See generally*, JOHN MAYNARD KEYNES, THE ECONOMIC CONSEQUENCES OF THE PEACE (1920).

62. FULLER, THE REFORMATION OF WAR, *supra* note 60.

63. B.H. LIDDELL HART, STRATEGY 338 (2d rev. ed., 1968).

battle" military doctrine, which so deleteriously affected military conduct during World War I. It was his "hardening conviction that the chief cause of the futile holocaust had been adherence to a false military doctrine, namely Clausewitz's interpretation of Napoleonic warfare."[64] He therefore argued that the function of grand strategy should be to identify the enemy's "Achilles' heel" and then strike it, rather than fight the enemy at his strongest points.[65] This conception of military operations, known as "the strategy of indirect approach," was not an original creation of Hart's.[66] As mentioned above, it in fact appeared thousands of years ago in the writings of Sun Tzu, who wrote that "He who knows the art of the direct and the indirect approach will be victorious. Such is the art of maneuvering."[67]

The historic presentation thus far has demonstrated the argument that when it comes to military doctrine and strategy, at the time of the UN's establishment in 1945 and the signing of the 1949 Geneva Conventions, Napoleon's bloody model of total war, as expressed by Clausewitz, did not enjoy a monopoly. Clausewitz's vision (in its extreme version[68])—despite being widespread and consistent with the buildup of mass armies in the nineteenth century and the industrialization of war, as reflected in the two World Wars—was not the only one extant. Indeed, as Luttwak points out, there is no one model of optimal war[69] and everything depends upon the specific circumstances of the military terrain and the adversaries. Whatever view one may hold, the Napoleonic model has never been accepted as the sole archetype of ultimate war between states.

---

64. Brian Bond, Liddell Hart: A Study of His Military Thought 37 (1977).

65. B.H. Liddell Hart, Paris, Or the Future of War 22 (1972).

66. It should be noted, however, that even in the framework of a Clausewitzian total war, a sophisticated military can still operate indirectly. For example, in executing the blietzkrieg in Europe, at the beginning of World War II, German commanders operated indirectly while still fighting a total war. *See, e.g.*, John J. Mearsheimer, *Hitler and the Blitzkrieg Strategy*, *in* The Use of Force: Military Power and International Politics 138, 146 et sq. (and the illustrations therein) (Robert J. Art & Kenneth N. Waltz eds., 6th ed. 2004).

67. TZU, *supra* note 57, at 106.

68. Indeed, Bond and others have argued that "Liddell Hart was so emotionally involved in attacking the inept conduct of the First World War . . . and its legacy, that he was unable to approach its more general causes with detachment. Instead he found a plausible scapegoat in what he mistakenly believed to be Clausewitz's notion of strategy." Bond, Liddell Hart: A Study, *supra* note 64, at 51. This debate among military historians is beyond the scope of our discussion; presenting the conflicting approaches will suffice.

69. *See* the discussion in Luttwak, Strategy: The Logic of War and Peace, *supra* note 25, at Chapter 7.

3.2.3 The Effectiveness of the Total Destruction of an Adversary's Military: The American Lesson

From a utilitarian military perspective, the critique of the Napoleonic total war model as the archetype of war concentrates primarily upon its lack of effectiveness. In this context one may look at the experience of the two World Wars from a critical perspective. The next example focuses upon the American military experience before and after the two World Wars.

The American strategy has traditionally favored the use of overwhelming force, a preference influenced by the country's size, wealth, and production capabilities.[70] During the later stages of the American Civil War, Abraham Lincoln insisted that the only way to victory was through the complete destruction of the Confederacy's forces, despite objection to the idea by some of his officers—which led to his dismissal of some of them whom he saw as conciliatory.[71] As Eliot Cohen notes, Lincoln insisted that in order to achieve ultimate victory, the Union armies would have to crush their Confederate adversaries: "'The strength of the rebellion is its military' . . . The war would not be won by maneuver but by hard fighting; it would not end with the fall of Richmond or any other geographical location, but with the collapse of the enemy's army."[72]

The American military's strategic thinking continued along the same lines during the two World Wars and in the post-World War II era as well. In Vietnam, for example, "[s]ome of the early air-war concepts (for example, an extensive program of bombing of industrial targets in North Vietnam) reflected an unthinking application of World War II-era concepts to a very different enemy."[73] Indeed, the poor strategic thinking in Vietnam reached one of its lowest levels in its obsession with the "body count" industry.

> "The best way to defeat the enemy and to protect the South Vietnamese people was to utilize maximum force against the entire Communist system," wrote Lieutenant General Julian J. Ewell and Major General Ira A. Hunt in a study promoting the use of the body count and a counterinsurgency strategy based on attrition. "Once one decided to apply maximum force, the problem became

---

70. *See supra* Chapter 2 note 89.

71. Eliot A. Cohen, Supreme Command 38–41 (2012).

72. *Id.* at 31 [citations omitted].

73. *Id.* at 179.

> a technical one of doing it efficiently with the resources available." Not entirely coincidentally General Ewell, commanding general of the 9th Division in the Mekong River delta, acquired the nickname "The Butcher of the Delta" for his obsession with the body count.[74]

Not surprisingly, the body count industry—indeed, the quantified strategy—was not very effective; in many cases, it triggered a countereffect. Its lack of success challenged the American military's way of thinking. In new military theories introduced in the 1970s, the tendency of the American military was to move away from quantitative destruction, carried out by means of a linear confrontation of masses, to operational maneuvers.[75] This tendency was demonstrated in the First Gulf War. General Powell's argument against the complete destruction of the Iraqi army and in favor of ending the ground war after one hundred hours was grounded, inter alia, on utilitarian grounds: affording an "exit strategy" to an adversary affects its determination to continue fighting.[76]

This strategic modification, fine-tuned to adversaries' interests, draws further support from the current American strategy, which relates not to conventional inter-state wars but to the totally different challenge of counterinsurgency. The Counterinsurgency Doctrine (COIN)[77] imposes greater constraints upon American combatants than those "externally" required by the laws of armed conflict. It requires the military, as a professional matter, to minimize civilian casualties. "Combat in counterinsurgency often obligates leaders, Soldiers, and Marines to apply force in a precise manner to accomplish the mission without causing unnecessary loss of life or suffering."[78] In the following discussion I shall present the argument that constraining military force reflects a contemporary trend, substantiated by both contemporary strategic reality and legal evolution, and then go on to present the paradox that the legal rules, in many cases, trail behind the strategic reality in humanizing the arena of war.

---

74. *Id.* at 184 [citations omitted].

75. Freedman, Strategy: A History, *supra* note 27, at 198–201. *See also* Shimon Naveh, In Pursuit of Military Excellence 251 (1997).

76. *See supra* Chapter 1 note 96.

77. *See supra* text accompanying Chapter 1 notes 19–24.

78. U.S. Marine Corps, Warfighting Publication 3-33.5/U.S. Dep't of Army, Field Manual 3–24, Counterinsurgency paras. 1–36 (May 13, 2014).

3.2.4 Internalization of the Limitations of Force by Law-Abiding States

The American COIN Doctrine is not an isolated episode, and its constraining message is not limited to asymmetric wars. On the micro level it reflects the current military perception of what constitutes an effective counterinsurgency campaign. On the macro level, however, it reflects the internalization of the limits of military power. This self-imposed doctrine exposes a new reality of utility of force in general, the duty of a military to construct rather than destruct in particular.[79] Indeed, the COIN Doctrine dictates greater constraints upon American combatants than those "externally" required by traditional interpretations of the law of armed conflict. In this unique war environment the belligerents are fighting not against the domestic civilians but for their "hearts and minds,"[80] as well as to win over international public opinion.[81]

In contemporary times, the traditional total war model, though still relevant, has become less prevalent even in wars between states. Totality in terms of unlimited scope of violence is absolutely forbidden currently, and totality related to the political objective of war is, in many cases, neither practical nor desired. Furthermore, totality in terms of the means used in a war might, in certain cases, not be desirable due to reciprocal deterrence considerations;[82] in other cases, it might be prohibited (i.e., chemical weapons)[83] or unacceptable due to the devastating effects (i.e., nuclear weapons).[84]

---

79. *See supra* text accompanying Chapter 1 notes 20–24.

80. *See, e.g.*, Paul Dixon, *"Hearts and Minds"? British Counter-Insurgency from Malaya to Iraq*, 32 J. STRATEGIC STUD. 353 (2009).

81. *See supra* text accompanying Introduction notes 89–90.

82. *See* the Korean War example, *infra* text accompanying Chapter 4 note 16.

83. *See* Protocol for the Prohibition of the Use in War of Asphyxiating, Poisonous or Other Gases, and of Bacteriological Methods of Warfare, June 17, 1925, 94 L.N.T.S. 65. For earlier (prior to 1925) and later developments, *see, e.g.*, YORAM DINSTEIN, THE CONDUCT OF HOSTILITIES UNDER THE LAW OF INTERNATIONAL ARMED CONFLICT 80–82 (2d ed. 2010), and *see* his discussion on prohibited weapons in general. DINSTEIN, *supra*, at 62–88.

84. Mutual deterrence probably prevented a nuclear war between the two superpowers during the Cold War. *See generally* THOMAS C. SCHELLING, ARMS AND INFLUENCE (1966); LAWRENCE FREEDMAN, DETERRENCE 10–13 (2004). Regarding the legality of nuclear weapons, *see* Legality of the Threat or Use of Nuclear Weapons, Advisory Opinion, 1996 I.C.J. Rep. 226 (July 8).

The civilian dimension of total war—one people fighting against another—has been totally rejected by the prevailing rules. Historically, between the contradictory definitions of adversaries, as reflected in the two models of war—between states or between peoples—the law explicitly chose to limit the scope of war to the combatants, and to limit the damage caused to noncombatants.[85] Another dimension of total war, its absolute political aim—the total surrender of the adversary (and often a regime change)—is, in many cases, neither attainable nor preferred.[86] Such a total political objective is usually contingent upon achieving the traditional military aim of a total war, namely a decisive victory.[87] Total and unconditional surrender—such as in the case of the Allies' war aim against the Nazi regime in World War II—is the most extreme political aim of a self-defendant against aggression.[88] A relatively less ambitious aim than regime change, but still total in its results, would be an absolute incapacitation of the aggressor's military capabilities.[89] Both total aims are counter to the current trend of limiting a self-defendant's war aims. In the modern environment, governing an adversary's land and people, once

85. Indeed, though the law has accepted the Clausewitzian all-out war strategy as a lawful prototype, the legality of the other part of this war vision, dealing with war between the civil populations of the rival states, was rejected. *See supra* text accompanying Chapter 1 note 80.

86. Limited wars can be limited in other dimensions, for example, their timing. The timing variable, however, seems to be problematic in characterizing a war as limited. Short wars might be restricted, indeed "limited," as was common before the French Revolution, to a single daylong pitched battle. *See supra* note 53. On the other hand, even very short wars (especially currently)—for example, potential nuclear wars—can be devastating. *See also* the Lieber Code's statement: "The more vigorously wars are pursued, the better it is for humanity. Sharp wars are brief." The Lieber Code, *supra* note 48, at art. 29.

87. Under the Clausewitzian legacy, war is aimed at preventing an adversary from carrying on the fight, by destroying its military capabilities and undermining its psychological will to continue it. Von Clausewitz, *supra* note 4, at 90.

88. Due to the widespread legacy of the Nazi doctrine and beliefs within German society and the absence of a strong democratic tradition, the perception was that only the displacement of the entire ruling system and the transformation of the entire German society could be the desired end result of this war. *See infra* text accompanying Chapter 4 notes 100–104.

89. The case of Japan in World War II might serve as an example. In contrast to the German case, the Japanese circumstances are more disputed. Michael Walzer, for example, criticized the morality of the American "unconditional surrender" request from Japan: "[U]nconditional surrender [of Japan] should never have been asked. Japan's rulers were engaged in a more ordinary sort of military expansion, and all that was morally required was that they be defeated, not that they be conquered and totally overthrown." Michael Walzer, Just and Unjust Wars 267–68 (4th ed. 2006).

considered a desirable prize for the victor in war, has become a strategic burden and legal liability.[90] Incapacitation, too, has its own deterring price, both strategic and legal, for the winning law-abiding belligerent.[91] Indeed, the currently inflated price of total and decisive victory, which is not offset by any tempting prize (except the promise of one's own self-defense), may explain why many contemporary wars are not total (nor, as noted earlier, were they such in the past).

The strategic trend of limited wars of self-defense is consistent with the UN Charter's aim and rules. Under the Charter, the unilateral proactive exercise of military force (or threat of use of force) is prohibited,[92] subject to two exceptions: in cases of individual or collective self-defense against an armed attack, or pursuant to a Security Council authorization.[93] The lawful self-defensive exercise of military force is subject to legal limitations and its natural aim would be a return to the status quo ante. For example, when territory is lost to an aggressor in an armed attack, a proportional military response by a self-defendant is expected to be aimed, according to the common view, at "halting and repelling" the ongoing attack and restoring the territorial status quo.[94] Though legally the "halt and repel" formula seems to represent an optimal generic self-defensive response, there are cases in which it is actually not practical. For example, where the attacker does not hold any territory, or if it is a repeat offender, as reflected by its actions and declarations, adopting the "halt and repel" strategy against it may only drive it to further acts of armed attack. The self-defendant is entitled to restore its security following any such armed attack. If the Security Council cannot deter the aggressor, as originally intended by the Charter, it may be expected that the lawful paradigm of self-defense would allow secondary deterring tools against it. The legal challenge—though it is indeed disputed—is to tailor the deterrent effect as integral to the lawful

90. *See, e.g.*, Eyal Benvenisti, The International Law of Occupation (2d ed. 2012).

91. A relatively recent American example of avoiding incapacitation was presented in the First Gulf War (1991), where the ground war was ended after one hundred hours. *See supra* Chapter 1 note 96.

92. U.N. Charter, art. 2(4).

93. *See* U.N. Charter, Chapter 7.

94. *See, e.g.*, Judith Gardam, Necessity, Proportionality and the Use of Force by States 156–57 (2004). For an elaborated discussion of the "halt and repel" formula—the minimal in-scale response—*see infra* text accompanying Chapter 4 notes 81–85.

self-defense considerations, while rejecting any retroactive, illegal punitive measures.[95]

Although the current strategic and legal preference is for limited wars, there are circumstances in which both the "halt and repel" strategy and deterrence are impractical. In such cases, a decisive victory aimed at total incapacitation of an adversary, or even regime change in extreme cases, might be justified within the self-defense paradigm. In cases of armed attack where deterrence cannot work—for example, in a dictatorship because of agency problems,[96] or due to religious jihadi motivation, or where an aggressor's lack of assets makes him unafraid of losing any—a desirable end result, probably within the contours of lawful self-defense, may be to eliminate the aggressor's substantial military capabilities. In other words, if a self-defendant cannot deter an aggressor from continuing its armed attack against it, an alternative—though legally disputed—might be to totally disable it. The most extreme and contentious scenario on the lawful self-defense scale involves regime change. If at all lawful, it should be applicable where only the transformation of the entire society, as in the Nazi case, can promote peace and security for the self-defendant. Though any of these potential war aims within the self-defense paradigm may be strategically desirable, legally some are in dispute due to a lack of consensus on the legitimate ends of force in self-defense whenever the generic "halt and repel" formula is inapplicable.[97] In sum, the current trend favoring limited self-defensive measures—over total incapacitation of an adversary (or even regime change), which has become a residual alternative, applicable only in extreme cases—is a combined product of the new strategic and legal environment.

Furthermore, the current trend is supported by the change in social perceptions of heroism and killing in the modern period. The willingness

95. Indeed, deterrence might be legally perceived as an inherent part of punitive measures, which are not considered compatible with the right to self-defense. *See, e.g.*, David Kretzmer, *The Inherent Right to Self-Defence and Proportionality in* Jus ad Bellum, 24 Eur. J. Int'l L. 235, 257 (2013). The ICJ, while dealing with the legality of nuclear weapons, has nonetheless stated: "The Court does not intend to pronounce here upon the practice known as the 'policy of deterrence.'" Legality of the Threat or Use of Nuclear Weapons, Advisory Opinion, *supra* note 84, ¶ 67.

96. In dictatorships, there is no correlation between the rewards and risks to an aggressor's leaders; for example, they usually do not pay with their lives, but rather their citizens do.

97. *See* Kretzmer, *The Inherent Right to Self-Defence and Proportionality in* Jus Ad Bellum, *supra* note 95, at 260–76. For the view that regime change should now be considered an unlawful

of societies, primarily liberal ones, to face the consequences of wars and to pay their price is limited, too. Neither the sacrifice of their own soldiers' lives nor (to a limited extent) their acceptance of the need to kill the adversary's combatants (or civilians, albeit collaterally) can any longer be taken for granted as before. Indeed, the current reality, dubbed by Luttwak the "post-heroic era,"[98] is characterized by a lessening tolerance of casualties on both adversarial sides.[99] Besides the combined effects of these social changes and public expectations, especially in Western democracies, the various media now have relatively easy access to conflict zones, and the images of carnage they transmit further escalate the moderating trend. Add to that counterinsurgency operations, where the struggle is to win the "hearts and minds" of the local population, and we get a reality in which how a war is perceived by public opinion and reflected in the media becomes very significant. The relative departure from the total war paradigm that now prevails also draws support from the development of new technologies. Though they have enhanced the lethality and devastating consequences of weapons of war, they have also triggered developments in intelligence gathering and precise weaponry, the combination of which allows much more surgical strikes than before. With the precise strike option, a window of opportunity has opened for accepting a strategy of limited war as the most effective one. Indeed, at a time when the strategic scales are turning toward limited wars, the new military capabilities make it possible to conduct such wars with limited (relatively speaking) hazards. On the demand side, the strategic call for limited wars in their aims may now find, on the supply side, an improved technology enabling such wars in terms of the devastation caused by them but, at the same time, more effective in its targeting effects.

In sum, though the contemporary strategic and legal environment, especially in Western democracies, tends to restrict the scope of military power and violence, the law of armed conflict ignores substantial segments of this strategic development. This blind spot and its effects will be the subject of the coming discussion.

---

political goal, *see, e.g.*, Janina Dill, *The 21st-Century Belligerent's Trilemma*, 26 Eur. J. Int'l L. 83, 90–91 (2015). For an elaborated discussion of the incapacitation of an adversary, or even regime change, *see infra* text accompanying Chapter 4 notes 97–104.

98. *See supra* Chapter 1 note 90.

99. Luttwak, Strategy: The Logic of War and Peace, *supra* note 25, at 72.

3.3 Turning a Blind Eye to Military War Aims: The Silence of the Law Promotes the Roar of the Cannons

The modern law of armed conflict—while adopting the distinction rule and rejecting the civilian dimension of total war—has tacitly accepted the *in bello* prototype of total war between armies carried out in a bloody, industrial manner and aimed at the complete destruction of the adversary's armed forces. There is no formal prohibition of such warfare and it is actually considered a legitimate alternative in a lawful inter-state war of self-defense.[100] Currently, the law does not deal with strategic issues and limits itself to an important yet consequential and residual role. Once war has begun, it seeks to reduce and contain its flames and limit its hazards. It usually takes the aims and pattern of modern wars as given, and only then steps in, ex post, with a limited *in bello*[101] goal: to reduce their damages—by limiting the use of marginal weapons—or the combatants' suffering to the bare minimum,[102] and to reduce the unintended, collateral damage caused to noncombatants. The formal *in bello* response is currently provided by the fundamental principles of the law of armed conflict: distinction, proportionality, necessity, and humanity, and the specific norms derived from

---

100. Franck, for example, points out that "the great wars of the past, up to the time of the San Francisco Conference, were generally initiated by organized incursions of large military formations . . . " Thomas M. Franck, *Who Killed Article 2(4)? or: Changing Norms Governing the Use of Force by States*, 64 Am. J. Int'l L. 809, 812 (1970). Therefore, he concludes, "[b]ecause it was so familiar to them, it was to aggression of this kind that the drafters of Article 51 [recognizing the right of self-defense] addressed themselves." *Id.*

101. Under the prevailing rules, the *jus ad bellum* and the *jus in bello* bodies of law are independent of each other. Indeed, there are a few exceptions, for example, the ICJ decision with regard to the legality of nuclear weapons. *See* ICJ. Legality of the Threat or Use of Nuclear Weapons, Advisory Opinion, *supra* note 84, ¶ 105. Under the current dichotomous paradigm, one might have expected that whereas the cause of "self-defense" legitimizes the defendant's war (an *ad bellum* consideration), the question of legitimizing nuclear weapons would be confined solely to the realm of *in bello* considerations—that is, considerations regarding which tools are legitimate in the course of fighting—with equal rules applicable to both sides, aggressor and defendant alike. Such a traditional way of thinking is not dependent upon any *ad bellum* considerations. However, the Court's "extreme circumstances of self-defense" exception—which might affect, according to the majority view, the legality of the use of nuclear weapons—conflates the two types of considerations.

102. *E.g.*, "It is prohibited to employ weapons, projectiles and material and methods of warfare of a nature to cause superfluous injury or unnecessary suffering." API, *supra* note 5, at art. 35(2). A similar rule was established in Hague Convention (IV) Respecting the Laws and Customs of War and its Annex: Regulations Concerning the Laws and Customs of War on Land, Oct. 18, 1907, 187 C.T.S. 227, art. 23(e) [hereinafter 1907 Hague Regulations].

them. The humanity requirement forbids the use of means and methods of warfare that cause superfluous injury or unnecessary suffering. "The principle of humanity is based on the notion that once a military purpose has been achieved, the further infliction of suffering is unnecessary."[103] The necessity rule is perceived as imposing a restraint upon the exercise of military power beyond what is necessary to attain the military goal.[104] Though the rhetoric of the necessity principle is impressive, its performance is not. It can be very easily manipulated and circumvented.[105]

Facing a reality in which the *in bello* rules seem to deliver only partial restrictions, the prevailing law has preferred, nonetheless, not to deal with militaries' doctrinal choices and their strategic and operational ways of fighting. Indeed, the prevailing legal rules turn a blind eye to the more crucial issue of a war's aims and doctrinal dimensions, which actually determine how militaries fight and the brutal scope and effects of any given war. The current rules' disregard of military strategic preferences related to the scope of war means that the law deals mainly with the two extremes—the *ad bellum* rejection of proactive wars on the one hand, and the mitigation of war's consequential hazards at the tactical (*in bello*) micro level on the other.

Theoretically, the *ad bellum* proportionality requirement might have served as a potential strategic constraint. A common view in the academic literature—which to some extent can be traced to the judgments of the International Court of Justice—is that the requirement of proportionality in the exercise of self-defense sequentially regulates the choice of means and methods of warfare, thereby affecting war's conduct and scope. According to this view, the fact that a state's initial use of military force was justified as lawful self-defense and that its conduct of the war was lawful according to the *in bello* rules is not enough from a legal standpoint; such a state should demonstrate that all military measures taken by it, during the war, were also *ad bellum* proportionate.[106] Such a proportionality requirement

---

103. U.K. Ministry of Defence, The Manual of the Law of Armed Conflict 23 (2005).

104. For the dual legal function of military necessity, being both an enabling and a constraining principle, *see* Gabriella Blum, *The Laws of War and the "Lesser Evil"*, 35 Yale J. Int'l L. 1, 3, at note 5 (2010).

105. *See supra* Chapter 1. *See also* Eyal Benvenisti, *Rethinking the Divide Between* Jus ad Bellum *and* Jus in Bello *in Warfare Against Nonstate Actors*, 34 Yale J. Int'l L. 541, 544 (2009).

106. *See, e.g.*, the discussion and references in Gardam, Necessity, Proportionality and the Use of Force by States, *supra* note 94, at 162–79 (arguing that "proportionality in *jus ad bellum* requires a consideration of such matters as the geographical and destructive scope of

could restrict the operational scope of a military and affect its war aims. In the actual practice of states, however, the application of this potential constraint seems to face substantial challenges. First, according to Dinstein's conflicting view, *ad bellum* proportionality is not a continuing requirement, but rather is limited to the moment of decision whether resort to war is justified in response to an armed attack. Relying, inter alia, on the (pre-UN Charter) examples of the 1941 Japanese attack on Pearl Harbor that triggered the Pacific War with the United States and the 1939 German invasion of Poland that sparked World War II, he argues: "There is no support in the practice of States for the notion that proportionality remains relevant—and has to be constantly assessed—throughout the hostilities in the course of war."[107] Second, even according to the widespread view—according to which the *ad bellum* proportionality requirement remains relevant during the entire conflict—the essence of this proportionality, a legal term that has multiple meanings, is disputed. It might be viewed as a sort of objective, quantitatively based "counter-force meter," as explained by Thomas Franck: "Put formulaically, most proportionality discourse occurs when A has done (or threatens to do) X to B, and B responds by doing Y to A. The issue then crystallizes as an inquest into whether countermeasure Y is 'equivalent' (i.e., *proportionate*) to X."[108] However, there is no strategic reason to expect proportionality relating to the amount of force exercised

---

the response, the duration of the response, the selection of means and methods of warfare and targets and the effect on third states." *Id.* at 162); Christine Gray, International Law and the Use of Force 148–55 (3d ed. 2008). Gray points out, however, that the ICJ's judgments treat the limitation of necessity and proportionality as "marginal considerations"—that is, they first declare that the use of military force is not legal (does not amount to a lawful self-defense) and then add that the actions were not proportionate. Gray, *supra*, at 151. Indeed, the ICJ in its *Congo v. Uganda* judgment held that in the absence of an armed attack, the preconditions for the exercise of self-defense do not exist. In an obiter dicta, however, the Court added: "the taking of airports and towns many hundreds of kilometers from Uganda's border would not seem proportionate to the series of transborder attacks it claimed had given rise to the right of self-defence, nor to be necessary to that end." Case Concerning Armed Activities on the Territory of the Congo (Congo v. Uganda), Judgment, 2005 I.C.J. Rep. 168, ¶ 147 (Dec. 19).

107. Yoram Dinstein, War, Aggression and Self-Defence 262 (5th ed. 2011); *see also* the remainder of his discussion at 262–67. It should be noted, however, that Dinstein distinguishes between the proportionality requirements in "war" versus "short of war" scenarios. In the latter, he advocates an approximation in scale and effects between the unlawful attack and the lawful response. *Id.*

108. Thomas M. Franck, *On Proportionality of Countermeasures in International Law*, 102 Am. J. Int'l L. 715, 715 (2008) (emphasis in the original) (explaining that in dealing with "categories of proportionality discourse that are paradigmatic . . . [t]he conflict may be one entailing a state's recourse to military force to retaliate against an actual or putative attacker").

by an aggressor in the military counter-response taken by a self-defending army in a full-scale war. Nor should there be any realistic expectation of quantitatively proportionate use of means and methods in such a war (as long as they are lawful under the law of armed conflict). For example, if one state mounts a full-scale military invasion of another state's territory, on realpolitik and military-professional grounds the self-defendant should not be expected to restrict itself to a "tit for tat" type of response. The preferred military strategy of the self-defendant would likely be to exercise overwhelming force whenever and wherever possible, thus ensuring its victory.[109] Indeed, this was the American (Colin Powell's) doctrine, applied successfully in the First Gulf War, advocating the exercise of "overwhelming force quickly and decisively."[110]

The potential exists, however, for creating a legal-strategic constraint through a broad interpretation of the *ad bellum* proportionality requirement in relation to a war's aims. Indeed, David Kretzmer and others argue that proportionality in the use of military force should be evaluated and judged against the legitimate ends of the self-defendant state exercising this force.[111] Such "means-ends proportionality," substantially connecting strategy to tactics, could perhaps reach the desired legal result: limiting the scope and hazards of wars. The legal problem with this interpretation, however, is the uncertainty relating to the legality of both its "ends" and "means" segments: "Even when it is accepted that the appropriate test of

---

109. Indeed, one of nine professional principles of war of the U.S. armed forces, for example, is *mass; see supra* text accompanying Chapter 2 notes 100–101. The British Army's manual addresses this issue as "concentration of force," defining it as an action that "involves the decisive, synchronised application of superior fighting power (physical, conceptual and moral) to realise intended effects, when and where required." U.K. MINISTRY OF DEFENCE, ARMY DOCTRINE PUBLICATION, OPERATIONS 2A-4 (Nov. 2010), https://www.gov.uk/government/uploads/system/uploads/attachment_data/file/33695/ADPOperationsDec10.pdf (last visited Aug. 24, 2016) [hereinafter U.K. OPERATIONS MANUAL]. Legally too, even the "halt and repel" formula does not oblige any equivalence between the force used and the self-defendant's response. *See, e.g.*, GARDAM, NECESSITY, PROPORTIONALITY AND THE USE OF FORCE BY STATES, *supra* note 94, at 160–61.

110. Colin Powell, *US Forces: Challenges Ahead*, 71 FOREIGN AFFAIRS 32, 37 (1992). It should also be noted that although the Allies' aim in the 1990–1991 Gulf War was to expel Iraq from Kuwait, the war was not restricted to the latter's territory. *See also infra* text accompanying note 176.

111. Kretzmer, *The Inherent Right to Self-Defence and Proportionality in* Jus ad Bellum, *supra* note 95 (arguing that the "means-ends proportionality" is applicable in human rights law as well, where "proportionality judges the harm caused by restrictions on a protected liberty when weighed against the legitimate ends those restrictions are meant to serve." *Id.* at 238).

proportionality is a 'means-end' test, in the absence of agreement on these ends it is obviously impossible to agree on the necessary means to achieve them."[112]

In the absence of a consensus on the legitimate ends of exercising force in self-defense, the legal discourse's failure to address the predictable results of the choice of any given military strategy and the war aims deriving from it invites the question: Was there any legal alternative? The suggested answer is a positive one. In case the visionary prohibition on starting a war were to fail, a practical "second line" of legal defense might have been expected to moderate all dimensions of war. Indeed, the founders of the modern law relating to armed conflict had a wide spectrum of theories of war to choose from. They had a model of a modest international arrangement: the 1868 St. Petersburg Declaration, which restricted the aim of war, stating that "the progress of civilization should have the effect of alleviating as much as possible the calamities of war; That the only legitimate object which States should endeavor to accomplish during war is to weaken the military forces of the enemy."[113] Our previous discussion demonstrated that there is a broad spectrum between total wars and limited ones. Wars can be limited, and the law of armed conflict should have a say about it. Within its stated agenda, it could exhibit a preference for channeling belligerent parties into limited rather than total wars and, within each type of war—with a given military aim—into the military course of action that may be expected to pose the least danger to human lives, of combatants and noncombatants alike. That expectation as a whole, however, has not been fulfilled.[114] An open question, which is beyond the scope of this chapter, is why: Do the prevailing rules represent a genuine legal failure (related to the very ability to regulate belligerents' strategic conduct)? Or do they rather, on a more forgiving view, reflect a realpolitik arrangement or compromise, internalizing the huge gap between rhetoric

---

112. *Id.* at 282. For the alternate *ad bellum* necessity suggestion, *see* the discussion *infra* text accompanying notes 172–178.

113. Declaration Renouncing the Use, in Time of War, of Explosive Projectiles under 400 Grammes Weight, Saint Petersburg, 29 November–11 December 1868, www.icrc.org/IHL.nsf/FULL/130?OpenDocument (last visited Feb. 23, 2015) [hereinafter The St. Petersburg Declaration].

114. With regard to civilians, however, API Article 57(3) determines that when a choice is possible between several military objectives for obtaining a similar military advantage, the objective to be selected shall be that where the attack is expected to cause the least danger to civilians. API, *supra* note 5, art. 57(3)

and practice in the international arena and aimed at the maximal attainable challenge: to partially mitigate the *in bello* consequences of war and help its victims?[115]

Whichever answer one prefers, the current law implicitly accepted and legitimized the Clausewitzian model of total war between militaries, with all its implications. The international community in the post-World Wars era was decisive enough to dictate a legal prohibition on the proactive use of military force, yet at the same time chose not to deal with the most crucial *in bello* issue—the strategic, operational, and tactical dimensions that derive from a war's aims and dictate the way wars are carried out in practice. Precisely on this point, the laws fall silent, allowing the cannons to roar and the blood to be spilled. Indeed, what obtains is a reversal of Cicero's famous saying: "In times of war, the law falls silent" (*Inter arma enim silent leges*).[116] Here, the silence of the law is antecedent to—and in fact allows—the most brutal type of war, with substantial implications for combatants and civilians alike. With regard to combatants, the acceptance and legitimization of total wars has its price in terms of soldiers' lives. Combatants on both sides simply become the most expendable commodity on the battlefield.[117] With regard to civilians, the prevailing proportionality criterion is relative to the magnitude of military force actually exercised. The greater the scope of the war, the more collateral damage might be lawful. Indeed, the current acceptance of total war as a lawful prototype of war triggers, as a default, a wide range of lawful targets. This

---

115. Such explanations may relate to state sovereignty regarding the choice of strategy (and grand strategy): states want to shield their leaders—both civilian and military—from any third-party legal scrutiny of matters relating to the designation of a war's aims and their choice of strategy in a given campaign. Added to that is the interest of states' militaries in maintaining their independence in designating a war's aims and in adopting doctrines and strategies to be applied on the battlefield that are suitable to them, without external intervention. Another explanation does not concentrate on states' interest in immunity, per se. Instead it points out that states' behavior in general, that of their militaries in particular, to a large degree reflects their cultural background. Ultimately, it is the culture of a given society that largely dictates its military doctrine and strategy. The patterns of war, the way militaries fight, and their doctrines and even military tactics "are usually the product of social and economic factors rather than of purely military ones." VAN CREVELD, supra note 33, at 19. *See also supra* Chapter 2 note 76.

116. Or in a different translation: "For among [times of] arms, the laws fall mute." Cicero's actual wording was "*Silent enim leges inter arma.*" M.T. CICERO, PRO MILONE 5, § 11 (F.H. Colson ed., 1980).

117. Indeed, Napoleon's saying that "soldiers are made to be killed" reflected his attitude of treating them as an expendable means in the battlefield. WALZER, JUST AND UNJUST WARS, *supra* note 89, at 136.

in turn legitimizes inflated collateral damage to civilians. This creates a vicious circle: the killing of more soldiers—so long as their killing is part of a stated "military advantage"—justifies, under the prevailing rules, the killing of a "proportional" number of innocent civilians as collateral damage.[118]

To conclude, the implicit adoption of total war between militaries as an archetypal pattern of war invites a twofold criticism. From a moral perspective, the required mass killing is unacceptable. Professionally, as we have just seen, such killing is of dubious effectiveness. Ironically, it is only in legal thinking that one finds an apparent acceptance of this strategic prototype of bloody war. The legal regime, which should have been the first to reject this bloody paradigm, still holds it to be valid and untouchable. Instead of leveraging military strategic constraints, it merely tries to contain war's hazards at the tactical level by limiting war's consequential hazards and suffering, to a limited degree.

Having surveyed this contemporary strategic and legal reality, I shall now turn to the prevailing, and later to the normatively desirable, targeting rules. The discussion will begin with the two conflicting schools regarding the lawful scope of military advantage that allows objects to be characterized as military targets. It will be argued that both schools are inconsistent with strategic reality. Through this analysis I shall later suggest a tool—indeed, pour new substance into an existing tool—that has the potential to moderate all dimensions of war: the *ad bellum* necessity.

3.4 Tactical "Military Advantage" or Strategic?

3.4.1 The Two Dichotomist Schools

In interpreting the concept of military advantage—a key component in the definition of both military objects and proportionality—two different schools have developed. The tactical school "applies a more restrictive interpretation with a goal of limiting lawful targets to those most directly linked to military personnel and material. This view puts particular emphasis on a temporal limitation on targeting and focuses on the 'tactical' level of war."[119] By contrast, the strategic school takes a wider view. It "accepts a broader and more indirect connection between military forces and the

118. *See* Gabriella Blum, *The Dispensable Lives of Soldiers*, 2 J. LEGAL ANALYSIS 115, 131 (2010).

119. Watkin, *Targeting in Air Warfare*, supra *note* 2, at 65.

resources of the State in supporting them."[120] The current fighting practice of law-abiding states and their targeting policy—which usually includes, for example, war industry and dual-purpose infrastructure—is consistent with the broader strategic approach. In fact, it is the strategic nature of warfare that dictates this practice.

The military advantage, whether "concrete and direct" (in the proportionality equation) or "definite" (as required for military objectives), should be certain and substantial. The law requires a clear, definite nexus between the targets of an attack—whose destruction is aimed at—and the military advantages gained.[121] Although the causality nexus—requiring a concrete rather than a hypothetical connection—is well accepted, the timing nexus—requiring a short-term advantage—is controversial. The ICRC Commentary to Additional Protocol I, Article 57(2)(a)(iii)[122] presents an extreme view, requiring that the connection be "relatively close, and that advantages which are hardly perceptible and those which would only appear in the long term should be disregarded."[123] Indeed, the last part of this statement is much disputed as "long-term effects may be both direct and concrete."[124]

If we put aside the timing nexus (if any), the geographical dimension and the level of war at which the military advantage should be examined are substantially disputed by the two schools. While some limit the military advantage that might justify collateral damage (if proportional) to the "on the spot" tactical advantage, others call for a wider strategic perspective of the desired military goal: the entire operational picture.[125] The wider perspective in defining military advantage in targeting reflects states' practice

120. *Id.*

121. In fact, there are two causality criteria required by API Article 52(2): an "effective contribution to the military action" along with the "definite military advantage." API, *supra* note 5, art. 52(2). *See infra* text accompanying note 159.

122. API Article 57(2)(a)(iii) requires as a precautionary measure that states "refrain from deciding to launch any attack which may be expected to cause incidental loss of civilian life, injury to civilians, damage to civilian objects, or a combination thereof, which would be excessive in relation to the concrete and direct military advantage anticipated." API, *supra* note 5, art. 57(2)(a)(iii).

123. Claude Pilloud & Jean Pictet, *Protocol I Article 57–Precautions in Attack, in* Commentary on the Additional Protocols of 8 June 1977 to the Geneva Conventions of 12 August 1949, at 684 para. 2209 (Claude Pilloud et al. eds., 1987).

124. Dinstein, The Conduct of Hostilities, *supra* note 83, at 134.

125. *See, e.g., id.* at 94, 133–34.

not only in theory but in their actual fighting. This is attested to by Western democracies' reservations upon signing the Additional Protocol I,[126] and by their targeting policy in contemporary wars.[127] Similarly, it was also the perspective adopted by the Rome Statute of the International Criminal Court, defining unacceptable collateral damage as "clearly excessive in relation to the concrete and direct overall military advantage anticipated."[128] (This preference, however, might be explained by the criminal law's unique attributes and the higher threshold required by it.)

The conflicting views can be illustrated, for example, by way of their divergent interpretation of the "by nature" criterion of military objects, which are limited by API Article 52(2), inter alia, to "those objects which by their nature, location, purpose or use make an effective contribution to military action." The strategic approach to interpreting "military objectives" by their "nature" broadly also includes "[i]ndustrial plants (even when privately owned) engaged in the manufacture of arms, munitions, military supplies and essential parts for military vehicles, vessels and aircraft . . . "[129] Similarly, the HPCR Manual on International Law includes, among the objects meeting this criterion, subject to the circumstances ruling at the time, inter alia, "factories, lines and means of communications (such as airfields, railway lines, roads, bridges and tunnels); energy producing facilities; oil storage depots; transmission facilities and equipment."[130]

---

126. *See* the Reservations and Declarations Made at the Time of Ratification of Protocol I by Australia, Belgium, Canada, France, Germany, Italy, Netherlands, New Zealand, Spain, and the United Kingdom, *available at* https://www.icrc.org/applic/ihl/ihl.nsf/States.xsp?xp_viewStates=XPages_NORMStatesParties&xp_treatySelected=470 (last visited Nov. 22, 2015); *see also* Int'l & Operational Law Dep't. The Judge Advocate General's Legal Center & Schools, U.S. Army, JA 422, Operational Law Handbook 13 (2014) (stating that "'military advantage' is not restricted to tactical gains, but is linked to the full context of one's war strategy. Balancing between incidental damage to civilian objects and incidental civilian casualties may be done on a target-by-target basis, but also may be done in an overall sense against campaign objectives").

127. *See infra* text accompanying notes 132–134.

128. United Nations Diplomatic Conference of Plenipotentiaries on the Establishment of an International Criminal Court, *Rome Statute of the International Criminal Court*, art. 8 (2)(b)(iv), U.N. Doc. A/CONF.183/9 (July 17, 1998) [hereinafter ICC Statute].

129. Dinstein, The Conduct Of Hostilities, *supra* note 83, at 97.

130. The Program on Humanitarian Policy and Conflict Research at Harvard University [HPCR], Manual on International Law Applicable to Air and Missile Warfare rule 23 (2009) (referring to Rule 22(a) dealing with the "by nature" criterion), *available at* http://www.ihlresearch.org/amw/manual/section-e-military-objectives/e-general-rules/rule-23 (last visited Nov. 22, 2015) [hereinafter HPCR Manual]. As to targets

By comparison, the same "by nature" criterion is interpreted much more narrowly by the restrictive school. For example, the *ICRC Commentary* defines it as "all objects directly used by the armed forces: weapons, equipment, transports, fortifications, depots, buildings occupied by armed forces, staff headquarters, communications centres, etc."[131] The reality, however, is that the strategic approach prevails among states, as reflected in their actual practice of broadly interpreting the "by nature" criterion, as well as the other criteria of "location, purpose or use." For example, in NATO's 1999 Kosovo air campaign the targets included, inter alia, broadcasting stations; bridges, railways and oil storage depots; and economic facilities and civilian political leadership compounds, such as government ministries.[132] Similar targets were attacked in Afghanistan[133] and Iraq.[134]

The controversy between the two schools does not stop at classifying military objects and is reflected in the interpretation of the phrase "direct military advantage" in the proportionality equation, as well. The limited approach was adopted, for example, in the ICRC Commentary, which states that the prohibition on "excessive" collateral damage[135] "is not concerned with strategic objectives but with the means to be used in a specific tactical operation," and that "[a] military advantage can only consist in ground gained and in annihilating or weakening the enemy armed forces."[136] State

---

that according to the HPCR should be classified as lawful, even though they do not directly take part in the actual fighting, *see infra* notes 161–162.

131. Claude Pilloud & Jean Pictet, *Protocol I Article. 52*, *in* COMMENTARY ON THE ADDITIONAL PROTOCOLS OF 8 JUNE 1977 TO THE GENEVA CONVENTIONS OF 12 AUGUST 1949, at 629, 636 para. 2020 (Claude Pilloud et al. eds. 1987).

132. ICC Office of the Prosecutor, *Final Report to the Prosecutor by the Committee Established to Review the NATO Bombing Campaign against the Federal Republic of Yugoslavia*, paras. 45–46 and 55 (June 13, 2000) [hereinafter OTP Report] www.icty.org/x/file/About/OTP/otp_report_nato_bombing_en.pdf (last visited Apr. 24, 2016).

133. In the Afghan case, Operation "Enduring Freedom" called for the bombing of three types of targets: (1) "infrastructure" (power plants, roads, etc.); (2) "industry"; and (3) a class of targets associated with the Taliban leadership said to have had "political implications." *See* BENJAMIN S. LAMBETH, AIR POWER AGAINST TERROR: AMERICA'S CONDUCT OF OPERATION ENDURING FREEDOM 311 (2005).

134. Barton Gellman, *Allied Air War Struck Broadly in Iraq: Officials Acknowledge Strategy Went Beyond Purely Military Targets*, WASH. POST, June 23, 1991, at A01.

135. API, *supra* note 5, at art. 57(2)(a)(iii).

136. Pictet & Pilloud, *Additional Protocol I art. 57, supra* note 123, para. 2218. It should be noted, however, that even this tactically oriented approach accepts that "it goes without saying that an attack carried out in a concerted manner in numerous places can only be judged in its entirety." *Id.*

practice in applying the proportionality requirement in contemporary war arenas is, however, much wider, following the strategic school.[137] In the following discussion, I shall present each school's mistake and suggest a novel, hybrid approach aimed at constraining the scope of lawful targets.

3.4.2 The Prevailing Schools' Mistakes and the Suggested Hybrid Approach

States' rejection of the tactical approach in their actual practice reflects reality, as strategy dictates how wars are fought. War aims and the targeting policies deriving from them—especially the "industrialized" ones, exercised primarily by modern air forces—are determined at the strategic level.[138] Each war has its own course, an azimuth, determined by its strategy; it cannot be judged by strictly looking at every single step taken along this course on its own. The mistake of the tactical school lies in its effort to "tacticize" the battlefield. Such an effort, even for the sake of legality only, is doomed to fail on realpolitik grounds. Furthermore, the notion that focusing upon the tactical level can minimize civilian suffering—which is the main rationale behind the current disregard of strategy in the targeting context[139]—is mistaken, as well. Ignoring the fighting level that matters most in the conduct of war triggers a counter-effect. Those who want to humanize the arena of war, to the most feasible extent, cannot entrench themselves in the tactical zone; rather, they must face reality and think strategically.

The mistake—or, one might say, the manipulation—of the strategic school is its disregard for the built-in constraining elements of a strategy. A war strategy will always be enabling in some aspects, but constraining in others. Indeed, due to the current blind spot of the law—its explicit disregard for the direct consequences of war strategy and the aims that derive from it—the prevailing strategic school leverages war strategy in a partial and biased way. It uses it strictly as an enabler, to widen the scope

137. According to this approach, what needs to be taken into account is the entire military campaign, taken "as a whole," for the purpose of assessing the military advantage gained. Nonmilitary (e.g., political or economic) advantages are considered irrelevant. *See, e.g.*, Dinstein, The Conduct of Hostilities, *supra* note 83, at 95.

138. *See generally*, Watkin, *Military Advantage*, *supra* note 29.

139. *See, e.g.*, Judith Gardam, *Proportionality and Force in International Law*, 87 Am. J. Int'l L. 391, 407 (1993).

of a war and its lawful targets list, while ignoring its constraining attributes. A side effect of this disregard is the dehumanization of the war arena. Familiarity with the constraining element of a given strategy, however, might be helpful in this regard. The focus upon concrete military advantages gained at the tactical level of war is aimed at restricting civilian damage at the retail level; its wholesale restriction, however, can be achieved mainly through the limiting attributes of the strategic level. A main strategic constraint might be adherence to a war's aims, especially in limited wars. (The application of another potential strategic constraint, the *ad bellum* proportionality requirement, is problematic and doubtful, as discussed earlier.[140]) The suggested hybrid approach requires adherence to strict and definite war aims in targeting, substantially affecting the scope of lawful targets. Currently, states can lawfully cross the legal *ad bellum* Rubicon only in their own (or collective) self-defense.[141] Were the law to require such ostensibly self-defensive states to publicly define their strategic war aims, at every stage of the conflict, their militaries' targeting practice would thereon derive from, and be evaluated in light of, this policy. (Indeed, a war's strategy is dynamic, and its aims may mutate through its evolving stages. Therefore, the suggested requirement of defining a war's goals at each stage does not deny a belligerent state the freedom to define and change its goals evolutionarily, subject only to the prevailing law.) It would dictate a coherent targeting practice consistent with the selected strategy. Since many, if not most, contemporary wars are limited rather than total, such a coherent targeting requirement would usually impose effective, substantial restrictions upon the scope of lawful targets. Although this coherency requirement, reflecting military professionalism, seems to be consistent with the interest of well-trained militaries, it will be elaborated below that mandatory declaration of a war's aims has to be externally imposed upon states, because of the ex-post disadvantages it entails from a grand strategy perspective.[142]

The prevailing rule does not require the fighting states to declare their specific war aims, but is satisfied with popular rhetoric that pays lip service to self-defense. Even for a "real" self-defendant (let alone a masquerading

140. *See supra* text accompanying notes 106–112.

141. *See supra* text accompanying note 93.

142. As for the advantages and disadvantages of strategic ambiguity, *see* the discussion *infra* text accompanying notes 188–199.

one), it allows militaries excessive discretion in their target selection for the sake of their own self-defense, especially when the war is a limited one. This discretion is consistent with the military legacy of Napoleon and Clausewitz and the acceptance of total war, albeit by default, as a lawful prototype. The current potential lawful targets bank is a natural product of the total war legacy. Put differently, by the same default that accepts total war as a lawful prototype, a wide spectrum of targets is considered as generically lawful military objectives "by their nature, location, purpose or use." Indeed, a prototype of a generic all-out war triggers a wide generic list of apparent military objects. If the model of lawful war is that of total warfare between mass armies, carried out in a bloody, industrial manner, the legal threshold—determining that lawful targets are such that make "an effective contribution to military action and whose total or partial destruction, capture or neutralization, in the circumstances ruling at the time, offers a definite military advantage"[143]—is bound to reflect it and be very low.

Paradoxically, focusing upon the tactical level affords both the boots on the ground and their commanders, at all levels, a wide range of potential military advantages to pick and choose from. Furthermore, its dependency upon the subjective soldier's perspective—including his or her perception of "the circumstances ruling at the time" (though this requirement has objective attributes, as well[144])—widens the scope of potential dual-purpose objects that surpass the legal threshold of military objective. The

143. API, *supra* note 5, at art. 52(2).

144. Indeed, one could argue that the contextual basis—"in the circumstances ruling at the time"—relates not only to the "nature, location, purpose or use" of the object, but should be interpreted broadly to include, in a given war, its strategic aims. Under this interpretation, a limited war is an important "circumstance" that will directly affect the targets list and moderate its spectrum. *See, e.g.*, Fenrick's statement: "[t]he definition [of military objective, by API] is situation-dependent. A core of objects will be military objectives in virtually any conflict. Other objects may become military objectives in certain conflicts depending upon various factors, including the strategic objectives of the parties to the conflict and the degree to which the conflict approaches total war." William J. Fenrick, *Targeting and Proportionality During the NATO Bombing Campaign Against Yugoslavia*, 12 Eur. J. Int'l L. 489, 494 (2001). Though such an interpretation is welcome, it should be remembered that the "circumstances" requirement seems to relate to the attributes of the object: their nature, location, purpose, or use. While the criteria of location, purpose, or use are totally dependent on "circumstances": even the "by nature" criterion depends upon them. For example, even a tank or warship, a military objective by nature, might not be considered so if it turns out to be a war museum piece. Furthermore, the specific aims of a war are currently not (always) public domain, and as argued above, the perception of circumstances is subjectively biased.

lawful targets are largely subject, currently, to the reasonable[145] beholder's perspective. In an apparent generic total-war strategic environment—and this is the legal world we live in, in light of the lack of a legal obligation to declare a self-defendant's specific war aims—it is relatively easy to assume a clear, definite nexus between the potential targets of an attack, whose destruction is sought, and the generic military advantages to be gained. Due to this generality, the requirement of a causality nexus is a low threshold. Every tank or machine gun, each military bunker, might easily surpass it due to its "nature"; many geographical points might be considered crucial due to their "location"; and the intended "purpose" or even actual "use" of a potential target might be either bona fide mistaken or easily manipulated. Furthermore, this too broad a scale of potential lawful military advantages in fact triggers a wider scope of lawful collateral damage, as the proportionality equation links the two by legalizing civilian damage not considered excessive. It is therefore necessary to adapt the potential generic lawful targets bank—which currently derives from the total war prototype—to actual wars, which are generally limited.

3.4.3 Adapting Lawful Targets to Limited Wars: The Shrinking of the Potential Targets Bank

The suggested approach takes the doctrinal choices and war aims of a military as a given, as long as they are lawful. It calls, however, for controlling the selected strategy and its effects, including the collateral ones. It therefore advocates that states be required to publicly declare their concrete aims when engaging in a war, and to adjust the targeting rules of their war to its specific aims. If declaring the war aims of a belligerent, adjusted at every stage of the belligerency, becomes mandatory, in many cases—probably most—such statements will define the practical, attainable goals of a limited rather than total war. Any restricted strategic aim would naturally generate a war with a limited spectrum of objectives. This, in turn, would substantially reduce the potential number of lawful targets—especially the dual-purpose objects—and might create the desired wholesale effect

145. In the legal assessment of the *in bello* proportionality—requiring that an expected "military advantage" be balanced vis-à-vis collateral damage—it has been accepted that the criterion of reasonableness should pertain to the reasonable commander. *See supra* Chapter 1 note 98.

of reducing civilian damage.[146] Consider, for example, the UK's military reaction to the Argentine conquest of the Falkland Islands in 1982. This conflict was mainly over the sovereignty of the Islands. It did not create an actual threat to the lives of British citizens. The explicit *ad bellum* aim of the UK government was the expulsion of the invader.[147] Any *in bello* military activity aimed directly at "halting and repelling" the invasion would have been lawful. However, bombing Argentinean homeland infrastructure not related to the military action (either actually or potentially)—such as bridges and railroads not used for the transfer of supplies and reinforcements to the front—would have been unlawful.

The expected diminution of the potential targets bank in limited wars, correlating a war's aims with its lawful targeting list, is expressed in the 1994 San Remo Manual's statement that "the legal rules should remain the same in both general and limited war situations but that the application of these rules to the facts should result in a more restrictive approach to targeting in limited conflicts."[148] This process of adaption, however, should not be perceived as being imposed externally by a rigid legal formula; rather, under the suggested approach, it is a natural professional practice of adapting the targeting rules to the changing strategic reality. It would reflect the internal professional military process, linking all levels of military activity, including targeting, in a coherent way toward a strategic directive.[149] The suggested mandatory declaration by a self-defendant of its

146. In fact, due to the necessity principle it would reduce the killing of combatants as well. *See supra* Chapter 1.

147. The Falklands Campaign, which was the culmination of a 200-year long dispute between Argentina and the United Kingdom over the islands, began on April 2, 1982. The campaign lasted for approximately two weeks and cost over 1,000 lives. *See* U.K. Ministry of Defence, Falklands 25: Background Briefing, http://archive.today/grTy (last visited Aug. 16, 2017).

148. International Institute on Humanitarian Law, San Remo Manual on International Law Applicable to Armed Conflict at Sea 116, ¶ 40.8 (1995) [hereinafter San Remo Manual]. For a general call for adjusting the targets list in a limited conflict, *see* Watkin, *Targeting in Air Warfare, supra* note 2, at 48–50 (arguing, inter alia, that "the scope of the conflict and the objectives being sought by its participants will act to set boundaries concerning the types and numbers of targets struck to obtain a legitimate strategic purpose. Given the relatively limited strategic objectives of most inter-State and non-State conflict in the 21st Century the scale of targets hit should also logically be reduced as both means and desired ends of the attacks must be linked to those objectives." *Id.* at 50).

149. The *San Remo Manual* seems to reflect such a view regarding the imposition of an external legal formula: "some participants had distinguished between general and limited war situations because they believed that in the latter case *more legal restrictions had to be applied* than in the former." San Remo Manual, *supra* note 148 (emphasis added).

concrete war aims would facilitate this new legal expectation of a restrictive approach to targeting at all levels of war.

3.4.4 Reasoned Declaration of War: Revisiting an Old Neglected Practice

The demand that the aims of war be made public is not absolutely new; however, the old practice, dealing with the reasons for war but not its aims, has fallen into neglect.[150] In the era before World War II, the practice regarding reasoned declarations of war—or a conditional declaration of war in the form of an ultimatum that, if not met, would unleash hostilities[151]—was enshrined in the Hague Convention (III) of 1907:[152] "The contracting Powers recognize that hostilities between themselves must not commence without previous and explicit warning, in the form either of a declaration of war, giving reasons, or of an ultimatum with conditional declaration of war."[153]

The benefit of this state of affairs was clear: a scenario was laid out regarding how to prevent hostilities without use of force or at least minimize their scope.[154] The disadvantage was also clear: states could open

---

150. For a description of the moral aspects of a declaration of war in a public, reasoned, and conditional statement, *see* Eric Grynaviski, *The Bloodstained Spear: Public Reason and Declarations of War*, 5 INT'L THEORY 238, 240 (2013) (arguing that "in any reasonable interpretation of just war theory, an undeclared war is usually simply unjust").

151. *See* James Brown Scott, *The Work of the Second Hague Peace Conference*, 2 AM. J. INT'L L. 1, 16 (1908).

152. Hague Convention (III) Relative to the Opening of Hostilities, Oct. 18, 1907, 205 C.T.S. 264 This feature was introduced by the Convention, following the Russian-Japanese conflict of 1905, to prevent cases of surprise attacks of bad faith. James L. Tyron, *The Hague Conferences*, 20 YALE J. INT'L L. 470, 481 (1911); Edward G. Elliott, *The Development of International Law by the Second Hague Conference*, 8 COLUM. L. REV. 96, 103 (1908).

153. Hague Convention (III), *supra* note 152, at art. 1.

154. The idea behind the French proposition for the addition of reasons to the declaration of war was twofold. First, with regard to the would-be attacked country, said country would be able to know the reasons for the attack and thus decide in advance whether to lay down its arms and submit to the terms, or it would know what was required of it to put an end to hostilities without force. Second, with regard to neutral countries, the statement of reasons in a declaration of war would allow those countries to consider their position with regard to the belligerent countries' conduct and act accordingly should they desire to. *See Annex B—Opening of Hostilities, Report to the Conference, in* DIVISION OF INTERNATIONAL LAW OF THE CARNEGIE ENDOWMENT FOR INTERNATIONAL PEACE, TRANSLATION OF OFFICIAL TEXTS OF THE PROCEEDINGS OF THE HAGUE PEACE CONFERENCES, THE CONFERENCE OF 1907, VOL. I, PLENARY MEETINGS OF THE CONFERENCE 131, 132 (1920). *See also* Arthur Eyffinger, *A Highly*

hostilities for any reason.[155] In the aftermath of the two World Wars, however, with the UN Charter's prohibition on the proactive initiation of wars,[156] this practice seems to have fallen into neglect. The Charter limits lawful belligerency to only two clear-cut justifications for war: either reactively in self-defense in response to an armed attack,[157] or proactively due to a Security Council resolution.[158] Given these new, limited justifications, the former practice of ex-ante explicit warning has come to be perceived as unnecessary and even counterproductive. (The old practice is currently replaced in art. 51 by an ex-post statement: "Measures taken by Members in the exercise of this right of self-defence shall be immediately reported to the Security Council.")

What is called for is not the revival of the obsolete formal declaration, but a concrete and definite statement by belligerent states—arguing self-defense in all types of wars—which specifies their war aims right from the start. The mere argument of self-defense—though commonly employed by overt aggressors and innocent victims alike—should not suffice.

Though the discussion thus far has focused upon a demand for an explicit statement of the strategic goals in any belligerency, it should be emphasized that the public declaration is merely a means to transparency, whereas the more substantive and essential requirement is coherency in a military's activities, including targeting, across all levels of war. Indeed, the declaration of a war's aims is mainly a procedural requirement, a way of applying professional and legal constraints through the *ad bellum* necessity to moderate all dimensions of war. This substantive demand therefore remains relevant, though more difficult to prove, when the aims of war have not been publicly declared but are only implied (e.g., through statements of politicians, actions actually taken, and other circumstantial evidence). Such a coherency requirement invites us to examine, in the coming discussion, what the desired nexus should be between a potential target and the military operation that legalizes it as a military objective.

Critical Moment: Role and Record of the 1907 Hague Peace Conference, 54 NETHERLANDS L. REV. 197, 207 (2007).

155. *See generally* Charles G. Fenwick, *War Without Declaration*, 31 AM. J. INT'L L. 694 (1937).

156. U.N. Charter, art. 2(4).

157. U.N. Charter, art, 51.

158. U.N. Charter, ch. VII.

3.5 The Required Nexus—Connecting Targeting to Strategy

3.5.1 The Prevailing Nexus: "Effective Contribution to Military Action"

In order to turn a potential target into a military objective, API Article 52(2) requires a clear nexus between the objects—characterized "by their nature, location, purpose or use"—and the military action. A preliminary question concerns the relation between the two causality criteria required of the objects by the API: the effective contribution to the military action and the definite military advantage to be gained upon their destruction. On this point, "[m]any commentators simply assume that the two criteria logically presuppose each other,"[159] and I shall adopt this practical assumption.[160] The main question concerns the "closeness" of the connection between the ongoing military operations and the potential target. The simple case is whenever an actual connection exists relating to objects that take part in the fighting (such as tanks or guns) or those that contribute to it (by supplying, for example, intelligence or logistics to the fighting forces). It is commonly accepted, however, that even if the current connection between the target and the military action is not direct, it may be considered close enough due to its future potential use ("purpose").[161] The HPCR Manual demonstrates this nexus threshold by the following examples of targets that are lawful, even though they do not directly take part in the actual fighting: "storage depots or barracks far from the battlefield because such assets constitute reserves for further military action by the enemy . . . factories producing munitions and military equipment . . . a port, railroad, road or airport used in the transport of supplies necessary for the production by the factory of military items."[162] An indirect connection, however, might be too remote to surpass this threshold if the object,

---

159. Dill, *The 21st-Century Belligerent's Trilemma, supra* note 97, at 85 (at note 7, and the references noted there).

160. Dill further argues that "it is the connection of an object to the conduct of combat operations—those of the enemy belligerent (effective contribution) and one's own (military advantage)—that puts an object into the category of military objectives." *Id.* at 85. This interpretation does not change the substance of our discussion—with regard to connecting a military's targeting to its strategy—but restricts it to the military advantage nexus requirement.

161. HPCR Manual, *supra* note 130, rule 24 commentary para. 1; Dinstein, The Conduct of Hostilities, *supra* note 83, at 95.

162. HPCR Manual, *supra* note 130, rule 24 commentary para. 1.

though relevant to the fighting, does not actually have the potential to be used either at present or in a future belligerency. Thus, an object of a civilian nature might yield resources that enable future fighting, but it itself is not part of the military action. The common approach is that it would be unlawful to target objects whose sole contribution to the fighting is the financial resources they produce, which may be used to finance the fighting. Their indirect contribution, though effective, does not seem to be closely connected to the military action.

By contrast, the American approach is to treat "war-sustaining" targets as lawful military objectives. It does not accept the common nexus, defined by the API as "effective contribution to military action," but rather widens it by replacing the words "military action" with the expression "war fighting or war-sustaining capability."[163] In the American view, the broadening of the nexus legalizes the targeting of objects whose proceeds would be used to fund the armed conflict.[164] This unique approach is rooted in the precedent set by the Union's destruction of the Confederate states' raw cotton during the American Civil War.[165] It represents the extreme view and is usually considered by many states to posit a nexus that is "too remote."[166] Indeed, economic warfare is no stranger to the prevailing law. If carried out through military blockade—the obstruction of approach to the enemy's land for the purpose of preventing ingress and egress of vessels or aircraft[167]—it is lawful, in spite of the harsh "collateral" consequences

---

163. "The term 'military objective' means combatants and those objects during hostilities which, by their nature, location, purpose, or use, effectively contribute to the war fighting or war-sustaining capability of an opposing force and whose total or partial destruction, capture, or neutralization would constitute a definite military advantage to the attacker under the circumstances at the time of an attack." Military Commission Act of 2009, 10 U.S.C. § 950p(a)(1) (2009). *See also* U.S. Dep't of Defense, Manual for Military Commissions, IV-1 (2010), http://www.loc.gov/rr/frd/Military_Law/pdf/manual-mil-commissions_2010.pdf (last visited Nov. 22, 2015).

164. *See generally* Watkin. *Targeting in Air Warfare, supra* note 2, at 37.

165. Dinstein, The Conduct of Hostilities, *supra* note 83, at 95. For a contemporary example of targeting the financial resources of an adversary, *see* the 2008 dispute over targeting the drug industry of the Taliban in Afghanistan. Michael N Schmitt, *Targeting Narcoinsurgents in Afghanistan: The Limits of International Humanitarian Law*, 12 Y.B. Int'l Humanitarian L. 301 (2009).

166. HPCR Manual, *supra* note 130, at the commentary to rule 24 para. 2. In support of the U.S. view, *see, e.g.*, Ryan Goodman, *Targeting "War-Sustaining" Objects in Non-international Armed Conflict*, 110 Am. J. Int'l L. 663 (2016).

167. *See, e.g.*, San Remo Manual, *supra* note 148, at 176–80.

there may be for civilians.[168] Nonetheless, the intentional targeting of civilian objects, due to the use of their yields for financing military activities, is perceived, under the common approach, as illegal. According to this conventional wisdom, the distinction rule, the basic pillar of the law of armed conflict,[169] should be diligently respected, not contingent upon secondary distinctions related to the use of the proceeds of civilian objects.[170]

The current discussion is focused on the nexus between the object and the military action, as required by API Article 52(2). There is agreement that the distance between the two—that is, the horizontal nexus between object and military action—should not be too remote; what that means is, however, disputed. If the generic war prototype—total war—were the only one available, such a distance measurement might be sufficient. In each total war, it would suffice to ascertain which objects are "by their nature, location, purpose or use" making "an effective contribution to military action." In limited wars, however, the potential horizontal "closeness" of the object to the military action should not be enough to turn it into a lawful military objective. The targeting of this object has to be relevant and effective—indeed, "close"—to the strategic goal, as well. The suggested "vertical nexus" will be dealt with in the coming discussion.

3.5.2 The Vertical Nexus

The suggested approach would require states to select and publicly define their strategic war aims—out of a wide spectrum of lawful strategic courses of action available to them—at every stage of the war, and to remain faithful to the professional corollaries of their preference, as long as the aims remain the same. The operational and tactical maneuvers and targeting practice would then have to be consistent and coherent with the strategy selected. (Although an explicit statement of the strategic goals in belligerency is preferable, the suggested approach is valid even when the

168. According to the *San Remo Manual*, the declaration or establishment of a blockade is prohibited if "it has the sole purpose of starving the civilian population." *Id.*, Rule 102(a), at 179. *See also* API, *supra* note 5, at art. 54(1) ("Starvation of civilians as a method of warfare is prohibited.").

169. *E.g.*, the heading of Article 48 of the API—establishing the distinction rule—is "Basic Rule."

170. Although, practically, "there appears to be little difference in terms of scope between attacks directed at the war sustaining capacity of a State and a blockade." Watkin. *Targeting in Air Warfare, supra* note 2, at 48.

aims of war have not been publicly declared but only implied.) Thus, in extreme cases, a decisive victory may be a self-defendant's strategic choice, and if that is justified—as was the case with Nazi Germany[171]—the entire spectrum of lawful targets ("military objectives") should be available to it. However, in many, probably most, cases a limited strategic goal—for example, stopping an armed attack or deterring further acts of aggression (indeed, as a matter of lawful self-defense)—would require adjustment of the potential lawful targets bank. Here, though, a substantial constraint on targeting is strategic: not every potential lawful target would be relevant and effective in a given war with limited aims. For example, the destruction of dual-purpose objects or the killing of a large number of the adversary's combatants, though possibly lawful, might be strategically useless and even counter-effective. At this point, law and strategy should meet: the law of armed conflict should contain and internalize constraining strategic considerations. The implicit paradox—why this manifest self-interest of a military should be codified and externally imposed upon it—will be dealt with next.

The legal ground for the vertical nexus is the necessity principle. Indeed, under the suggested approach, the necessity principle should be revised. This principle—one of the fundamental principles of the law of armed conflict—is theoretically perceived as imposing a restraint at the tactical level upon the exercise of military power beyond what is necessary to attain a military goal.[172] The suggested approach calls for upgrading the same *in bello* necessity constraint to the strategic level; to combine the tactical constraint with the suggested strategic one, through a revised reading of the *ad bellum* necessity. Although the *ad bellum* necessity is currently usually perceived as a precondition for the lawful exercise of military force in self-defense, as a matter of last resort,[173] under the suggested reading, it should also be crucial in defining the contours of the belligerency. The targeting of military objectives should be contingent upon, and consistent with, the strategic aims of a war. The *in bello* law of targeting cannot remain indifferent to the latter, even though strategy is decided first at the *ad bellum* level—before engaging in war, whenever the decisive

171. *See infra* text accompanying Chapter 4 notes 100–104.

172. *See supra* note 104.

173. *See, e.g.*, Dinstein, War, Aggression and Self-Defence, *supra* note 107, at 231–32, 262; Gardam, Necessity, Proportionality and the Use of Force by States, *supra* note 94, at 6, 148–53.

echelon (in democracies, the civilian one) decides that it has no choice but to fight—and then adjusted *in bello,* during the entire belligerency. From this perspective, the suggested vertical nexus[174] connects the *ad bellum* and *in bello* discourses; to some extent it breaks down the wall currently standing between the two.[175] Indeed, the distortions caused by the choice made by the prevailing law—not to deal with the strategic issue of a war's aims and to limit itself to the residual role of limiting the *in bello* hazards of war—should be revisited.

The expectation that a quantitatively based *ad bellum* proportionality requirement might restrict the *in bello* operational scope of a military was presented above, and rejected. I argued that quantitative proportionality has neither been fulfilled in states' practice nor, on realpolitik grounds, could it be. Proportionality in relation to the amount of force or means exercised by an aggressor will not be accepted by self-defendant states on strategic grounds. The desire to ensure their victory will channel them to adopt the Powell doctrine of exercising "overwhelming force" whenever militarily possible[176] and permissible *in bello.* Furthermore, even the means-end reading of the *ad bellum* proportionality, evaluating the use of military force against its legitimate ends, cannot accomplish the task of restricting the operational scope of a military, due to the inherent uncertainty relating to both its "ends" and "means" segments.[177] Indeed, even if one accepts the argument that the means and methods of warfare should be *ad bellum* proportionate,[178] how does one measure the *ad bellum* "excessiveness" or reasonableness of targeting?

By contrast, the suggested vertical nexus requirement, connecting strategy to tactics through the suggested reading of the *ad bellum* necessity, is consistent with and to a large extent reflects reality. The fact is that wars are fought strategically. A law-abiding self-defendant selects its strategic war aims from the spectrum of potential lawful strategic courses of action available to it, at every stage of the war, and consequentially

---

174. *See supra* text following note 16.

175. *See supra* note 101.

176. *See supra* notes 109–110 and accompanying text.

177. *See supra* text accompanying notes 111–112.

178. *See, e.g.,* Gardam, Necessity, Proportionality and the Use of Force by States, *supra* note 94, at 169 (demonstrating her argument: "an electricity grid may meet the definition of a legitimate military target in IHL but its destruction in the particular circumstances pertaining at the time may be excessive in terms of achieving the aims of self-defence").

adapts—as a natural military professional exigency—its targeting rules to the changing strategic reality. Taking the current legal acceptance of a state's selected strategy and the war aims deriving from it as a given, as long as it is within the lawful self-defence paradigm, invites the introduction of sequential necessity—imposing a restraint upon the exercise of military power beyond what is necessary to attain a military goal, at all levels of a military's activities and during all stages of a belligerent conflict. The suggested vertical nexus would constrain the scope of lawful targets; it reflects an internal professional military process, linking all levels of military activity in a coherent way toward a strategic directive. In contrast to the unrealistic requirement of quantitatively based *ad bellum* proportionality, and the uncertainty relating to the means-ends reading of the *ad bellum* proportionality, the suggested sequential necessity derives from fine-tuned strategic thinking. As it is qualitative and professionally based, it would probably be accepted by militaries if introduced legally.

How can these strategic constraining elements actually be exercised? The answer lies in military professionalism that prescribes the way wars are conducted. Military planning is not a black box: it is a professional system, aimed at selecting the optimal courses of action in a due process, with its own manifest rules and procedures, most of which are in the public domain. For example, the wartime decision-making model used in the U.S. military[179] consists of six steps, including Intelligence Preparation and Mission Analysis.[180] Preparing the targets bank in advance and updating it throughout the belligerency is an integral part of this professional process. Intelligence, from all available sources, is the main vehicle for validating military objectives and evaluating their relevance and effectiveness in the given battle (their "target value").[181] Although "war is the realm of uncertainty," as suggested by Clausewitz,[182] and the "fog of war"[183] is a crucial factor in understanding military reality, intelligence gathering is the main tool to clear this fog, to the extent possible. A shortage

179. *See* U.S. Naval War College, NWC 4111H, Workbook on Joint Operations Planning Process (Jan. 21, 2008), www.usnwc.edu/getattachment/Departments---Colleges/Joint-Military-Operations/NWC-4111H-21-Jan-08-Final.pdf.aspx (last visited Feb. 23, 2015).

180. *Id.* at 1-1.

181. *See* Watkin, *Military Advantage*, *supra* note 29, at 289–96 (dealing with high-value targets).

182. *See supra* Chapter 1 note 51.

183. *See supra* Introduction note 87.

of intelligence and problems in its interpretation are regular phenomena in the battlefield; nonetheless, it is a professional challenge to a military to study the culture and interests of its adversaries, their preferred patterns of war, and the way their militaries fight (their military doctrines). Militaries are required to maintain a quasi-industrial apparatus, aimed at producing an intelligence map of their adversary in general and validating their targets bank in particular.[184] This apparatus should be adjusted to the distinctions between total and limited wars and required to remove from the generic lawful targets bank irrelevant and ineffective targets vis-à-vis a given limited mission. This process of limiting targets should be carried out bona fide and in a professional and reasonable manner,[185] based upon the available data and an understanding of the adversary's strengths[186] and weaknesses.[187] Indeed, it is this apparatus's task to conduct an ongoing process, through trial and error, yet always professionally based. The reduction of targets should always be guided by the strategic considerations, as adjusted throughout a given war, and it should gain support from the current development of new technology, allowing both accurate intelligence and precise targeting.

3.5.3 Losing Strategic Ambiguity: Costs and Benefits

This chapter has suggested introducing a mandatory statement of a belligerent state's concrete war aims—aimed at linking all levels of military

---

184. *See generally* Watkin, *Military Advantage, supra* note 29.

185. The criterion of reasonableness (and the reasonable sphere) is no stranger to the law of armed conflict. *See supra* note 145.

186. Though the Clausewitzian concept of "center of gravity" is disputed—because the military struggle is between dynamic maneuvering forces, whereas the physical concept relates to a static object—it may nonetheless demonstrate militaries' desire to attack their enemies' sources of strength. *See* Von Clausewitz, *supra* note 4, at 258, 260, 391, and *see* the American definition of this concept as "The source of power that provides moral or physical strength, freedom of action, or will to act," Joint Pub. 1-02, *supra* note 2, at 29.

187. *E.g.*, if the adversary is ruled by a dictator, striking "regular" military objectives might not deter it from its aggression, whereas economic sanctions aimed specifically against the ruler's echelon, or striking specific military objectives that are important to it, in some cases might. Another example, though more controversial and legally much disputed, relates to targeting an adversary's morale. Military advantage might be physical, affecting actual military capabilities—for example, by killing or injuring combatants or destroying or damaging military objectives—or mental, affecting an adversary's willingness to fight. Eroding the willingness of an enemy to continue fighting constitutes a military advantage. Objects whose targeting would definitely produce such an effect might constitute lawful military objectives. *See* William H. Boothby, The Law of Targeting 506 (2012).

activity in a coherent way toward a strategic directive—due to the humanitarian advantages to be gained from this clarity. In the following discussion, I shall present an interim balance of costs and benefits related to the suggested approach. In solving the paradox—why this professional self-interest of a military should be legally imposed upon it—the benefits of strategic ambiguity will be introduced. Later, the countervailing advantages—favoring strategic clarity—will be presented. Though transparency in belligerency might be perceived as less popular, its moderating effect and long-term benefits should not be ignored.

If coherency in targeting is professionally desired by militaries, as suggested, why transform it into a legal rule? As trained militaries tend to respect their own professional norms, ostensibly there should be no need to turn autonomously working and effective internal norms into mandatory ones. The answer to this perplexity lies in the tension between the grand strategy considerations of a state, dealing with its "policy," and its military strategy relating to on-the-ground military activities.[188] Indeed, the discussion thus far has focused upon the humanitarian advantage of the suggested requirement and its effect in reducing war's hazards, while pointing to its consistency with the military's interests. However, it has its disadvantages as well, mainly at the grand strategy level. Requiring self-defendant states to publicly define their war aims, at every stage of the war, comes at a cost. It damages the flexibility that strategic ambiguity affords.

Most grand-strategic relations are complex. Every message sent by a state is aimed at more than just its direct adversary. There are larger, multiple audiences, both domestically within the state's own national political system (constituents), and abroad (i.e., allies, friends, and foes, and the international community as a whole); none of these groups is homogenous. For example, there are scenarios involving deterrence strategy in which ambiguity is intentional. In some cases where secrecy is of the utmost importance, the party exercising deterrence does not want to disclose its strategy in full to the adversary being deterred (thus allowing it to intentionally circumvent it). In other cases, intentional ambiguity, expressed through vague demands, is aimed at inducing the recipient to comply without causing it undue embarrassment. Realpolitik considerations may dictate ambiguity as well, reflecting the deliverer's preferences regarding to whom among its multiple audiences it wants to be precise

---

188. *See supra* text accompanying notes 18–20.

and clear. In many scenarios this is precisely the case, especially in open and democratic societies. Indeed, deterrence threats may primarily be issued to reassure allies rather than to affect actual opponents.[189]

From this perspective, one could classify the transparency suggestion as naïve, as was American general Stanley McChrystal's request for clarity as to what the American policy in Afghanistan was in 2010. Although we enjoy the academic freedom to request transparency and coherency from fighting states, the highly decorated general was forced to submit his resignation after his criticism became public in a newspaper article.[190] Though he was formally relieved of his command due to what was perceived as a challenge to the constitutional norm of civilian control over the military, the essence of his criticism concerned the president's probable desire to enjoy the benefits of ambiguity and maintain flexibility—by hiding essential policy information related to the war's aims from his own leading commander and from the American Congress and people.[191]

Though there are cases in which grand-strategy clarity is preferred by leaders[192]—for example, when conveying a deterrent message to either a potential or actual adversary—this chapter has suggested introducing a mandatory statement of a belligerent state's concrete war aims even where such clarity is not the preferred course. The cost (if any) incurred by giving up grand-strategy ambiguity is residual to the humanitarian advantages gained.

Indeed, although the suggested clarity is motivated by humanitarian considerations, it has ex-post strategic advantages even when it is imposed upon states. It may reduce the anomaly associated with limited wars. It

---

189. Patrick M. Morgan, Deterrence Now 214 (2003) (citing Freedman: "Yet describing what is to be deterred and how it is to be deterred in terms that are fully understood by friends, allies and constituents makes perfect strategic sense, especially if their support may be vital in a coming trial of strength—even if the net effect on the actual opponent may be to confuse rather than to clarify, to provoke rather than to dissuade. Multiple audiences are being addressed all the time." *Id.*). For an elaborated discussion of deterrence in general, *see infra* Chapter 4.

190. *See* Scott Wilson & Michael D. Shear, *Gen. McChrystal Is Dismissed as Top U.S. Commander in Afghanistan*, Wash. Post, June 24, 2010, http://www.washingtonpost.com/wp-dyn/content/article/2010/06/23/AR2010062300689.html.

191. As to the constitutional effects of this ambiguity, *see infra* text accompanying note 198.

192. An analysis of the advantages incurring to a leader who "commits" herself to a specific course of action is beyond the scope of this chapter. For the sake of the current discussion, however, a commitment might reflect the leader's desire to influence third-party choices, or to be bound in the future by its current preferences. *See generally* Thomas C. Schelling, Strategies of Commitments (2006) (especially, Chapters 1 and 6).

might help to bridge the gap between the stark rhetoric—which is common in the case of a self-defendant state, reflecting domestic public opinion's desire to see a decisive victory in the old style, for example in the "war against terror"—and the strategic reality, which usually does not grant knockout opportunities or decisive victories in such wars. By publicly stating its war aims, at every stage of a war, a law-abiding self-defendant would convey, in advance, a moderate message regarding the diminishing utility of its military force. The politician's intuitive temptation to join the crowd in its preference for unnecessary brutality, in the futile search for knockout opportunities, would be overridden by the strategist's recognition of what is militarily actually achievable.[193] Indeed, a transparent commitment by states' leaders to be judged by (relatively) moderate war aims would force them to be more precise when declaring them to their constituents. Furthermore, this threat of public scrutiny minimizes the risk of leaders who might manipulate their war aims just for the sake of expanding their actual targets bank. The apparent benefit (if any) of inflated targets, due to the widening of a war's aims, would be offset by the inflated expectations and the ex-post frustration of their constituents.

In addition, requiring a country's leaders to state their war aims and demonstrate the connection between these aims and their militaries' actual targeting would help the self-defendant state face the legitimacy demand of both domestic and international public opinion. Indeed, many current wars are characterized by relatively easy access by the media to conflict zones, with all of the parties involved fighting for the public's "hearts and minds,"[194] both domestically and internationally. Transparency of the war's declared aims and consistency between those aims and the actual fighting might help to reassure public opinion.

Furthermore, the requirement of strategic clarity is consistent with the prevailing trend toward transparency and accountability in the international arena. The requirement of transparency may be motivated by both domestic and international pressures. For example, there may be a demand to compensate for the rise in the influence of intergovernmental

---

193. Such clarity might prevent a potential slippery slope during wars when political leaders come under huge pressure, from their voters and other domestic political parties, to fulfill their obligation to defend their citizens by granting them full protection. For the discussion of the temptation to please constituencies and the frustration due to the limited number of lawful targets, *see* the discussion *supra* text accompanying Chapter 1 notes 76–77.

194. The phrase "hearts and minds" is generally associated with the importance of using "minimum force." *See, e.g.*, Dixon, *"Hearts and Minds"?*, *supra* note 80.

institutions on national public policy, or increasing involvement by national governments in setting international law and criticism of governmental policy decisions, by both the public and NGOs, may require a response in the form of such transparency.[195] The demand for transparency is coupled with a demand for accountability, backed by international intervention in the decision-making processes of national governments.[196] In the law of armed conflict, this phenomenon is being manifested by the "criminalization" of breaches of its core values.[197] In light of these trends, it is perfectly fitting to require a belligerent state (even one that appears to be a self-defendant) to publicly declare its war aims.

The suggested approach may have domestic constitutional advantages as well. For example, the American lesson demonstrates that the "war on terror," declared in reaction to the 9/11 attacks, can be perceived as having a perpetual life of its own. In the U.S. conflict in Iraq, "Congress self-consciously restricted the war's aims to narrow purposes—expressly authorizing a limited war. But the Bush Administration evaded these constitutional limits and transformed a well-defined and limited war into an open-ended conflict operating beyond constitutional boundaries."[198] Indeed, although clarity and transparency in one's own fluctuating war aims do not really promise anything regarding one's adversary (because it takes two to tango or make war), they may have, at least, their own domestic advantages.

Finally, a side effect of the suggested approach is a lifting of part of the veil from the popular, yet problematic, argument that the law ties Western liberal democracies' hands when fighting limited wars, especially

---

195. Megan Donaldson & Benedict Kingsbury, *The Adoption of Transparency Policies in Global Governance Institutions: Justifications, Effects, and Implications*, 9 ANN. REV. L. & SOC. SCI. 119, 127–29 (2013).

196. Eyal Benvenisti, *The Potential and Limits of Global Regulation of Sovereign Discretion* (GlobalTrust Working Paper Series 6/2014). Intervention is carried out for various reasons, such as making sure that governments comply with what they agreed to, promoting global welfare through cooperation, compensating for democratic failures, and more. *Id.* at 6, 8, 11.

197. *See generally* WILLIAM A. SCHABAS, AN INTRODUCTION TO THE INTERNATIONAL CRIMINAL COURT (2007).

198. Bruce Ackerman & Oona Hathaway, *Limited War and the Constitution: Iraq and the Crisis of Presidential Legality*, 109 MICH. L. REV. 447, 447 (2011). *See also* President Obama's statement in his 2013 speech at the National Defense University: "[o]ur systematic effort to dismantle terrorist organizations must continue. But this war, like all wars, must end . . . " President Barrack Obama, Remarks at National Defense University, 2013 D.C.P.D. No. 201300361, https://www.gpo.gov/fdsys/pkg/DCPD-201300361/pdf/DCPD-201300361.pdf.

asymmetric ones.[199] An implicit message of this tied-hand argument is that it is the law that bears the blame for the mixed results of such wars and that in a "free world," not subject to legal constraints, militaries would have the knowledge, skills, and capabilities to deliver a decisive victory. In reality, however, the problem of these wars is not legal, but rather mainly strategic. The strategic ambiguity is rooted, in many cases, in strategic blindness and operational difficulties in fighting this type of war. Rather than admit the inherent difficulties of fighting limited wars, leaders may find a convenient scapegoat in the law that allegedly ties their hands. Requiring consistency between the strategic aims of a state, its actual military operations and its lawful targets list would oblige leaders to define these aims and not take shelter in the fog of strategic ambiguity. The more transparent the reality, the more the actual strategic difficulties will surface in (both domestic and international) public consciousness, and the less the legal constraints will be perceived as an impediment to a self-defendant's victory. A transparent process of public internalization of this type of war's special strategic attributes would create awareness of a reality in which neither the law nor lawyers should be blamed for its enduring unresolvedness.

3.6 Concluding Remarks

The prevailing law rejects the strategic discourse when it comes to defining the contours of the law of armed conflict. However, when it comes to determining military advantages and the potential lawful targets, reality prevails and states' practice demonstrates that their targets bank in a given war reflects, inter alia (and in many cases, mainly), their strategic war aims. Contrary to the common legal perception, this chapter has called for the adoption of the strategic discourse and leveraging its constraining force, in order to minimize both civilians' and combatants' suffering.

The suggested approach offers a new stage in the evolution of the law of armed conflict. The current phase is characterized by the distinction rule, which utterly rejects the civilian dimension of total war. War is no longer perceived—as it used to be, under Napoleon's legacy—as people

199. *See, e.g.*, the Supreme Court of Israel's ruling with regard to the ban on the use of torture in security interrogations, stating that a democracy must sometimes fight its non-law-abiding adversary "with one hand tied behind its back." HCJ 5100/94, *The Public Committee Against Torture v. The Government of Israel and Others* (1999), 53(4) PD 817, [39] (Isr.).

fighting against people. The law explicitly chose to limit the scope of war and channel its hazards to the combatants, while prohibiting intentional damage to noncombatants. Despite that rejection, however, the same prevailing law chose total war between militaries, by way of default, as its prototype of an inter-state war. This chapter calls for taking the legal evolution a step further and recognizing the legal implications of the strategic phenomenon of limited wars. The classification of a war as a limited one should have its own legal consequences, as demonstrated in this chapter, through the law of targeting. It should affect all of war's dimensions with respect to both combatants and noncombatants.

Is the above discussion purely normative, or does it have some positive roots in the prevailing law? The suggested answer tends toward the latter. The demand for a vertical nexus—connecting strategy to tactics and requiring operational and tactical maneuvers and targeting practice to be consistent with the former—can be perceived as purely normative, or, as implied, as a call for connecting the *ad bellum* and the *in bello* discourses. Indeed, the suggested reading of vertical necessity may echo the call in the literature for a broad interpretation of *ad bellum* proportionality, evaluating the use of military force against its legitimate ends.[200] I have deemed such a reading, though consistent with the main argument of this chapter—connecting strategy to tactics—to be less preferable than the suggested vertical necessity.[201]

Finally, the main theme of this chapter has surfaced an issue that requires further elaboration. The suggested call—for coherency between strategy and a military's operations and targeting—follows the current legal acceptance of a state's selected strategy and the war aims deriving from it as a given. The paradox is that the implicit acceptance of the Napoleonic-Clausewitzian model, as the archetype of war, is inconsistent with the underlying humanizing rationale of the contemporary law of war. In the face of this paradox, I will suffice with offering only preliminary clues regarding two initial alternatives that might be considered in the future, in light of our discussion. The first and more ambitious, though less realistic, would be to challenge the implicit adoption of the Clausewitzian "killing madness" as a lawful archetype of war. Another, albeit less ambitious, legal alternative would be to accept the current reality and take the reluctance

---

200. *See supra* text accompanying notes 111–112.

201. *See supra* text accompanying notes 177–178.

of the law to interfere with the macro issues of selecting military doctrine and strategy as a maxim. Even so, the micro affairs of actual fighting are not immune to legal intervention. The protection granted, under this maxim, to the military strategy selected should not cover the operational and tactical aspects of war. Under this approach, a new imperative would be added to the contemporary law of armed conflict, requiring a military to select the course of action that is least harmful to its adversary's combatants and civilians while in pursuit of its given military aims within its selected strategy.[202]

This chapter has focused upon the *ad bellum* necessity, calling for the introduction of a restraint upon the exercise of military power beyond what is necessary to attain a military goal, during all stages of a conflict and at all its levels. It takes the current legal acceptance of a state's selected strategy and the war aims deriving from it as a given, as long as they are within the lawful self-defense paradigm. The next chapter takes a step further to open this apparent black box by evaluating the circumstances that might legalize four generic war aims. It will suggest the tool of deterrence—indeed, a much disputed strategic concept and legally a relatively rejected one—when relevant and applicable, as a criterion for evaluating the need to escalate the strategic war aim of a self-defendant. From this perspective, the following chapter will revisit the contested concept of *ad bellum* proportionality.

202. Currently, with regard to military objectives, while obtaining a given "military advantage", the least harmful alternative should be adopted, but only with respect to civilians. *See* API, *supra* note 5, at art. 57(3).

4

Defensive Deterrence

LEGALIZING THE STEPCHILD OF INTERNATIONAL LAW

DETERRENCE CONSTITUTES AN essential tool in keeping peace and order. From a strategic-military perspective, it cannot be renounced. It plays a substantial role in the management of global security and is "woven into many elements of foreign and national security policy."[1] In contemporary international law, however, deterrence, if not actually rejected, is nonetheless a concept that attracts suspicion. This chapter offers normative suggestions for introducing defense-oriented deterrence within the current contours of the international law relating to the use of military force.

Deterrence consists of a deliberate attempt to manipulate the behavior of others through credible threats.[2] It is a natural phenomenon in everyday human interaction, in both the domestic and international arenas. It may be viewed as "negative," as in the case of a frightened neighborhood deterred by a local gangster; or "positive," as might be the case regarding the influence of domestic law enforcement authorities. In the international arena, which is characterized by the absence of strong law enforcement authorities, deterrence has to a large extent been privatized and left, in fact, at the state (or collective of states) level. It discourages "the enemy from taking military action by posing for him a prospect of cost and risk outweighing his prospective gain. [. . .] the deterrent value of military forces is their effect in reducing the likelihood of enemy military moves."[3]

1. PATRICK M. MORGAN, DETERRENCE NOW xix (2003).

2. *See, e.g.*, LAWRENCE FREEDMAN, DETERRENCE 6 (2004).

3. GLENN HERALD SNYDER, DETERRENCE AND DEFENSE: TOWARD A THEORY OF NATIONAL SECURITY 3 (2015).

Military Professionalism and Humanitarian Law. Yishai Beer.

Naturally, a credible threat by a self-defender has deterrent value only if the potential attacker believes it has the will and capabilities to exercise it, if aggressively attacked.

Legally, the unilateral use of force in the international arena, in order to affect an adversary's will, is usually considered illegal. Under the UN Charter, the exercise of military force (or threat of use of force) is prohibited, subject to two main exceptions: in cases of individual or collective self-defense against an armed attack, or pursuant to a Security Council authorization.[4] Prevention by a self-defendant of an ongoing "armed attack" is legal, if it is necessary and proportional,[5] whereas the punishment of the aggressor by it is not. Under this paradigm, deterring aggressors is the task of the Security Council.[6] Generally speaking, direct deterrence-oriented tools are not currently considered lawful, but rather fall into the category of prohibited punishment. Not only does deterrence currently not have a high standing in the legal discourse, but the deterrence theory, per se, does not enjoy a very good reputation in international relations either. It suffers from inherent problems in both its (lack of) coherency and its application.

This chapter suggests developing a lawful defensive deterrence standard, as an integral part of a defensive doctrine aimed at preventing a potential aggressor from initiating an armed attack, by the self-defendant threatening to harm (and, if necessary, harming) him through lawful (necessary and proportional) self-defense measures. Of course, in essence the threat should be consistent with the aim of the *ad bellum* rules—to maintain international peace and security—and coherent with the *in bello* rules. Indeed, the aim of the suggested defensive deterrence would be consist ent with that of the Charter: to preserve the international status quo by prohibiting aggression aimed against it.[7] This goal can be sustained in a legal system that promotes the containment of potential conflicts and

---

4. *See supra* Introduction notes 59–60.

5. *See supra* Chapter 2 note 6.

6. Even lawful self-defense must be suspended or regulated once the Security Council takes the measures necessary to maintain international peace and security. U.N. Charter, art. 51.

7. Aggression has been defined by the UN General Assembly: "[a]ggression is the use of armed force by a State against the sovereignty, territorial integrity or political independence of another State, or in any other manner inconsistent with the Charter of the United Nations, as set out in this Definition." G.A. Res. 3314 (XXIX), at the annex, art. 1 (Dec. 14, 1974). Indeed, article 7 of this Resolution allows an exception in cases of use of force to promote self-determination. The Rome Statute's review conference in Kampala also adopted a similar definition of aggression for the purposes of criminal prosecution of individuals at

deters aggressors. If containment fails and a war starts, a focused deterrence against *in bello* transgressor militaries seems to be consistent also with the overall aim of the law of armed conflict: to allow for lawful self-defense with the targeting of only "military objectives,"[8] thus sparing innocent lives and preventing, or at least minimizing, unnecessary suffering.

The suggested standard is not subject to preliminary recognition by any third party of the "righteousness" of the parties (i.e., determining who the aggressor is and who the victim), in the same way that its mother right—the right of self-defense—is not contingent upon any such. Its introduction should be universal: applicable to all states, law-abiding and transgressors alike. It would provide, however, an essential tool, which is currently missing, to law-abiding states. Indeed, defensive deterrence, like self-defense, could be abused and manipulated by an ostensible defendant, using it as pretext for the illegal use of force—especially due to its subjective variables and in the absence of effective central international law-enforcement. The suggested answers to these challenges will be based, consistent with this book's paradigm, on adherence to military professionalism and transparency requirements. They would minimize bona fide reckless mistakes and reduce any opportunistic misuse of deterrence as a pretext for aggression.

This chapter proceeds as follows. Part 4.1 presents the importance of deterrence and the inherent difficulties in its application. Part 4.2 presents the positive law and demonstrates the current rejection of deterrence considerations by the law as it stands. (The first two introductory parts deal with deterrence in general and relate to both *ad bellum* and *in bello* examples.) Part 4.3 explains the normative need for introducing deterrence considerations into lawful self-defense, pointing to deterrence as an efficient tool to enforce compliance with the law. Part 4.4 deals with the practical application of the suggested norm: how to tailor a lawful defensive deterrence suit. As deterrence is not a magic formula, effective in all military campaigns, Part 4.5 deals with four generic war aims, explicating the role of deterrence, when applicable, and its relations with each of them. In fact, it suggests using deterrence as a tool to evaluate the need for a self-defendant to escalate its strategic war aim. From this perspective,

---

the ICC. *See* ICC Kampala Review Conference, *Resolution RC/Res. 6 on Crime of Aggression*, annex I, para. 2, concerning art. 8 bis (June 11, 2010).

8. Protocol Additional to the Geneva Conventions of 12 August 1949, and relating to the Protection of Victims of International Armed Conflicts (Protocol I), art. 52(2), June 8, 1977, 1125 U.N.T.S. 3 (API).

it suggests a novel tool for evaluating the *ad bellum* proportionality in the strategic sphere. Part 4.6 presents the balance of contradictory arguments, in favor of and against introducing deterrence into the legal discourse; it concludes that, in many cases, defensive deterrence should be legally preferred over the reactive self-defense that is currently lawful.

4.1 Deterrence: An Essential—yet Problematic—Strategy

The modern use of strategic deterrence is due to the development of nuclear weapons. Indeed, deterrence strategy reached its climax during the Cold War.[9] A divided world, heavily influenced by the two superpowers, was faced with a prolonged conflict that could be resolved by neither diplomacy nor war. Diplomacy could not resolve the ideological conflicts between East and West ("Socialism v. Capitalism"), whereas war was considered taboo due to its high cost to mankind. Adversaries, primarily the superpowers who possessed nuclear weapons, internalized the fact that it is better for them to contain their disputes and manage their conflict, inter alia, through the use of mutual deterrence, than to use the destructive power of their armies. The superpowers' militaries, long taught to win full-scale wars, started looking for ways to avoid them, at least in a direct full-scale manner.

Deterrence affects the relationships and understanding (or misunderstanding) between actual or potential belligerents and has a spillover effect; there are consequences for third parties as well. At the mutual level, its effects should be looked upon from two perspectives: that of the deliverer of the deterring threat and that of its direct target. The first relates to the way the deliverer understands the recipient's construct and perception of reality and then finds an effective way to manipulate it by using threats; the other relates to the actual understanding and response of the target state. This is true for both the threat of the use of force per se, where the threat serves as a bargaining chip, as well as its actual realization. This bargaining, like any ordinary commercial bargaining process, has both explicit and implicit parts. Thus, if an aggressor attacks a defendant, the defendant's response reflects its acceptance of the message, while delivering a counter-message to the aggressor. Indeed, "it is even more necessary

---

9. *See generally* THOMAS C. SCHELLING, ARMS AND INFLUENCE (1966).

to think of warfare as a process of violent bargaining," keeping in mind that actions "speak louder than words on many occasions."[10] Such a process is consistent with Clausewitz's famous observation: "[W]ar is simply a continuation of political intercourse, with the addition of other means. [. . .] Is war not just another expression of their thoughts, another form of speech or writing? Its grammar, indeed, may be its own, but not its logic."[11]

Deterrence is, initially, aimed at preventing wars. Indeed, a nuclear war between the two superpowers during the Cold War was avoided. Many thinkers credit this achievement, at least partially, to mutual deterrence.[12] But once a war has started, it does not mean that deterrence "is dead," or that it has no validity between the adversaries and third parties involved (if any). It is a sequential process, relative rather than absolute. *In bello* deterrence is an integral part of the ongoing violent "bargaining"; despite being relative, it plays a substantial role in restricting the scope and magnitude of the violence. In this relative form of deterrence, the use of force does not reflect its failure (as is the case with absolute deterrence), but is an essential tool for sustaining it. No chemical weapon was used in World War II, even though the fighting parties had used such weapons extensively during World War I.[13] Merely the illegality of chemical weapons,[14] however, does not seem to offer a persuasive explanation why they were not used. Bearing in mind the general lack of abidance by legal rules and moral standards of all parties who participated in the war, it seems reasonable to assume that reciprocity considerations prevailed in this case.[15] Another example is the Korean War, which demonstrated that even during a bloody war in which the superpowers are totally involved, military destructive power can be restricted to conventional means and precise and concrete channels: "The Korean War was furiously 'all-out' in the fighting, not only on the peninsular battlefield but in the resources used by both sides. It was 'all-out' though, only within some dramatic restraints: no

10. *Id.* at 33 and 88 respectively.

11. Carl Von Clausewitz, On War 605 (Michael Eliot Howard & Peter Paret trans., indexed ed. 1984).

12. *See* Freedman, Deterrence, *supra* note 2, at 10–13.

13. *See, e.g.*, Augustin M. Prentiss, Chemicals in War: A Treatise on Chemical Warfare 647–84 (1937).

14. Indeed, the European parties in World War II were bound by the Protocol that prohibits the use of chemical weapons. *See supra* Chapter 3 note 83.

15. Schelling, Arms and Influence, *supra* note 9, at 131.

nuclear weapons, no Russians, no Chinese territory, no Japanese territory, no bombing of ships at sea or even airfields on the United Nations side of the line."[16]

In spite of its practical importance as a tool of defensive strategy, deterrence cannot be relied upon as its exclusive, or even main, component. Communication through threats—which is the essence of deterrence—is a problematic way of delivering messages in general and reflects a poor standard of inter-human relations in particular. One of the first documented deterrent threats is God's warning to Adam and Eve not to eat the fruit of the Tree of Knowledge.[17] The dramatic failure of this documented case of deterrence—aggravated by "the identity" of the divine messenger—may serve as an example of its limits. In practice, most earthly strategic relations are complex. Every message sent by a state is aimed at more than just its direct adversary. There are larger, multiple audiences, both domestically within the state's own national political system (constituents), and abroad (i.e., allies, friends and foes, and the international community as a whole); none of these groups is homogenous. Any language used in this context has both explicit and implicit content, and the understanding of both is subjective and, to a large extent, dependent on culture and context. The double-language used can be demonstrated by the resumption of nuclear testing by India in 1998; India explicitly claimed that this was prompted by concern over China. Lawrence Freedman doubts this notion and points at Pakistan as being the more reasonable addressee of the implied threat.[18]

If messages and words are neither always taken solely at face value nor understood in exactly the same way, it is understandable why attempts to communicate a threat clearly using the language of deterrence have so often failed. Those who are supposed to be deterred do not always receive an effective message of the kind intended by the deliverer. The Korean War—presented earlier as a "positive" example of relative mutual deterrence regarding, for example, the use of weapons of mass destruction[19]—demonstrates some of its failures as well. There were misunderstandings, or perhaps miscalculation, when the American military misread the

---

16. *Id.* at 31.

17. This biblical example is taken from FREEDMAN, DETERRENCE, *supra* note 2, at 7.

18. *Id.* at 48.

19. *See supra* note 16.

Chinese warnings during its advance toward the Yalu River. Similarly, "the Soviets (or Chinese, or whoever made the decision) miscalculated."[20]

Furthermore, there are scenarios involving deterrence strategy in which this ambiguity is premeditated and does not reflect a misunderstanding or miscalculation. Rather, it exactly reflects the aim of the party exercising deterrence. Intentional ambiguity might be preferred where the party exercising deterrence does not want to disclose its strategy in full to the adversary being deterred, or wants to induce the recipient to comply without causing it undue embarrassment. I have already mentioned that realpolitik considerations may dictate the ambiguity as well, especially in open and democratic societies, where the deliverer has a preference regarding to whom among its multiple audiences it wants to be precise and clear.[21]

But even in cases where the deterring message seems to be clear and precise, with well-established "red lines," it may be challenged and gradually eroded by the so-called "salami tactics" of its recipient. Any rule can be challenged, any norm confronted. Salami tactics demonstrate how dangerous it is to constantly rely upon a threatening message, as well as the inherent weakness of deterrence maintenance. As Thomas Schelling argues, these are the kind of tactics used by children: "[t]ell a child not to go in the water and he will sit on the bank and submerge his bare feet; he is not yet 'in' the water . . . [later] he will start wading. . . . Pretty soon we are calling to him not to swim out of sight, wondering whatever happened to all our discipline."[22] Schelling goes on to offer another example that, in fact, touches on the heart of our discussion: "No matter how inviolate our commitment to some border, we are unlikely to start a war the first time a few drunken soldiers from the other side wander across the line and 'invade' our territory . . . There is some threshold below which the commitment is just not operative, and even that threshold itself is usually unclear."[23] These examples show the inherent difficulty in any reliance upon deterrence. Any line, rule, or norm can easily be circumvented. Every small child checks and redefines her parents' or teacher's boundaries on a daily basis. In the vast majority of cases, when the red line is

20. Schelling, Arms and Influence, *supra* note 9, at 54.

21. *See supra* Chapter 3 note 189 and accompanying text.

22. Schelling, Arms and Influence, *supra* note 9, at 66–67.

23. *Id.* at 67.

vague from the very beginning, the recipient has a twofold motivation to use salami tactics: first, to manipulate the situation in order to define and discover the line that, from the defendant's original perspective, the recipient is not allowed to cross; and second, to push the envelope by making the defendant redefine its thresholds and boundaries, and through this erosion process to damage its credibility.

This short presentation has dealt with only a few illustrations of the inherent difficulties of deterrence theory and its application. I have not dealt with its problematic underlying assumption of rationality—that adversaries are guided only, or mainly, by cost-benefit analysis—or the problems related to each of its basic concepts, such as retaliatory threat, unacceptable damage, and credibility.[24] Furthermore, as presented above, the mere notion of manipulating, and even controlling, an adversary's will is not (fully) attainable. In reality, however, despite all of its flaws, deterrence is pivotal in strategic thinking, and, in some cases, an essential component of the defense strategy of law-abiding states. In the coming discussion, I shall show that the tension relating to the importance and scope of deterrence strategy seems to be missing from the legal discourse.

4.2 The Rejection of Reciprocal Deterrence Considerations by the Prevailing Law

International law has rejected monitoring the international peace and order through mutual deterrence. Legally, deterrence per se is generally perceived as an inherent part of punitive measures, which are not considered compatible with the right to self-defense. For example, dealing with the prohibition on armed reprisals, David Kretzmer concludes: "The majority of writers take it as settled law that use of force following an armed attack that has been completed, and the only object of which is deterrent rather than protective, will amount to an armed reprisal that is not a legitimate exercise of the right to self-defence recognized under Article 51 of the Charter."[25]

Indeed, deterrence considerations might serve as effective built-in guarantors in containing and restricting war's hazards, especially in the

24. *See generally* MORGAN, *supra* note 1.

25. David Kretzmer, *The Inherent Right to Self-Defence and Proportionality in* Jus ad Bellum, 24 EUR. J. INT'L L. 235, 257 (2013). *See also supra* Chapter 3 note 95.

absence of strong law enforcement authorities in the international arena. Thus, mutual deterrence could have been created by contingent *in bello* rules, allowing a price to be paid for their being breached. Such relative deterrence could affect the duration of a war, its scale and consequences, the weapons used and the targets, as well as its territorial dimensions. Indeed historically, mutual deterrence has functioned as a very substantial promoter of adherence to the *in bello* rules. An empirical survey of the record of compliance with the law of armed conflict, throughout the twentieth century, explains its mixed results to a large extent by reciprocity considerations; where mutuality exists, the trend is positive.[26] However, the current law demonstrates a backlash against the reciprocity paradigm. Obedience to the law is usually required unilaterally from each belligerent, in most cases not contingent upon the behavior of its adversary. The prevailing *in bello* rules have shifted from their historic contractual model (based mainly upon reciprocal considerations) to largely a regulatory model (starting with the 1949 Geneva Conventions, followed by the 1977 Additional Protocols to the Conventions).[27] Similarly, the prevailing *ad bellum* rules explicitly ignore deterrence considerations. Reciprocity, the natural built-in guarantor of obedience to the law, currently is largely missing from both segments of the law. I shall present this reality first in the *in bello* sphere (the law of armed conflict) and then move on to the *ad bellum* sphere.

The current main restrictions of the law of armed conflict, based on both treaties and customary international law, are relevant to all parties, regardless of their record in abiding by the law. A law-abiding state is currently obliged to respect the rules of the law of armed conflict, even if its adversary does not. Thus, under the common view, a belligerent has to do its utmost to spare its adversary's civilians, even if its own civilians are being targeted indiscriminately.[28] "The obligation to respect and ensure respect for international humanitarian law does not depend on

---

26. *See* James D. Morrow, *When Do States Follow the Laws of War?*, 101 Am. Pol. Sci. Rev. 559, 560 (2007).

27. *See* Samuel Estreicher, *Privileging Asymmetric Warfare (Part II): The "Proportionality" Principle Under International Humanitarian Law*, 12 Chi. J. Int'l L. 143, 144 (2011). This is not to say that currently there are no reciprocity components in the Geneva Conventions. For example, article 2 of the Third Geneva Convention indicates that when dealing with belligerents not party to the Convention, a party to the Convention is obliged to the rules as long as the nonparty belligerent "accepts and applies" them too.

28. API, *supra* note 8, at art. 51(6).

reciprocity."[29] This disregard of reciprocity considerations can be demonstrated further by the grave restrictions imposed in the specific niche of reprisals by a victim military. Under the *in bello* rules, lawful reprisals are very limited in their scope; in any case, they are not allowed as a retaliatory or penal measure, even in the course of war, and are completely forbidden once the war has ended. Reprisal in wartime, that is, "belligerent reprisal," is only allowed when it is aimed at preventing the transgressor of the *in bello* rules from continuing to breach them.[30] In this "educational process," which takes place in real time, a victim state is allowed to push the envelope, only temporarily, by way of an exceptional act of reprisal, which is illegal per se, yet lawful when proportional and pinpointed.[31]

Thus, the humanitarian considerations usually prevail under the prevailing rules and reciprocity between states' militaries is, to a large extent missing; the mutual selfish interest to observe the rules is almost gone (although there are indeed "selfish" reasons why a state might comply with the rules unilaterally: for example, a desire to instill higher morale and discipline within its military, a concern over domestic and international public opinion, or the wish to "win hearts and minds").[32] When the mutual interest is no longer valid, however, the deterrent effect against a breach declines dramatically. It incentivizes the transgressor and creates a disincentive for the law-abiding state. The transgressor of the *in bello* rules (who may also be an aggressor, breaching the *ad bellum* rules) thus enjoys

29. International Committee of the Red Cross [ICRC], *Study on Customary IHL*, rule 140, http://www.icrc.org/customary-ihl/eng/docs/v1_rul_rule140 (last visited Aug. 29, 2016).

30. *See supra* Introduction note 16 and the accompanying text.

31. As to the conflicting views relating to the disputed norm prohibiting reprisals against civilians, *see supra* Introduction notes 16–27 and the accompanying text. Under the prevailing norm, however, the aim of a lawful reprisal is strictly to harm the transgressor's soldiers (except for its wounded soldiers, prisoners of war, and any other person or object specifically protected from reprisal by the Geneva Conventions and the API) in a very selective and limited way. Nonetheless it is agreed that the reprisal aim should be limited to deterring the transgressor from further breaches of the law of armed conflict, while the war between the parties rages on. According to the U.S. Army Field Manual, lawful reprisals are a residual, proportional tool of last resort, subject to approval by the highest available commanding officers on the field, and should never be adopted "merely for revenge" but, rather, "to induce the enemy to desist from unlawful practices . . . For example, the employment by a belligerent of a weapon the use of which is normally precluded by the law of war would constitute a lawful reprisal for intentional mistreatment of prisoners of war held by the enemy." DEP'T OF THE ARMY, FIELD MANUAL 27-10, THE LAW OF LAND WARFARE, para. 497 (July, 1956) [hereinafter FM 27-10].

32. *See supra* Introduction note 90.

both worlds. It enjoys the benefits granted by the legal rules in times of war, whereas its law-abiding adversary is denied their enjoyment, but has to pay the premium for them in its own fighting.[33]

The legal rejection of reciprocity is not limited to the *in bello* sphere and is valid in the *ad bellum* arena as well. Under the prevailing rules, a law-abiding state enjoys the right of self-defense, but cannot unilaterally punish an aggressor who has started an illegal war against it, nor can it punish that aggressor's soldiers. The soldiers of an aggressor army enjoy all the benefits of the law of armed conflict; combatants are not responsible for their state's aggression. Thus, under the prevailing rules, the *jus ad bellum* and the *jus in bello* bodies of law usually do not intermix and are entirely separate.[34] Under this twofold approach, the circumstances leading to the outbreak of a war bear no relevance to the legal rules dictating the way a war is to be conducted. The aggressor's military is allowed fair treatment, similar in every way to that of the defendant's army.[35]

The current separation between the *ad bellum* and the *in bello* rules has a counter-effect in terms of deterrence. A self-defending army does not enjoy any "offsetting" legal privileges in its fighting, even where its relative position may be inferior due to the illegal armed attack it is facing. It must obey the same rules and standards applicable to its aggressor. The legal system does not compensate it for any operational or tactical loss it might incur as a result of its opponent's armed attack. An aggressor's army that crosses the *ad bellum* Rubicon and initiates an armed attack—in defiance of the legal threshold set by the UN Charter—is not legally punished, nor are its soldiers, by having any special constraints set on its fighting. The *in bello* rules relating to the way it fights are not influenced by its preliminary sin. The legal rules applicable to the aggressor's soldiers are neutral, allowing them to fight on the battleground against the defendant's soldiers in an atmosphere of "fair play," regardless of the "unfair"—indeed, illegal—cause for which they are fighting.[36]

---

33. Indeed, the transgressor's incentives might be inflated due to the changes in the prevailing pattern of war in general and in the strategy and tactics adopted by nonstate actors in particular. The lack of a concrete battlefield and the interfusion of civilians and combatants challenge the underlying assumptions of the *in bello* rules.

34. *See supra* Chapter 3 note 101.

35. This well-established principle has been codified, for example, in the API's preamble; *see supra* text accompanying Introduction notes 7–8.

36. Discussing the full justification for the independence of the *ad bellum* and *in bello* rules from each other goes far beyond the scope of our discussion. Indeed, morally speaking,

From this perspective, there is no penalty for violence, but quite the opposite: it offers actual operational rewards. For example, if a self-defendant who plays by the rules is surprised by an illegal attack, the aggressor's army may enjoy strategic, operational, and tactical advantages—all dependent, of course, on the general circumstances and on the aggressor's ability to realize those advantages and the defendant's ability to overcome them.[37] No legal offsetting mechanism is granted in real time to a self-defendant, who has been maneuvered into an inferior operational position by an aggressor's surprise attack. The aggressor has better cards in its hands at the start of the war, yet the game continues under the same rules even though the operational cards were not distributed fairly. The aggressor's felony cannot be leveraged by the defendant. Nor can its advantage be offset by it. Indeed, from the perspective of fairness, the aggressor is rewarded at the law-abiding self-defendant's expense. On this point, instead of deterring aggression, the current law seems to incentivize it.

The above presentation of the positive law and its rejection of reciprocity, due to humanitarian and utilitarian considerations, invites a normative discussion regarding its alternatives. In an international arena in which the central law enforcement apparatus of the UN does not function (at least, properly), there should be an effective shield for law-abiding states. In a world where wolves hunt for prey, states need powerful and effective protection against aggression. In the following discussion,[38] defensive

---

one might favor a legal environment that prefers a military fighting a just war, as does John Rawls: "Where a country's right to war is questionable and uncertain, the constraints on the means it can use are all the more severe. Acts permissible in a war of legitimate self-defense, when these are necessary, may be flatly excluded in a more doubtful situation." JOHN RAWLS, A THEORY OF JUSTICE 379 (1971). For the sake of the current discussion, however, it should be noted that this separation creates a reciprocal incentive for soldiers of both sides to fight "fairly" and obey the law. From this perspective, it reflects a "reciprocal incentive niche" in the new legal paradigm that has generally supplanted the old reciprocity paradigm. This set of rules is applicable not only in cases where one can easily recognize the innocent party, but also in the more common case where each side accuses its opponent of being the aggressor.

37. When calculating the expected risk to a victim state of a surprise attack, the balance of power between the adversaries in all dimensions (military, economic, social, and cultural) should be taken into consideration. Indeed, the endurance capacity of a victim state depends upon a combination of both physical and mental considerations, for example, whether the defendant has a territorial buffer zone to mitigate the offensive blow; *see* the discussion *supra* text accompanying Chapter 2 notes 140–142.

38. Although the discussion till now has dealt with the lack of deterrence in both the *ad bellum* and *in bello* rules, the normative discussion that follows will concentrate mainly upon the former.

deterrence will be suggested as an efficient tool to enforce compliance with the law.

4.3 The Potential Benefits of Introducing Defensive Deterrence Considerations into Lawful Self-Defense

4.3.1 Deterrence—An Efficient Tool to Enforce Compliance with the Law

The legal challenge is to provide the tools and environment promoting the preservation of the international law relating to war. (Though the law is universally applicable to all adversaries, such tools are, naturally, more appealing to law-abiding states or to marginal states: those standing on the edge and vacillating over which path to choose that would serve their best interest, inducing them to law-abidance.) Defensive deterrence, aimed at maintaining the status quo and containing potential conflicts in the international arena, might serve as an appropriate method of fulfilling the UN Charter's prohibition on the unilateral exercise of military force.

In theory, maintenance of the current international peace is supposed to be carried out by the UN's organs. In the same way that the domestic law-enforcement apparatus is based, to a large extent, on the state's monopoly on the use of force, the international vision was that the Security Council would exercise this sort of effective centralized monopoly. In practice, this expectation has usually not been realized. In light of the Security Council's current impotency,[39] one available substitute for the universal preservation of the status quo would seem to be by introducing deterrence considerations into the determination of the scope of lawful self-defense. A strong law should have inherent incentives for its preservation. Introducing deterrence considerations into individual or collective self-defense might provide the required counter-aggression vector to the law-abidance scales. The following discussion addresses the benefits and drawbacks of doing so.

Allowing a credible threat for the deterrence of a potential or actual aggressor may offer a peaceful alternative to the self-defendant. Containment of the aggression should usually be preferred over actually

39. Even though the UN would appear to be a perfect representative of a collective security system—and notwithstanding its exceptional actions in the Korean War, in Somalia, and in the First Gulf War—generally, it hasn't functioned effectively. *See, e.g.*, Anthony Clark Arend & Robert J. Beck, International Law and the Use of Force 52–57 (1993).

fighting against it. In such a case, deterrence has a moderating or cooling effect, replacing actual wars with cold ones, which should be endorsed. It can elevate the lawful threshold for actual war by offering a realistic alternative to the self-defendant. Threatening to severely harm a potential aggressor through lawful measures, aimed against military objectives, raises two legal questions. The first relates to the precise substance of the threat, the second to its timing. Both, however, involve the risk of miscalculation of the threat, which might escalate the conflict rather than prevent it.[40] In fact, shaping an actual defensive response is analogous, to a large extent, to tailoring the contours and substance of a preliminary threat, as the threat, in case the deterrence fails (either in whole or in part), might actually be exercised. The delicacy of the timing—given the requirement for the actual "occurrence" of an armed attack to justify self-defense[41]—invites an analytical process that is, to a large extent, analogous to the discussion of the preemptive strike above, in Chapter 2. To avoid the premature exercise of a threat, it is necessary to determine its lawful timing by a combination of the explicit intent of the potential aggressor to initiate an armed attack against the self-defendant and a substantial degree of active preparation by it that makes that intent a real and present danger.[42]

4.3.2 Introducing Defensive Deterrence Considerations into the *ad Bellum* Proportionality: Challenging Its Quantitative Basis

A proportional military response by a self-defendant to an "armed attack" should be aimed, according to the common view advocated by prominent writers and judges, at "halting and repelling" the ongoing attack and restoring the territorial status quo.[43] The self-defendant is required to respond moderately, exercising the minimal and strictly necessary force required for this purpose throughout its entire defensive military campaign.[44]

---

40. *See infra* text following note 108.

41. *See supra* Chapter 2 note 7.

42. *Cf.*, the three conditions creating a sufficient threat that according to Walzer legitimizes a first strike. Michael Walzer, Just and Unjust Wars 81 (4th ed. 2006).

43. *See supra* text accompanying Chapter 3 notes 94–95.

44. *Cf.*, Dinstein's conflicting view—arguing that "There is no support in the practice of States for the notion that [*ad bellum*] proportionality remains relevant" throughout the entire hostilities—*supra* text accompanying Chapter 3 note 107.

An extreme version of the soft reading of proportionality interprets proportionality as requiring a linear, in-type response by a law-abiding self-defendant.[45] In a previous discussion, the difficulties related to the quantitatively based *ad bellum* proportionality were presented.[46] I will now elaborate upon the criticism of this common—yet problematic—reading of the *ad bellum* proportionality.

Indeed, at first glance, the linear reading of proportionality seems to offer nothing but advantages—both moral and practical. Under "laboratory conditions," due to reciprocity considerations, it might even be seen as the most efficient response. Indeed, the intuitively simple "tit for tat" strategy does have its own advantages: "A famous computerized game in game theory has demonstrated 'tit for tat' to be the most effective strategy that a player can adopt. He ought to reciprocate positive actions in the interest of mutually beneficial co-operation, and retaliate when his partner fails him in order to persuade his partner that he cannot get away with it."[47]

However, the in-scale principle of response strategy is based, to a large extent, upon reciprocity, which currently, as mentioned above, is largely missing from the international law arena. Furthermore, real life is not a game. In reality, there are too many variables and uncertainties involved, relating to both sides. The simple in-scale proportionality approach requires adjustment, especially when it has been demonstrated that an actual aggressor is not deterred by the threat of "tit for tat." Furthermore, if one looks at the correlation between the risks assumed by a potential rational aggressor and its potential rewards, this formula seems, prima facie, to be less than convincing, as it minimizes the potential risks to an aggressor in relation to its potential rewards. Indeed, the soft proportionality convention—requiring an equivalent, in-kind, linear and sequential defensive response—rewards an aggressor who takes the initiative in attacking a law-abiding state. From the aggressor's perspective—assuming that it isn't concerned about abiding by the law—in the upside scenario, its reward will be the defeat of its victim enemy, with no (or fewer) legal limits. In the downside state of affairs, if it is defeated, it will not suffer a total loss, but only limited, "proportional" damage from the limited, in-kind (sequential and proportional) response allowed to its law-abiding

45. *See, e.g., supra* text accompanying Chapter 3 note 108.

46. *See supra* text accompanying Chapter 3 notes 107–110.

47. Azar Gat, War in Human Civilization 94 (2006).

self-defendant opponent. The smaller the proportional response allowed by the legal system to the defendant, the greater the aggressor's incentive to attack its adversary. Having taken the minimal response of its law-abiding adversary for granted, a rational aggressor may even attack if it realizes that its chances of winning the war are equal to or lower than those of its defendant adversary, as it is the "expected value"[48] of its aggression—based upon the probabilities of the belligerency's anticipated results (results contingent, inter alia, upon the defendant's potential response and its magnitude)—that matters. Thus, although the demand for an in-scale type of response is aimed at reducing the hazards of war and humanizing its environment, it paradoxically creates a clear incentive for aggressors to fight law-abiding states.

The fallacies presented above, relating to the quantitative dimension of the *ad bellum* proportionality, invite rethinking about adding a qualitative dimension to it, indeed, reshaping the cost-benefit calculation of a potential aggressor. This is the rationale behind the call for introducing defensive deterrence considerations into the *ad bellum* proportionality. The magnitude of military force required for a proportional response by a self-defendant—one that, if exercised at such a scale, should be lawful—is neither minimal, nor should it be "equal" to the force used by the aggressor; it should be effective by allowing the self-defendant to realize its defense. Indeed, there is no objective measure ("aggression meter"), nor is there a consensus, regarding the quantification of allowable military force in the context of a counter-response taken by a state acting in its own self-defense. However, demanding that the response be proportionate to the injury inflicted[49] is too simple by far; the quantification of force should not be based exclusively on such an objective criterion as it is affected, inter alia, by the self-defendant's war aim.

The war aims of the self-defendant directly affect the scope of force used.[50] In an ongoing state of armed conflict, the expulsion of an aggressor and the restoration of the territorial status quo may not always be the desired end result for all law-abiding self-defendants. In some cases—for example, in an isolated case of aggression that crosses the armed

---

48. *See supra* Chapter 2 note 155. *See also* Brian Angelo Lee, *Preventive War, Deterrence Retaliation, and Retrospective Disproportionality*, 2009 BYU L. Rev. 253, 262 (2009).

49. *See, e.g.*, John Lawrence Hargrove, *The Nicaragua Judgment and the Future of the Law of Force and Self-Defence*, 81 Am. J. Int'l L. 135, 136 (1987).

50. *See* the discussion *infra*, Part 4.5.

attack threshold—it might be enough.[51] In others—for example, in the case of continuous aggression—such restoration might be analogous to a cosmetic treatment that does not deal with the substantive core problems. Forestalling any further aggression and creating (relatively speaking) long-term stability is the desired goal of a self-defendant rather than an unstable status quo ante. Merely the fact that the status quo was not kept by the aggressor, in the first place, shows that an automatic return to square one—the situation as it was prior to the aggression—is not always the optimal result. It depends on whether this status quo is, or at least has the potential of being, a solid ground rather than an unstable basis of shifting sands.

Regrettably, under the current positive law, quantitative measurement has been selected as the main yardstick for evaluating proportionality in some Security Council decisions,[52] whereas the ICJ holds that lawful measures taken in self-defense leave no room for any "measure of discretion."[53] Such a mechanical approach is wanting when it comes to determining a conclusive threshold. Instead, in appropriate cases, a qualitative assessment of a certain measure's deterrent effect should accompany the prevailing quantitatively oriented proportionality. It is not the magnitude of the aggressor's military force that should determine, exclusively, the scope of the lawful response; rather, this response should be reasonably and professionally designed in accordance with its effect upon any other act of belligerence by the aggressor. This argument is further strengthened when the rationale behind the *ad bellum* proportionality requirement—minimizing the disruption of international peace and security[54]—is taken into consideration. It is not the formal status quo that should exclusively matter, but rather preventing any recurrence of this aggression. If one is interested in maintaining international peace and security, one should not deal solely with the limited management of conflicts but rather also with the reasonable option of preventing them. There should not be any

---

51. *See, e.g.*, the Falklands scenario, *supra* Chapter 3 note 147.

52. Oscar Schachter, *The Right of States to Use Armed Force*, 82 MICH. L. REV. 1620, 1637 (1984) (arguing, inter alia, that "[s]ome of the Security Council decisions that declared the use of force to be illegal reprisal rather than legitimate defense noted the much higher number of casualties resulting from the defense in relation to those caused by the earlier attack").

53. Oil Platforms (Islamic Republic of Iran v. U.S.), Judgment, 2003 I.C.J. Rep. 161, ¶ 73 (Nov. 6).

54. JUDITH GARDAM, NECESSITY, PROPORTIONALITY AND THE USE OF FORCE BY STATES 16 (2004) (referring to C. Greenwood).

confusion between ex-ante considerations, prevailing before an armed attack has begun, and ex-post considerations. Indeed, the underlying rationale of the UN Charter's general rule prohibiting the use of force is maintenance of the current international peace and preservation of the status quo. This prohibition is the ex-ante means derived from the chosen aim of the Charter—to maintain "international peace and security." Yet when this rule is not kept and war breaks out, the conclusion must be that the old means has failed and a new legal path, within the contours of lawful self-defense, should be considered ex-post. In this state of affairs, I suggest cautiously considering the addition of a qualitative element—based on the reasonable desire to prevent recurrence of the armed attack, currently or in the near future, under the specific circumstances of the case—to the prevailing quantitative approach. The focus should be not only on the measurement of the "amount" of force used, but also on its effect. As long as the aggressor is rational, the subjective deterrence-based element of proportionality should be cautiously added to the objective yardstick of the aggression-meter.

Introducing defensive deterrence considerations into proportionality would teach another lesson to actual or potential aggressors: they do not hold an option, to be exercised by them unilaterally, over the decision whether to initiate an armed attack and when to stop it. It takes two to tango. The monster of war, once released from its cage, cannot be contained and reconfined unilaterally, solely at the will of the aggressor. Otherwise, any such act of aggression would create a "win-win" situation for aggressors. They would be induced to adopt a strategy of let us start (a war) and see (its results), and then decide (whether to carry on with it or stop it). Allowing an aggressor to take the initiative throughout the war and to unilaterally decide when to resume or stop it, at its sole discretion, is totally mistaken. The argument that "where the aggressor state indicates a willingness to end hostilities . . . there is in principle a duty to end defensive measures"[55] is analogous to inviting an aggressor state to a "free lunch" at the expense of the defendant. It is an open-ended invitation to aggressors to free-ride on the shoulders of the victim states. It grants

55. Kaiyan Homi Kaikobad, *Self-Defence, Enforcement Action and the Gulf Wars, 1980–88 and 1990–91*, 63 Brit. Y.B. Int'l L. 299, 337 (1993) (arguing that: "a defending State would be justified in not accepting an offer to end hostilities where there was clear evidence to demonstrate that the offer was not a bona fide one"). *Cf.*, Yoram Dinstein, War, Aggression and Self-Defence 264 (5th ed. 2011).

them the initiative at every stage of the military campaign, illegally started with their armed attack, while allowing them to contain it at their earliest possible convenience. It insures them for free against the self-created risks deriving from their own act of aggression. One aspect of the problem is that the risk-takers, the aggressors, do not pay the real premium for their activity; the other aspect of the problem is that it is paid by the victims who bear the main risk! This is a clear incentive for lack of accountability on the part of actual and potential aggressors and, as such, is unacceptable: aggressors should not unilaterally have the power to decide either the scope of war or its duration.

There is a price for initiating an armed attack. The end of a war of self-defense doesn't come automatically when "the aggressor state indicates a willingness to end hostilities," nor will its scope always be linear and proportionate to the actual harm inflicted. Normatively speaking, it is the defendant state that has—and should have—the final say; and just to remove any doubt, this final say ought to be reasonable (by the strategic and operational professional standards adopted by law-abiding states) and proportional, finely tuned to the specific circumstances. This final self-defendant's say should be valid, under the prevailing law, as long as the Security Council does not adopt a binding ceasefire resolution. Thus, whenever an aggressor decides to cross the *ad bellum* Rubicon and initiate an armed attack, it will have to bear the unknown full consequences of its illegal activities. When potential aggressors internalize that there is a price—not fully known in advance—to be paid for their aggression, they may be deterred from starting hostilities in the first place; on rational players, motivated by cost-benefit calculations, it should have a substantial deterrent effect. The tailoring of this effect will be discussed in the next section.

4.4 Tailoring an Appropriate Defensive Deterrent Suit

The search for a proportional and deterring self-defensive response is a fine-tuning process involving both objective and subjective variables. If we were dealing with rational parties of a similar cultural background, and working in an efficient "international power" market—in which all information and outcomes are known in advance to all players—such an optimal *ad bellum* deterrence equation might have been precise. If such an equation existed, it would actually deter the potential aggressor in advance and no belligerence would ever take place. In fact, if all the relevant information, regarding all the variables determining the result of a potential war, were known to two rational adversaries in advance, war would be avoided (regardless of the law), and the parties would settle the conflict in light of the war's outcome without paying its price.[56]

However, as these are not the conditions under which we live, nor can we rely (at least, not exclusively) upon the collective security measures of the UN, aimed at deterring any would-be aggressors, we need to look for a type of "homemade" deterrence to be applied by a potential self-defendant state and its allies, if any. The substance of the deterring threat should be coherent with the merits of the *ad bellum* rules, aimed at maintaining international peace. Indeed, it must be tailor-made and fine-tuned ad hoc. It cannot rely solely on fixed rules with quantified objective measures that are precise and clear in advance, but rather should create, by professional means, deterrence against actual or potential aggressors. Indeed, tailoring a deterrent suit, when appropriate, aimed against military objectives, is a very challenging and delicate task that should be carried out by exercising professional, strategic, and operational military standards. From these standards, and based upon the professional use of military force in good faith, we can start thinking about and evaluating a specific, proportional response in a given conflict.

The search for the optimal concrete legal rules for the purpose of deterrence is not unique to international relations. The law and economics analysis of deterrence has much to say in the context of domestic law enforcement. For example, laws enforcing traffic limits, air pollution, or tax evasion and the extent to which they ought to be enforced are dealt with in this context. An efficient system of domestic law enforcement is one in which the deterrent fine is as large as possible, depending, of course, on the wealth of the individual whose illegal behavior is to be deterred.[57] Raising the amount of the fine drastically reduces the probability of detection, thus saving on enforcement costs. Optimal deterrence against such a potential transgressor can be achieved by adjusting the fine until the expected sum (the nominal amount of the fine multiplied by the probability of

---

56. *See* Eric A. Posner & Alan O. Sykes, Economic Foundations of International Law 170 (2013).

57. This principle was first formalized by Gary S. Becker, *Crime and Punishment: An Economic Approach*, 76 J. Pol. Econ. 169 (1968).

detection) adjusted to its subjective risk premium equals the harm caused to the public.[58] Criminological literature differs in that it prefers the certainty of punishment: "[c]hanging the marginal severity of punishments therefore appears to have far less effect than increasing the certainty that crime will result in some punishment."[59] Whatever level of detection is optimal, monetary sanctions against criminals are preferred economically over imprisonment, due to cost considerations; they are cheaper to implement. The use of force against criminals is justified when they do not have the financial capability (or will) to pay for the harm caused. As international aggression is perceived to be socially undesirable, deterrence should be designed at the level that will prevent the occurrence of the crime. In many cases, monetary sanctions do not work against transgressor states—due to their lack of assets, an agency problem,[60] or lack of international enforcement—and ex-post war crimes trials and imprisonment are usually impractical. "For these reasons, the use of force, or at least a credible threat of force, will often be essential to deter potential rogue states from unproductive acts or to incapacitate the states that cannot be deterred."[61]

Normatively speaking, in order to deter a rational aggressor, the expected return on its aggression should be negative[62] from its own perspective, with the expected total costs (losses) deriving from its aggression exceeding its expected gains. This will be the case if the actual reaction of the self-defendant (or the expected value of a potential reaction) to the aggression is large enough in magnitude to create negative value for the aggressor—all depending, of course, on the information known to both adversaries and their "objective" reality perceptions.

As the above discussion has shown, there is neither a universal proportionality rule nor an international fixed rate for deterrence. For each potential aggressor, its own professionally tailored and culturally based deterrence suit is required. This means that each adversary's unique attributes must be studied in-depth professionally in order to prepare the right suit. These attributes include, inter alia, each adversary's culture and

58. *See, e.g.*, A. Mitchell Polinsky, An Introduction to Law and Economics 75–86 (2d ed. 1989).

59. Freedman, Deterrence, *supra* note 2, at 64.

60. Usually, an aggressor's leaders do not pay the monetary penalties, but rather its citizens do. *See supra* Chapter 3 note 96.

61. Posner & Sykes, *supra* note 56, at 179.

62. *See supra* Chapter 2 note 155.

economy, and in many cases its dominant religion (if any); and also its military doctrine, which, as one might expect, is often connected to the adversary's culture and other relevant attributes.[63] This process requires studying the adversary's political regime, whether democratic or authoritarian, and especially in the latter case, the agency problem deriving from the gap between the interest of the dictator or ruling echelon and that of their constituents. It is necessary to analyze and understand the adversary's military "center (or centers) of gravity"[64] (which is not always an easy or attainable task, especially in asymmetric wars)—those sites that if substantially hit, as threatened, might deter it from further belligerent aggression. Indeed, it is an entire professional process requiring the self-defendant to analyze, from the aggressor's perspective, the cost-benefit balance of its aggression and the individual variables involved. This intelligence-based analysis should assess the value the aggressor attributes to all its assets and liabilities and ascertain how to leverage the military assets—out of the potential lawful military objectives—that the aggressor might lose due to its unlawful potential armed attack. It is mainly the assets that the aggressor does not want to lose—before and during the war—that may be leveraged to deter it. When it comes to dictators, for example, they are used to treating their citizens and soldiers as a means; it is their own wealth and safety or holding on to power that usually matters most to them. It is the credible threat of taking military action, when applicable, vis-à-vis a rational potential aggressor, that should provide the deterrence. In some cases, the cost-benefit analysis of an aggressor might sustain an absolute deterrence, but in others only a relative deterrence, preventing it, for example, from using certain types of weapons. When deterrence fails and the self-defendant is unable to contain the military conflict (or substantial segments of it), a requirement of total defeat and even regime change might be a condition for the self-defendant to realize its defense (these extreme scenarios will be elaborated below).

The product of this analysis of the aggressor's cost-benefit calculations, if carried out professionally and with due diligence by the self-defendant, is the basis for preparing a concrete deterrence suit in a given conflict. From the perspective of an outsider, who is not privy to the professional military way of thinking, such in-depth learning might be perceived as too

63. As to military doctrines, *see supra* text accompanying Chapter 2 notes 76–91.

64. *See supra* Chapter 3 note 186.

complicated and impractical. Intuitively, one might argue, from a legal perspective we cannot require a self-defendant to conduct such a complicated preliminary analysis. Yet this imperative—to know your enemy before counterattacking it in your own self-defense in an appropriate and precise manner, the action aimed at its main military assets and effective vis-à-vis its unique attributes—is a basic professional requirement of any military faced with an adversary. (In the rare cases where it is absent, the deterrence discourse has no substantial relevance in the realm of self-defense.) The argument advocated in this chapter is that this professional—strategic and operational—analysis should also have legal implications. Infusing deterrence considerations into the legal requirement of proportionality would accomplish the task.

Tailoring the suggested deterrence suit begins with the objective attributes of a lawful and proportional self-defense. Thus, in an ongoing armed attack "the harm inflicted" might serve as a benchmark against which to start tailoring a specific deterring yet proportional response. The challenge ahead of us is one of transformation: to add to the objective-quantitative benchmark of proportionality[65] a subjective-qualitative criterion for a deterrence-based response, without its being manipulated as a pretext for counter-aggression. It is, indeed, a strategic and operational challenge to a law-abiding state, requiring an adaptation process based, to a large extent, on trial and error. In light of this problem of not knowing the exact deterrence dosage needed in a given situation of belligerent aggression (which will usually be the case), it is desirable to allow the self-defendant to start from what might reasonably seem to be the minimal required dose to efficiently achieve its military deterrent aim.

Normatively, then, the discussion thus far indicates that the linear version of proportionality, as endorsed by its prominent advocates, ought to be rejected as the exclusive reading. From the defendant army's perspective, one of the best ways to achieve a "military advantage" is to break the linear chain and surprise its opponent. We should not expect there to always be an artificial linear equation between an aggressor's activities and the response of its victims. Thus, it is fully legitimate for a defendant army that has lawfully engaged in war—once its aggressor-adversary has crossed the *ad bellum* threshold of an armed attack against it—to surprise its opponent, inter alia, by the magnitude of force and the sites and dimensions

65. Dinstein suggests a standard of reasonableness as an appropriate criterion for measuring self-defense. DINSTEIN, WAR, AGGRESSION AND SELF-DEFENCE, *supra* note 55, at 233.

of its response. Indeed, this is the operational essence of the American (Colin) Powell doctrine that was exercised successfully in the First Gulf War,[66] and that requires overwhelming force to be precisely deployed in a decisive campaign, though not automatically aimed at the "wholesale destruction" of the aggressor's capabilities, per se. To meet the challenge of shaping the necessary and proportional deterrent suit without manipulating it, one must remain loyal to professional principles. The overwhelming force should be exercised professionally in the minimal-limited dose required—in combined terms of the force and means used, the objects targeted, and the duration and scope of the belligerency—toward achieving its war aim. Indeed, the moderating effect of exercising military force in a professional manner was demonstrated in the First Gulf War, where the "overwhelming" military campaign was stopped at a relatively early stage.[67]

4.4.1 Proportional Deterrence—Limited to the Specific Conflict

The effect of the desired deterrence against a specific act of belligerent aggression is not limited to the given conflict with its designated parties. Advocating for military resistance once aggression has begun, Michael Walzer provides a wider perspective on the universal effects of any aggression: "[r]esistance is important so that rights can be maintained and future aggressors deterred. . . . The victim of aggression fights in self-defense, but he isn't only defending himself, for aggression is a crime against society as a whole."[68] Similarly, the International Military Tribunal at Nuremberg declared: "War is essentially an evil thing. Its consequences are not confined to the belligerent states alone, but affect the whole world."[69] Despite this universal effect, however, the scope of a given proportional deterrence-oriented response to an armed attack should be limited to the specific conflict. Indeed, deterrence, like aggression, whether successful or failed, has a secondary effect that goes far beyond the given episode. Nonetheless, the limitation of its scope should be consistent with its direct rationale: to deter a specific aggressor in a given situation of *ad bellum* aggression (or

---

66. *See supra* Chapter 3 note 110.

67. *See supra* Chapter 1 notes 95–96 and Chapter 3 note 110.

68. Walzer, Just and Unjust Wars, *supra* note 42, at 59.

69. Trial of the Major War Criminals before the International Military Tribunal (Nuremberg, 1946), 1 I.M.T. 186.

to deter a specific transgressor from an *in bello* transgression). Looked at from this perspective, the dropping of the atomic bombs on Japan—if it was mainly motivated by deterrence considerations with regard to third parties (such as inducing Moscow's acceptance of postwar American objectives)—seems to depart from this moral and legal reasoning.[70] Signaling a threat to third parties, at the expense of an adversary (even if an aggressor) in general, of its innocent civilians in particular, is totally unacceptable. Deterring a third party, the Soviets, at the expense—indeed, over the bodies—of the innocent residents of Hiroshima and Nagasaki would have been neither moral nor legal. On the other hand, a proportional response to a specific belligerent aggression should also be realistic and take into account other conflicts, if any, in which the specific aggressor is currently actively involved.[71] Indeed, this was the case regarding the Third Reich, whose belligerent activities on all fronts should have been considered as a whole by the Allies when tailoring their unique response to it. The adjustment of the desired defensive deterrence reflects, in fact, the changing face and prototypes of wars and the belligerents' specific circumstances.

4.4.2 Deterrence-Oriented Proportionality in a Changing Reality—A Self-Adjustment Challenge

The argument that a lawful and proportional self-defense response should be adjusted to the general circumstances of a given attack may give new life to the reading of the prohibition on the use of force and its exceptions under the UN Charter. It may, in fact, not only lend relevance to the prohibition, but also challenge Thomas Franck's declaration, made in 1970, regarding the death of Article 2(4): "The most significant factor in

70. *See, e.g.*, Gabriella Blum, *The Laws of War and the "Lesser Evil"*, 35 Yale J. Int'l L. 1, 26–27 (2010) (arguing that "there is considerable evidence that the Soviets themselves viewed this as the primary American motivation for using the atomic bomb"); Gar Alperovitz, Atomic Diplomacy: Hiroshima and Potsdam—The Use of the Atomic Bomb and the American Confrontation with Soviet Power 270 (1966).

71. Indeed, although an aggressor has to "pay" only for its own sins (in terms of its deterrence), in some cases it might benefit (and enjoy a "discount" in the self-defendant's countermeasures that it has to face), due the defendant's need to deter other third parties who are potential aggressors as well. This "moderating function," motivated by realpolitik considerations, triggered Liddell Hart's rejection of the call for "unconditional surrender" of the Axis powers in World War II. Hart was motivated to prevent the Soviet Union from controlling substantial parts of Europe after it became clear that the Third Reich was going to be defeated. *See* Azar Gat, A History of Military Thought: From the Enlightenment to the Cold War 800–10 (2001).

complicating the 'simple' right of self-defense . . . has been the changing nature of warfare itself."[72]

Indeed, the pattern of wars has changed, to some extent dramatically. But this phenomenon, per se, should not be interpreted as signaling the death of the prohibition on the use of military force in the international arena, or as voiding its self-defense exception. It does require, however, a redefinition and adjustment of the self-defense exception, in particular its proportionality component, to the changing reality. The legitimacy of self-defense should not depend on any given pattern of war.[73] A lawful and proportional response by a self-defendant state ought to be specifically tailored and aimed, in appropriate cases, at deterring its aggressor. Similarly, a law-abiding state should have tools to deter a transgressor of the *in bello* rules. An adjustment process—based upon professional standards applicable to the specific circumstances of any given conflict—might morally and legally validate such a response in any type of armed conflict. Whatever asymmetric tactics and strategy the aggressor (or transgressor) adopts—be they sub-conventional (terror or guerilla warfare) or meta-conventional (weapons of mass destruction)—a tailor-made deterrence suit, when applicable,[74] should be fitted to it. This tailoring process requires readjusting the right of self-defense to a changing reality, thus vindicating its relevancy. A rigid reading of article 2(4), based upon objective fixed criteria, justifies declaring it dead, as Franck did in 1970, whereas its elastic adjustment, as suggested above, would maintain its vitality. Indeed, deterrence is not a magic formula to be applied in all military campaigns, nor is it effective in all cases; rather, it is a powerful strategy, to be applied only in appropriate circumstances. In the next Part of this chapter—revisiting the morally and legally desirable end results of wars—I will try to establish the basic framing for such circumstances. It presents the direct connection between the aggressor's explicit and implicit war aims and the self-defendant's spectrum of lawful proportional responses, including the deterrence component thereof. In fact, it looks at defensive deterrence—internalizing the

72. Thomas M. Franck, *Who Killed Article 2(4)? or: Changing Norms Governing the Use of Force by States*, 64 Am. J. Int'l L. 809, 811–12 (1970).

73. Indeed, the legality of self-defense by a state fighting against a nonstate actor is disputed. *See supra* Chapter 2 note 46.

74. The case of "undeterrable" leaders or terrorists will be partially dealt with in the following discussion.

need and probability of exercising it—as a tool for evaluating the legality of the self-defendant's war aim.

4.5 Defensive Deterrence: A Tool for Evaluating the Legality of a War's Aims

Introduction: Revitalizing the *ad Bellum* Proportionality

There is no fixed prescription how to conduct and end war morally or legally. Within the current contours of the law, however, the assumption should be that a self-defendant is entitled to realize its self-defense. This is based not only on realpolitik considerations but on a moral justification, as well. The current legal dispute relates to the scope of the lawful defense, as reflected in the current lack of consensus about a lawful war's aims in general and the "means-ends *ad bellum* proportionality" in particular.[75] Introducing, in fact legalizing, defensive deterrence, as suggested, might afford a tool for evaluating the legality of the aim of a given war: in particular, for evaluating the need to escalate the strategic war aim and to move along the spectrum of war aims from the "halt and repel" minimal response to a more powerful and aggressive one. From this perspective, the suggested defensive deterrence makes it possible to revisit the *ad bellum* proportionality and give this disputed concept[76] new life.

Let us turn back to the four generic war aims of self-defense, discussed above.[77] In all four, the fact of a belligerent aggression—the crossing of the legal *ad bellum* Rubicon by the initiation of an armed attack that allows for the defendant's self-defense—is taken as given; they vary, however, with regard to the lawful scope of defensive proportionality. The first scenario involves an ad hoc, isolated act of aggression, limited in its scope and intentions, with a low probability of recurrence. The "halt and repel" formula seems to present an optimal generic response to it by a self-defendant. Any deterrent effect of such a moderate response will be merely secondary. The second scenario deals with a repeat offender who should be deterred from further acts of aggression. Adopting the "halt and repel" strategy against such a raging bull might only drive it to further acts of aggression. The focus of the deterrence against such an aggressor

---

75. *See supra* text accompanying Chapter 3 notes 111–112.

76. *See supra* text accompanying Chapter 3 notes 106–112.

77. *See supra* text accompanying Chapter 3 notes 94–97.

should be on a credible threat (and if necessary, its exercise) that might moderate its belligerent intentions and activities. It should create an atmosphere in which the expected value of the aggression, from the aggressor's perspective, is negative, by signaling the loss he stands to sustain due to his aggression. This delicate strategy aims to keep important assets of the aggressor—from the bank of potential lawful military objectives—under threat, yet untouched (either in whole or in part), in order to create the "losing premium" and the incentive attached to it. Indeed, such a credible threat might prevent or at least delay a war or reduce its scope. In terms of reducing war's hazards, the notion that potential aggressors are entitled to an explicit warning would seem, in most cases, to create a win-win situation, as long as the threat is not used as a pretext for aggression.[78] Usually, even in the downside scenario, where the threat fails and a war starts, the carrying out of the military threat by the self-defendant does not increase the scope of the war and its hazards, as long as the merits of the original threat were within the contours of the lawful self-defense paradigm.

The third scenario involves cases of belligerent aggression where deterrence cannot work and the scope of the belligerency cannot be contained by it, for example, in a dictatorship because of agency problems,[79] or due to religious motivation, or where an aggressor doesn't have assets that he is afraid of losing. Here the desirable end result may be to eliminate the aggressor's substantial military capabilities. If a self-defendant, who has professionally tried to tailor a deterrence suit to the aggressor, cannot deter it from its aggressive will, it might be lawful for it to disable it. Moving from the containment of belligerent aggression to its elimination sends, from a deterrence perspective, a mixed message. Incapacitation means that deterrence has failed to a large extent, and also, especially in cases of complete incapacitation ("total defeat") of the aggressor, that the seeds of aggression may sprout again. On the other hand, the incapacitated aggressor (and its people) might internalize the lesson of deterrence, especially when the self-defendant leaves part of the aggressor's assets untouched, in order to incentivize it not to continue down the path of aggression.

The fourth scenario involves only the most extreme instances of aggression. Here the desirable end result, applicable in very rare cases, is regime

78. *See infra*, Part 4.6. As for the pre-Charter practice of reasoned declarations of war, requiring previous and explicit warning, even in clear cases of aggression, *see supra* text accompanying Chapter 3 notes 150–158.

79. *See supra* Chapter 3 note 96.

change. An example is the Nazi regime, where only the uprooting of the entire ruling system and the shake-up of the entire society could promote peace and security for the international community in general and the self-defendants in particular.

In the above discussion, while dealing with *ad bellum* necessity—and calling for the introduction of sequential necessity to impose a restraint upon the exercise of military power beyond what is necessary to attain a military goal, during all stages of a belligerent conflict—we took the current legal acceptance of a state's selected strategy and the war aims deriving from it as a given, as long as they are within the lawful self-defense paradigm.[80] It is now time to evaluate the legality of these war aims.

4.5.1 "Halt and Repel"—the Minimal In-Scale Response

The "halt and repel" formula, discussed earlier in regard to the traditional linear proportionality,[81] represents a moderate aim of self-defense. It seems to be the optimal response to an isolated event of belligerent aggression. To illustrate, consider the proportionality of the United Kingdom's military reaction to Argentina's conquest of the Falkland Islands in 1982[82] and its resumption of sovereignty over the Islands.[83] Indeed, as Higgins states: "[p]roportionality here cannot be in relation to any specific prior injury—it has to be in relation to the overall legitimate objective, of ending the aggression or reversing the invasion."[84] Punishing the Argentine government for its aggression was not lawful, nor was the desire to educate it ("teach it a lesson"). Any military activity aimed directly at "halting and repelling" the invasion should have been lawful.[85] Indeed, one may reasonably assume that the recapture of the Islands by the British

80. *See supra* text following Chapter 3 note 178.

81. *See supra* text accompanying notes 43–54.

82. *See supra* Chapter 3 note 147.

83. For the moral challenge of a war waged only for the sake of formal sovereignty, *see, e.g.*, Daniel Statman, *Targeted Killing*, 5 Theo. Inq. L. 179, 181–84 (2004).

84. Rosalyn Higgins, Problems and Process: International Law and How We Use It 232 (1995).

85. Higgins's conclusion that "any bombing of the Argentinian air force or navy while in Argentina or in port would have been regarded as disproportionate" (*Id.*) can be contested. Any bombing aimed directly toward achieving the expulsion of the invader should have

army, in a precise and professional manner, to some extent guaranteed that there would be no attacks by Argentina in the near future, although this deterrent effect was merely a residual result of the desired return to the status quo.

4.5.2 Deterring a Repeat Aggressor

When the belligerent aggression is not an isolated event and the aggressor is a repeat player, expecting to gain from its continued aggression—or, in the more problematic case, a potential aggressor, whose deeds, motivated by its stated cost-benefit analysis, and intentions are explicitly aggressive—the halt-and-repel formula might have a counter-effect. In such a case, the moderate formula, based upon a linear proportional response, might incentivize a rational aggressor to continue or intensify its aggression, even though the formula's declared aim is to discourage it.[86]

Deterrent proportionality is concerned with "the result to be achieved by the 'defensive' action and not the forms, substance and strength of the action itself."[87] To demonstrate, take for example an aggressor—either a state or nonstate actor—who wants to benefit from the use of salami tactics in its fight against a law-abiding state, by exercising modest acts of aggression, "slice by slice." Said aggressor, knowing that the right of self-defense is restricted as a legitimate tool solely against the "most grave" of armed attacks,[88] decides to embark on small-scale attacks—but none exceeding the armed attack threshold—against its adversary. Let us assume it fires only one shot or rocket, on a weekly or daily basis, such that under the current *ad bellum* rules each of its acts, on its own, does not justify the victim state's exercising its inherent right to self-defense. What, then, should a law-abiding defendant's proportional lawful response be?

---

been lawful, even if carried out on Argentina's mainland. For example, bombing of reinforcements "while in Argentina or in port" before departing to the Islands should have been lawful.

86. *See supra* text accompanying notes 43–49.

87. Int'l Law Comm'n, Addendum—Eighth report on State responsibility by Mr. Robert Ago, Special Rapporteur—the internationally wrongful act of the State, source of international responsibility, U.N. Doc. A/CN.4/318/Add.5-7, at para. 121 (1980).

88. *See supra* Introduction note 67.

Indeed, salami tactics challenge the *ad bellum* self-defense constraints of necessity and proportionality.[89] The aggressor intentionally and repeatedly provokes the self-defendant, while sheltering beneath the threshold of lawful response. To illustrate this legal challenge, consider the circumstances leading to the 2008–2009 conflict between Hamas and Israel in the Gaza Strip. Between the years 2001 and 2009 Palestinian armed groups launched approximately 8,000 rockets and mortar shells into southern Israel from (as of 2007, Hamas-controlled) Gaza, killing five civilians, physically injuring over 1,000 civilians inside Israel, and psychologically traumatizing thousands more.[90] The Goldstone Mission stated these numbers, concluding: "Where there is no intended military target and the rockets and mortars are launched into civilian areas, they constitute a deliberate attack against the civilian population. These actions would constitute war crimes and may amount to crimes against humanity."[91]

What should Israel have done under the circumstances? One of any sovereign state's primary obligations vis-à-vis its citizens is to protect their safety.[92] Having come under protracted armed attack by thousands of rockets and mortar shells—which would seem to have surpassed the "most grave" threshold, allowing Israel to exercise its right to self-defense[93]—Israel faced an explicit need to protect its citizens. No doubt the Israeli

89. *See* the discussion *supra* notes 21–23, regarding the erosion of red lines by these tactics. The argument that the *Oil Platforms* decision of the ICJ promotes aggression because it might encourage states to engage in a series of "small" attacks, entitling the aggressor to privilege from a defensive military response, was raised by (then) U.S. State Department Legal Adviser, William H. Taft. William H. Taft, *Self-Defense and the Oil Platforms Decision*, 29 Yale J. Int'l L. 295, 300–01 (2004).

90. *See* Human Rights Council, Human Rights in Palestine and Other Occupied Arab Territories—Report of the UN Fact Finding Mission on the Gaza Conflict, U.N. Doc. A/HRC/12/48, ¶¶ 103–105 (Sept. 25, 2009) [hereinafter "The Goldstone Report"].

91. *Id.* at ¶ 1950.

92. Thus, the Summary of the American National Security Strategy of 2006 states that "the first duty of the United States Government remains what it always has been: to protect the American people and American interests." White House, National Security Strategy section V (Mar. 2006) [hereinafter 2006 National Security Strategy] http://georgewbush-whitehouse.archives.gov/nsc/nss/2006/ (last visited May 5, 2016).

93. For the sake of simplicity, I shall refrain from dealing with the legal status of the Hamas regime in Gaza; neither shall I deal with the legal effects of the majority view in the ICJ'S decision in the Wall Advisory opinion, which limited the right to self-defense only against armed attacks by military forces of states. *See supra* Chapter 2 note 46.

response was subject to all legal and moral constraints.[94] However, when exercised, its proportional response should have been strong enough to deter Hamas from continuing to launch rockets, at least for a reasonable time. The proportional limitation placed on the magnitude of Israeli military force should not have been based exclusively upon equality considerations comparing Hamas's actions and Israel's response; nor should it have been based solely on any other quantitative measurement (such as "body count"). Instead, it should have been examined in light of its qualitative deterrent effect as well. For example, in an ongoing armed conflict, a self-defendant's proportional response might aim at shortening its duration and reducing its scope in the short run, and postponing (if not preventing) the eruption of the next round of belligerency in the long run. Indeed, a nation that wants to fulfill its obligation to its citizens and protect them—while strictly obeying the API's prohibition of "excessive" collateral damage to the adversary's civilians—ought to be provided with deterring tools against its adversary's military objectives.

An efficient way of fighting such salami tactics is by deploying uncertainty. If an aggressor opponent were to know that the self-defendant is not always obliged to a predetermined, expected, proportionally linear response to that opponent's belligerent aggression, the potential spectrum of risks the aggressor faces would grow wider. This would undermine its cost-benefit calculations. The aggressor should not know in advance whether the defendant will respond militarily to a specific small bite from the salami, or whether it will wait and defer its response until enough aggressive events have accumulated.[95] Thus, the aggressor will not have the privilege of knowing in advance whether a specific act on its part will be the straw that breaks the camel's back, nor will it be certain, in advance, what the camel's reaction to each such infraction will be. This uncertainty

94. Indeed, Israel was heavily criticized, including by the Goldstone Report, for the proportionality of its actions. Regarding its necessity, however, bearing in mind the scope of the rocket fire and the fact that the Hamas Charter rejects Israel's right to exist, no reasonable settlement of the conflict seems to have been attainable in a peaceful way. (*See* the Charter's preamble: "Israel will exist and will continue to exist until Islam will obliterate it, just as it obliterated others before it." The Covenant of the Islamic Resistance Movement, Aug. 18, 1988 (Hamas) http://avalon.law.yale.edu/20th_century/hamas.asp (last visited Aug. 29, 2016).

95. Indeed, the "accumulation of events" theory, advocating one large action in response to a series of small-scale attacks suffered by a state, is legally disputed; it is susceptible to allegations of disproportionality, depending on the circumstances. *See, e.g.*, DINSTEIN, WAR, AGGRESSION AND SELF-DEFENCE, *supra* note 55, at 206.

may teach the aggressor a very important deterring lesson: there are no free meals (or free risk-insurance) in the aggression business. Furthermore, neither the menu of these (aggressive) meals nor their price is fixed either. If, on the other hand, a self-defendant is constantly constrained to a linear and proportional response by law, the aggressor's spectrum of risks will be substantially reduced, incentivizing its aggression.

I have brought salami tactics into the discussion as a tricky example of how the *ad bellum* threshold can be challenged and eroded. Normatively speaking, in order to deter such a rational aggressor, the expected value of this daily or weekly "investment" of one or a few rockets should be negative,[96] whether the potential reaction to the aggression comes after the first or tenth rocket or after thousands of them. For such an aggressor, if the price of its aggression—the targeting of its own military assets—is higher than its rewards, it may be deterred from engaging in such tactics from the very beginning. Such an approach was advocated by Oscar Schachter: " 'defensive retaliation' may be justified when a state has good reason to expect a series of attacks from the same source and such retaliation serves as a deterrent or protective action."[97]

Although the need to deter a repeating aggressor might be justified in due circumstances, the escalation should be limited then only to this strategic aim of the war. The aim of deterrence—like any other aim on the spectrum of war aims, to be elaborated in the coming discussion—should be lawfully achieved in the most restricted and limited way.

4.5.3 When Deterrence Fails: Incapacitation or Regime Change

Deterrence is not a magic formula. There are cases in which it does not work in the sense that the desired result is not achieved (and the adversary is not deterred from acting) or, in some cases, could not be achieved from the get-go, for example, with respect to "undeterrable" leaders (or terrorists). In such cases, the self-defendant, who is entitled to realize its self-defense, should be allowed to aim even further by incapacitating its adversary's capabilities; if that does not work either, it might consider a regime change.

---

96. As to the law and economics analysis of deterrence in the context of domestic law enforcement, *see supra* text accompanying notes 57–58.

97. Schachter, *The Right of States to Use Armed Force*, *supra* note 52, at 1638.

What should have been the proportionate expected response of the United Kingdom to Germany's 1939 conquest of Poland by military force?[98] Should the British reaction to the German invasion of Poland, deriving from the guarantees Britain had given to Poland, have triggered a full-scale World War against an undeterred Germany? Or should it have been restricted, aimed simply at "ending the aggression or reversing the invasion"? In short, was the UK's declaration of war on September 3, after its ultimatum had expired, a proportional response to the concrete act of German aggression by current legal standards? Similarly, by contemporary legal rules, should the U.S. response following the Japanese attack on Pearl Harbor on the morning of December 7, 1941, have been restricted to the specific injury suffered, or was the formal declaration of war by the U.S. Congress the day after the Japanese attack[99] a proportional and therefore lawful response? Furthermore, even if the need of the self-defendants to declare the World War is taken as a given, what should have been its aims?

On August 20, 1940, British prime minister Winston Churchill, in his famous speech, "The Few" ("Never in the field of human conflict was so much owed by so many to so few"), delivered to the House of Commons, dealt with Britain's war objectives against Germany:

> I do not think it would be wise at this moment, while the battle rages and the war is still perhaps only in its earlier stage, to embark upon elaborate speculations about the future shape which should be given to Europe or the new securities which must be arranged to spare mankind the miseries of a third World War. [. . .] But before we can undertake the task of rebuilding we have not only to be convinced ourselves, but we have to convince all other countries that the Nazi tyranny is going to be finally broken.[100]

---

98. Indeed, the requirement of necessity was probably fully satisfied: there was no alternative to a military response by Britain and France after the failure of Prime Minister Chamberlain's policy of appeasement. For a general description of the road to war, *see, e.g.*, Jessica Talarico, *How Europe Went to War in 1939*, British Imperial War Museums, http://www.iwm.org.uk/history/the-road-to-1939# (last visited Aug. 29, 2016).

99. Congressional Declaration of War on Japan, S.J. Res 116, 77th Cong. Sess. 1 (1941).

100. Winston Churchill, The Few (Aug. 20, 1940), http://www.winstonchurchill.org/learn/speeches/speeches-of-winston-churchill/1940-finest-hour/113-the-few (last visited Aug. 29, 2016).

Indeed, the challenge of defeating Nazi tyranny represents the opposite pole of the spectrum of war aims. The ambition "to spare mankind the miseries of a third World War" requires the destruction of "the Nazi tyranny." Nevertheless, it should be noted that even this extreme uncompromising requirement is not quantitatively based. There is no reference to killing all or most of the tyrant's soldiers, or to causing any or a given amount of damage to its civilians or civilian infrastructure. There is no body count or any other measurable index. The desired result is explicitly formulated: the destruction of the "Nazi tyranny." When deterring a tyrant leader fails, the resort left to its victim state is to deny the tyrant state its military capabilities. In rare cases, however, even that is not enough due to the relatively temporary effect, and a total regime change is required.

The Allies' demand for Germany's unconditional surrender in World War II seems to have been not only morally justified but practically desirable, due to the widespread legacy of the Nazi doctrine and beliefs within German society and the absence of a strong democratic tradition. Indeed, the building of a new Germany seems to have required the destruction of the old: "[t]he outer limit is the conquest and political reconstruction of the enemy state, and only against an enemy like Nazism can it possibly be right to reach that far."[101] Even in this case, however, there is no consensus regarding the demand, made in 1943 in Casablanca by Roosevelt and Churchill, for the "unconditional surrender" of the Axis powers.[102] It was criticized, for example, by Liddell Hart who believed at that time "[t]hat once the odds have changed against Germany, a new German leadership might arise which, provided that German independence and national integrity were maintained, would seek peace on terms that could be acceptable to the West. Unconditional surrender, which closed the door to a negotiated end to the war, would leave no way out for the German people and opposition, thus playing into Hitler's hands."[103]

The more common view, however, is presented by Andrew Roberts. He justified the "unconditional surrender" requirement and the need to

---

101. Walzer, Just and Unjust Wars, *supra* note 42, at 113 (pointing out that "[i]n a sense, aggression was the least of Hitler's crimes." *Id.* at 116).

102. For a brief discussion of objections to the demand for unconditional surrender at the end of World War II, *see* John L. Chase, *Unconditional Surrender Reconsidered*, 70 Pol. Sci. Q. 258 (1955).

103. Gat, A History of Military Thought, *supra* note 71, at 800–01.

reconstruct Germany, claiming that it was based on the internal structure and beliefs of German society:

> The war had to be won by the Allies, of course, but it also needed to be lost, comprehensively and personally, by Hitler himself. His suicide in the bunker after the total collapse of his dreams had to be the last chapter of the tale, the crucial prerequisite for the decent, peace-loving Germany we know today. If Hitler had been killed by the generals in [the assassination plot of July] 1944—with or without British help—and a compromise peace had been arranged that way, present-day Germans would always have wondered whether the Fuhrer might have won the war. . . .
>
> A negotiated peace would have let the German people off the hook, although it would have saved millions of lives in Europe and, by presumably shortening the war against Japan, in the Far East too. Yet to have concluded an armistice on the demonstrable fallacy that the war was begun and carried on by one man's will, rather than through the wholehearted support and enthusiasm of the German people, would hardly have produced the most durable and profound period of peace Europe has ever known.[104]

The extreme example of the Third Reich, and the conflicting views of the end results of World War II, demonstrate the wide spectrum of lawful *ad bellum* proportionality in general, and the relativeness of its deterrence component in particular. Although the end result of a war might be contested, deterrence considerations, whether explicit or implicit, play a substantial role in framing it.

4.6 Defensive Deterrence: Advantages and Disadvantages—An Interim Balance

Deterrence aimed at preserving the status quo is generally a defensive tool, although it can be manipulated as a pretext for aggression. In the following discussion I compare the currently lawful self-defense against an armed attack with the suggested supplement of legalizing defensive

104. Andrew Roberts, The Storm of War: A New History of the Second World War 484–85 (2009) [footnotes omitted]. As regards Japan's "unconditional surrender," *see supra* Chapter 3 note 89.

deterrence, whenever appropriate, and conclude that defensive deterrence may be morally and legally preferable to reactive self-defense, in appropriate cases, due to the following reasons.

First, defensive deterrence is usually more effective; counterintuitively, if regulated, in many cases it should be less destructive. If the threat aimed against the potential aggressor's military assets works and deters it, the social benefit is clear: both adversaries (as well as third parties) will not suffer from this potential war's hazards. The more credible the threat the less need there is to exercise it, and indeed legalizing it would add to its credibility. If the threat fails and the aggressor crosses the legal threshold of an armed attack (including situations lawfully justifying a preemptive, anticipatory strike), the self-defendant is entitled to defend itself, subject to the legal constraints of self-defense. The scope of the military force used in such a case should not be greater than that which is lawful under the "regular" self-defense rules, on the assumption that the proportional response in the latter case should not always be linear but rather, as suggested earlier, adjusted to the threat. Once the qualitative flavor of deterrence is added to proportionality, as suggested in appropriate cases, trying to contain conflicts by deterrence may prevent wars or defer their start, and even when it fails, it usually will not worsen the war's hazards.

Second, defensive deterrence, due to its proactive nature, allows focusing the threat—and the actual use of military force, if necessary—on military objectives while sparing civilians, much more than in the reactive scenario.[105] In reactive self-defense, due to its responsive nature, the place, pattern, scope, and focus of the aggression are selected by the aggressor, and the self-defendant is dragged into an existing state of affairs. For example, an aggressor may choose to fight asymmetrically in an urban area as its preferred arena. In such a case, the expected lawful collateral damage caused by a law-abiding self-defendant[106] might be much greater than had it been proactive.

Third, due to the potential proactive alternative available to a self-defendant against an "imminent threat," defensive deterrent measures

105. Furthermore, even an aggressor's combatants unrelated to the closed circle of its center of gravity would be spared, to a greater extent, since targeting them would not be necessary for the sake of the lawful war aim.

106. *See supra* Chapter 1 note 59.

and an anticipatory strike are in many cases interchangeable.[107] Legalizing the former would, in many cases, eliminate the need to exercise the latter. Strategically, deterrence assumes that a credible threat might contain hostilities, whereas an anticipatory strike might unleash them; legally, an anticipatory strike might not be perceived as a natural course of self-defense in general; in particular, the "imminent threat" prevented might not be considered tantamount to an armed attack. Thus, its legality may be (very) controversial. Legally, defensive deterrent measures might be considered less speculative.

Last but not least, legalizing defensive deterrence would bridge the gap, so common in international law, between the actual practice of states and the legal rhetoric.[108] The law cannot ignore the reality in which deterrence is part of the explicit and implicit language in which belligerents talk to each other; deterrence should therefore find its place within the legal paradigm. If the goal for the laws of war is to be practical and effective, the strategic practice should be followed by integrating deterrence considerations in them.

There are two main arguments against legalizing the suggested deterrent component of a lawful self-defense. One, the slippery slope argument, is mainly applicative; the other argument is substantive. The slippery slope argument warns that ostensibly defensive deterrence can very easily serve as a pretext for aggression. Deterrence argumentation could be manipulated by potential or actual aggressors, pretending to be defendants, paying lip service to it in justifying their aggression through a self-defense discourse. The substantive argument relates to the deterrence doctrine's inherent drawbacks, discussed earlier. A legal system cannot rely on a strategy that might lead to a counter-effect. Steps intended to be defensive deterrent measures might mistakenly be perceived by an adversary as preparations for an aggressive attack, inducing it to attack first. Miscalculation could escalate atrocities rather than prevent them. In addition, miscalculation can occur on the self-defensive side as well: in

107. Indeed, there is no substitution between the two when deterrence does not work. *See supra* notes 97–103.

108. As an example demonstrating this gap, while dealing with the legality of nuclear weapons in general and their deterrent effect in particular, the ICJ's vice president Schwebel stated: "More than any case in the history of the Court, this proceeding presents a titanic tension between State practice and legal principle." Legality of the Threat or Use of Nuclear Weapons, Advisory Opinion, 1996 I.C.J. Rep. 226, 311 (July 8) (dissenting opinion of Judge Schwebel).

order to maintain its credibility, a self-defendant might be driven to start a war against an aggressor. The mere fact that an armed attack surpassing the legal threshold has occurred does not automatically oblige the self-defendant to respond with a war of self-defense. However, it might be drawn into a war of self-defense aimed, practically (though not formally), at maintaining its credibility and reputation. Indeed, it could be argued that this example demonstrates, in fact, the inherent fallacies of deterrence theory: that it is a non-coherent theory aimed against the unknown intentions of an adversary, yet which throws all of its weight into manipulating them. Indeed, a substantive objection to introducing deterrent defensive considerations into the legal discourse might argue against building a legal construction on such shifting sands.

These arguments should be taken seriously. Indeed, introducing the deterrence effect as an integral part of a self-defendant's proportional military response to an act of aggression might create the risk of abuse and manipulation by an ostensible defendant, using deterrence as leverage and as an excuse for the illegal use of force. However, such potential manipulation is a concern with any legal rule—indeed, self-defense per se is subject to abuse and manipulation, as well; yet due to the inherent weakness of the *ad bellum* rules, and in the absence of effective central enforcement, deterrence threats demand special attention. Furthermore, even bona fide defensive measures, from the defendant's perspective, might be perceived as aggression by its adversary and trigger a counter-effect.

The answer to these two challenges should be based on adherence to professional military standards and transparency requirements. Attention has been directed throughout our discussion to the substantive attributes of "real" deterrence in order to distinguish it from rhetoric and manipulation. The suggested tailor-made approach to proportionality should not be misinterpreted as promoting a wild-horses approach. On the contrary, as discussed earlier, every belligerent act by a self-defendant should be professionally militarily justified, in light of its alternatives. Transparency of the decision-making process, though required and common in liberal democracies, which are the typical law-abiding states, requires the self-defendant to provide to both the domestic and international public an accounting of the process of tailoring the deterrence suit to its specific aggressor, and of the way its deterrent components are actually exercised. It is this required professionalism from the deliverer of the deterrent threat that would minimize reckless mistakes, whereas the transparency requirement would reduce opportunistic misuse of deterrence as a pretext for aggression. Furthermore, any potential unprofessional, reckless, or opportunistic misuse of deterrence would have to contend with the same unconducive social changes, new liberal norms, and public expectations, especially in liberal democracies, together with relatively easy access by the different media to conflict zones.[109]

At the end of the day, it need be kept in mind that the suggested proactive defensive deterrence is mainly a defensive tool. Indeed, there are good arguments against its legalization; in many cases, however, it would be preferable to the currently lawful, reactive self-defense measures. When the contradictory arguments are balanced, my conclusion is that its adoption should be favored, in appropriate scenarios. In many cases, the promise it carries seems much more attractive than the downside effects it may trigger.

4.7 *Concluding Remarks*

Deterrence is an integral part of defensive strategy. In most cases, however, it should not and cannot be its only basis. Strategically, deterrence has a mixed reputation. Legally, it enjoys limited standing. Its limitations and fragility, as outlined above, crystallize a legal challenge: How can the positive effects of deterrence be introduced into the international legal discourse? This chapter has called for legalizing defensive deterrence when it is coherent with the aim of the *ad bellum* rules: to maintain international peace and security. Naturally, a military strategy that is aimed at preserving the prevailing status quo and containing conflicts is consistent with the UN Charter, which has the very same goal. Furthermore, if the goal is to promote adherence to the prevailing *in bello* rules, the legalization of some concrete deterrent measures should be sanctioned. Deterrence against transgressors' militaries should be legally endorsed rather than suppressed, as long as it is consistent with the overall strategy of the law, to allow for lawful self-defense while sparing innocent lives and preventing unnecessary suffering. The leverage suggested for overcoming the main disadvantages of legalizing deterrence is consistent with this book's paradigm: military professionalism and transparency. Indeed, as stated above, the suggested professionalism is not a black box deposited, and operated, solely by military personnel; rather it is public knowledge and should be

---

109. *See supra* text accompanying Chapter 2 note 176.

scrutinized by the public and by its appropriate domestic and international bodies and organs.

The suggested defensive deterrence might revitalize the disputed concept of *ad bellum* proportionality. In determining the amount of force that can be lawfully exercised in a given belligerency, I have suggested using the deterrence criterion when applicable, as a tool, to determine the lawfulness of a war's aims. The containment of conflicts, in whole or in part, by the use of deterrence should be preferable to actual fighting. Indeed, the *ad bellum* sphere is mainly strategic by nature, and in essence the suggested *ad bellum* proportionality, by reference to the spectrum of war aims, is also mainly strategic. From this perspective, this chapter closes a circle in this book. Although in previous chapters (1 and 3) I have called for revitalizing the necessity principle, this chapter has dealt with reviving the other basic principle, the requirement of proportionality, relating to the *ad bellum* laws.

Indeed, this interaction should have a moderating effect upon the hazards of war. Totality in terms of unlimited scope of violence is absolutely forbidden currently, and totality relating to the political objective of war is, in many cases, neither practical nor desirable. But even where a more aggressive war aim has been lawfully selected, that does not automatically trigger totality in terms of either the means used in that war, its targets, and duration; or its scope. The opposite is true: with regard to any strategic aim, along the spectrum of lawful war aims, the minimal force that can achieve it should be exercised. This is the combined legal effect of combining the necessity principle (at both the *ad bellum* and the *in bello* stages), as suggested earlier, and the *ad bellum* proportionality discussed here.

5

Conclusions

THE WRITING OF this book was triggered by a twofold desire: to bridge the unacceptable gap between the positive rules of the international law governing armed hostilities and actual state practice, and to reduce the humanitarian damage caused by this reality. The current law, which reflects the compromise reached between the two apparently rival camps, the military and the humanitarian, does not seem to be optimal in balancing the different interests of states' militaries and the humanitarian agenda. In response to this challenge, this book offers a new paradigm based on reality that may, in appropriate cases, elevate the humanitarian threshold by replacing the currently unsustainable or doubtful imperatives imposed upon militaries with professionally-based, therefore attainable, requirements.

The suggested paradigm seeks to revitalize the humanitarian mission of the international law governing armed hostilities, which is being frustrated due to states' actual practice. In order to achieve its two aims—creating an environment in which full abidance by the law becomes an attainable norm, thus facilitating the second and more important aim of reducing human suffering—it calls for the acknowledgment of realpolitik considerations that dictate states' and militaries' behavior. This requires recognition of the core interests of law-abiding states, fighting in their own self-defense—those that, from their militaries' professional perspective, are essential in order to exercise their defense. Internalizing the importance of existential security interests, when drawing the contours of the law, should not automatically come at the expense of the core values of the humanitarian agenda—for example, the distinction rule. Rather, it allows more room for the humanitarian arena. Indeed, it requires a dialogue

Military Professionalism and Humanitarian Law. Yishai Beer.

between the two camps, reflecting and delicately balancing both sides' core interests. The product of this dialogue should create a new equilibrium, allowing for more humanitarianism, which would still be acceptable to militaries.

The suggested tool to allow for such an improved dialogue is the standards and principles of military professionalism. Militaries function in a professional manner; they respect their respective doctrines, operational principles, fighting techniques, and values. Their performances are not random or incidental. Though it might sound counterintuitive at first, the essence of the suggested paradigm is, inter alia, to surface and leverage the constraining elements hidden in military professionalism. Talking professional language and adopting the professional way of thinking that underlies militaries' conduct makes it possible to identify and focus upon the core interests of a military in any given war—those that ought to be taken into consideration—alongside those that can be sacrificed for the sake of the humanitarian interests, while still achieving the military mission. Indeed, leveraging professional standards and norms would establish a reasonable modus vivendi for a military, while allowing substantial new space for the humanitarian mission of the law.

Indeed, military professionalism does not endorse excessive use of force, above the amount reasonably necessary to achieve a given, lawful military advantage. In performing a given military mission, a professional and well-trained military will exercise its force with minimal brutality. From a utilitarian perspective, efficient exercise of military force is in the self-interest of a professional trained military, and this utilitarian concern is buoyed by legal and ethical ones. Indeed, there are internal constraining forces within military professionalism, and this internal brake should be legally utilized.

Though the suggested paradigm is motivated by the desire to bridge the gap between the law and reality—allowing the humanitarian threshold, in many cases, to be elevated—it may have some side benefits, as well. It will clarify the contours of the law and offer criteria for judging the belligerents' conduct. If followed by transparency requirements, as suggested, it would reduce the risk of the law being manipulated. The suggested approach, which would impose greater responsibility upon soldiers and their commanders, would also reshape the roles played by them vis-à-vis courts, NGOs, and public opinion. Though the suggested criteria for shaping the contours of the law are based upon military standards and norms, militaries do not enjoy exclusivity in using them. They are not immune to external criticism or even punishment, if required, whenever they deviate from these norms. Indeed, the suggested role for the humanitarian community is not to apply the brake to the military's operations—a task that under the suggested approach is subject mainly to the professionals' responsibility and accountability—but rather to inspect its activities.

The contours of the suggested paradigm and its application have been drawn by presenting four, currently controversial issues and demonstrating how the suggested paradigm offers criteria for resolving them. The first issue is the scope of the *in bello* necessity principle. Although it is usually perceived as a permissive rule, justifying the mere use of lethal force, under the suggested approach it simultaneously would be a protective rule, shielding combatants and noncombatants alike from excessive brutality. The second issue relates to the criteria to be used in defining the timing threshold, vindicating the right of self-defense. It has been suggested that the legality of a preemptive strike be taken from the toolbox of military professionalism and defined as the last reasonable point, according to the self-defendant's military doctrine and circumstances, at which it can successfully face the aggressor's threat and still operationally defend itself—including, when necessary, by taking the initiative in its own self-defense. The third issue is the leveraging of military strategy as a constraining tool—this book has called on those who want to reduce war's hazards to think strategically, indeed professionally, especially when determining the legality of targeting in limited wars. The fourth controversial issue that was discussed is deterrence. Despite being a central concept in the management of global security and international peace, it is currently viewed with suspicion and, in many cases, considered an unlawful punitive measure. The suggested paradigm offers a normative framework for introducing deterrence within the current contours of the law.

Regarding all four issues discussed, there is no definite solution to the complicated challenge presented; however, the suggested paradigm offers the contours leading to a reasonable result. Indeed, military professionalism as determined through the prism of the reasonable commander is no stranger to the law of armed conflict. Paradoxically, it was introduced into balancing the *in bello* proportionality equation,[1] where the comparative advantage inherent in military knowledge is largely missing, as it relates

1. *See* the text *supra* accompanying Chapter 1 note 98 and Chapter 2 notes 127–128.

to only one side of the equation.[2] (Although military professionalism has a substantial say in defining "military advantage," it doesn't have an advantage in "quantifying" the moral values in the balancing required vis-à-vis expected collateral damage, on the humanitarian side of the equation.) What is called for here, however, is broadening the application of the professional criteria along the entire spectrum of the legal discourse related to war, especially in challenging cases where they have, or should have, a dominant role.

The suggested paradigm is subject to criticism. Even its assumption that the gap between the law and reality is undesirable and ought to be bridged can be disputed. It can be argued that this gap does not reflect an ex-post compromise, but rather an ex-ante desired arena in which states and politicians can maneuver. On such a cynical approach—one could call it a realistic one—the fog of war invites a parallel, sought-after legal fog. Although the suggested paradigm acknowledges realpolitik considerations, nonetheless it doesn't accept this gap as normatively desirable. However, even if one accepts that bridging the gap is desirable, as suggested, the methodology offered in this book could be criticized by both camps. Humanitarians may treat it as a naïve experiment, or even a vicious one, trying to leverage militaries' necessities at the expense of the innocent and the unprotected. According to such a view, it would be a mistake to grant more power to militaries; in fact, due to their problematic record worldwide, the opposite should be endorsed: the only moral and practical trend should be to reduce militaries' authority and discretion to act forcefully. Indeed, an underlying assumption of such an approach is the difficulty of controlling the exercise of military power—an obstacle that motivates the desire to constrain it in all dimensions—and mistrust of apparently existing internal forces, within militaries, that might restrain them voluntarily. Militaries, on the other hand, might see the notion of leveraging internal constraining forces as a Trojan horse aimed at trying to restrict their freedom to operate in the battlefield. Leveraging vectors based upon internal professional standards and norms, and transforming them into legal rules that might be regulated and inspected by third parties, might be perceived by some militaries as introducing a fifth column within their ranks. It might be considered as a legal takeover of their professional guild's conduct.

---

2. *See supra* Chapter 1 note 59.

To some extent, these critical arguments have some merit. The suggested paradigm might be used as a pretext for aggression and transgression of the law; it might be perceived as another manipulative tool of states and militaries, and it might even trigger counter-effects. On the other hand, if the professional standards and norms work in practice—why transform them into mandatory legal rules? Furthermore, both camps may argue that the tool suggested for bridging the gap between the law and reality, namely the standards of military professionalism, is neither stable nor universal, but rather too elastic. All of these arguments have been presented in the text above and were addressed, at least in large part. What is being suggested here, however, is not a utopian solution but rather a compromise—different from the existing one—that may actually accommodate more humanitarian requests. The argument that there are internal constraining forces within military professionalism neither ignores nor weakens the restraining legal and ethical vectors. Rather, it strengthens them by allowing their operation on more solid and stable grounds. Indeed, military professionalism should be a complementary force in fulfilling the humanitarian mission. The notion that power should be constrained first of all, as a professional matter, by the exercise of internal constraining forces to their full capacity and only afterward by legal rules, too, is well rooted in legal thinking. Indeed, any power holder is legally obliged, under domestic law, to constrain it. If the suggested approach is accepted, it would mean that the full humanitarian burden does not fall mainly, and to some extent exclusively, upon the thin shoulders of humanitarian norms and standards. Making these latter the last residual brake, rather than the main (if not the only) one, would strengthen the overall constraining forces of military operations.

The suggested paradigm has a long road ahead of it. If accepted, it could be applied in regard to other controversial issues not discussed above; for example, in confronting the challenge of exceptional, largely disputed, cases of extreme emergency situations. An example demonstrating this potential is the International Court of Justice's "extreme circumstances of self-defense" exception, relating to the threat or use of nuclear weapons.[3] The Court observed that none of the states advocating the legality of such weapons "has indicated what, supposing such limited use [of such a weapon, including tactical ones] were feasible, would be the precise

3. *See supra* at the Introduction note 85.

circumstances justifying such use."[4] Though the suggested approach does not offer a precise protocol for dealing with such a challenge—nor has this book suggested a detailed solution to any of the other challenges presented—it does offer the potential criteria for doing so.[5] Similarly, it could be applied in regard to any military activity that is otherwise unlawful but might fall into the categories of justification or excuse;[6] the contours of a justified or excusable military operation and its scope ought to be the mildest possible, and should be drawn, inter alia, based upon professional criteria.

The suggested paradigm and its potential application challenge current perceptions and paradigms relating to both segments of the laws of war. It contests, from a critical perspective, the law's basic pillars—that is, the proportionality and necessity principles. However, if accepted, it would still maintain the basic contours, rationale, spirit, and morality of the modern law. Though it relies heavily upon the positive rules and their appropriate interpretation, it invites, at some select points, a normative intervention as well. From this perspective, the suggested reform calls for an evolution of the prevailing system rather than revolutionizing it.

---

4. Legality of the Threat or Use of Nuclear Weapons, Advisory Opinion, 1996 I.C.J. Rep. 226, ¶ 94 (July 8).

5. *Cf.* Walzer's analysis of the carpet bombing of German cities in World War II, which started as a result of a "supreme emergency," to adopt Winston Churchill's description of Britain's predicament in 1939. According to Waltzer, the level, imminence, nature, and scope of the military threat of Nazi Germany required—as a measure of last resort—utilizing all means necessary to win, including unlawful ones. The decision made in November 1940 to bomb the German cities cannot be justified in his opinion as revenge or even reprisal, nor on utilitarian considerations of shortening the war, but only by military justifications, if any, relating to the mere ability to win the war. However, what might have been justified in the early stages of the war (1940–1942)—though even then, at the height of the Blitz, many British officers argued that Britain should bomb only German military targets—should have been totally rejected in its later stages (1942–1945), which Walzer defines as "allied terrorism" or "terror bombing." MICHAEL WALZER, JUST AND UNJUST WARS 251–61 (4th ed. 2006).

6. Whereas a justification usually relates to exceptional but warranted acts by law, an excuse relates to wrongful acts that are excused due to their special circumstances (i.e., mental illness of the wrongdoer). *See, e.g.*, Kent Greenawalt, *The Perplexing Borders of Justification and Excuse*, 84 COLUM. L. REV. 1897 (1984). *See also* Cassese's recommendation to consider anticipatory self-defense as legally prohibited, while admittedly knowing that there may be cases where it may be justified on moral and political grounds; *see supra* Chapter 2 note 20.

Index

Abdel Nasser, Gamal, 77–79
anticipatory strike, 70, 73–76, 85, 98
Afghanistan, 4, 148, 164
API (additional protocol 1 to the Geneva Conventions), 3–4, 12, 46
  Article 44, 8
  Article 49, 99
  Article 51, 4, 6
  Article 52, 6, 39, 147, 156, 158
  Article 57, 53, 146
  history of, 5
  and reprisals, 7
  and targeting, 147
  and United Kingdom, 6
  See also Geneva conventions additional protocols
armed attack
  and ICJ, 70
  and imminence, 72–3, 83
  and self-defense, 72, 113
  and terrorism, 105
Atlanta, 126–128
Austria, 102

Barak, Aaron (Israeli supreme court president), 10
Basra, 50
Benvenisti, Eyal, 2n2, 7, 10, 11n51, 39, 136n90, 140n105, 166n196
Blum, Gabriella, 17n81, 32n5, 32n8, 46n41, 49, 49n48–50, 140n104, 145n118, 195n70
"body count," 63, 132–133, 202, 205
Bonaparte, Napoleon, 44, 63, 100n141, 125, 128, 151, 167
Brussels Conference of 1874, 59
Bush, George H. W., 16n74, 64
Bush, George W., 83n52, 84, 104n152, 166

Carnahan, Burrus, 38
Caroline case, 76
"carpet bombing," 63, 218n5
Cassese, Antonio, 7, 16n75, 32n4, 59n80, 73n16, 74n20, 105n154, 218n6
Churchill, Winston, 204–205
Cicero, 144
Civil War (U.S.), 38, 126–127, 132, 157
COA (course of action), 54, 57
Cohen, Eliot, 64n96, 89n71, 92n89, 132
The Cold War, 79, 82, 92, 99–102, 174–175
collateral damage, 22n91, 25, 47, 52–56, 62, 65, 138–139, 144–148
combatants, classification, 46–47

"concentration of force," 93
Confucius, 91
counterinsurgency, 21, 37, 62, 64, 95, 132, 138
criminal law, international, 7
customary law, 3, 7, 73

deterrence, 27, 110, 163–164, 169
  advantages, 183–184, 207–208
  and ambiguity, 177
  and collateral damage, 207
  and containment, 174, 183, 198, 211
  and credibility, 178, 207–209
  defensive, 28–29, 171–174, 183–186, 188, 196–197, 206–211
  and deterrent suit, 173, 189–194, 196, 198, 209
  and dictatorship, 137, 162n187, 192, 198, 205
  effects of, 194
  and enforcement, 182–183, 190–192
  failure, 137, 175–176, 179, 182–184, 192, 194, 198, 203
  legal standing, 172, 178
  and manipulation, 173, 178, 208–209
  and military professionalism, 173, 209
  mutual, 174–176, 178–180
  and proportionality, 184–191, 193, 195–197, 199–203, 206, 209, 211
  and qualitative approach, 186–188, 193, 202
  and quantitative approach, 188, 193, 202
  and rationality, 178, 186, 189–192
  and reciprocity, 175, 179–182, 185
  and repeat offender, 197, 200
  and reprisals, 180
  role of, 171, 175
  self-defense, 173, 178, 181, 183, 196, 201
  shortcomings, 176–178, 208
  and spillover-effect, 174
  strategic, 174
  and third party, 195
  and timing, 184
  and transparency, 209
Dinstein, Yoram, 9, 13, 33, 74–75, 97, 141
distinction, rule of, 15, 19, 29, 44, 46–47, 167
  and collateral damage, 22n91
  and targeting, 118, 139
  and urban warfare, 62
doctrine
  and Counterinsurgency, 133–134
  definition of, 90
  development of, 91–92
  NATO, 90, 92
  Soviet, 51, 90, 92
DPH (direct participation in hostilities), 8
  and belligerent nexus, 9
  and ICRC, 9
  and revolving door, 9
dual-purpose objects, 59

economy of force, 35–37, 94
Egypt, 77

Falkland Islands, 153, 199
"fog" of war, 20, 50, 88, 161, 216
France, 5, 75
Franck, Thomas, 14, 79, 107, 141, 195–196
Freedman, Lawrence, 176
The French Revolution, 128
Fuller, J. F. C., 130

Gat, Azar, 125
Geneva Conventions, 2, 131, 179
  and law of armed conflict, 2
  and deterrence, 179

and law of armed conflict, 2
See also API
Germany, 5, 76, 101, 204–206
Glennon, Michael, 14
"grand battle," 131
Grant, Gen. Ulysses, 127
Greenwood, Christopher, 105, 111
Gulf War (1991), 50–51, 64, 133, 142, 194
Gulf War (2003), 83, 104

Hackett, Gen. John, 102
Hague Peace Conferences, 59
Hague Regulations (1907), 46, 139n102
"halt and repel," 184, 197, 199
Hamilton, Alexander, 129
Handel, Michael, 91
Hart, Liddell, 122, 130–131, 205
Higgins, Rosalyn, 199
"Highway of Death," 50–52
Hiroshima, 195
"horizontal nexus," 121, 158
HPCR manual, 147, 156
human shields, 62
humanitarian camp (school of thought), 1, 18, 213–214, 217
humanity, principle of
as a constraint, 32, 119
history of, 33
and necessity, 60, 64
and targeting, 139–140
Hungary, 111
Huntington, Samuel, 88
Hussein (king of Jordan), 77
Hussein, Saddam, 51, 84, 104

ICJ
and armed attack, 70
and *Nicaragua* decision, 72
nuclear weapons advisory opinion, 16n75, 18n84, 86, 217
and *Oil Platforms*, 187
and proportionality, 140
and self-defence, 19, 217
and Wall Advisory Opinion, 81n46, 201n93
ICRC, 8, 39, 46
and DPH, 10
ICTR (International Criminal Tribunal for Rwanda), 7
ICTY (International Criminal Tribunal for the Former Yugoslavia), 7
IHL camp (school of thought), 10
IMT (International Military Tribunal), 194
incapacitation, 135, 203
India, 176
"indirect approach," 131
The Industrial Revolution, 63
initiative, principle of, 94
intelligence, 104–105, 138, 161–162
Iraq, 148, 166
Israel
and anticipatory self-defense, 78
and Hamas, 201–202
and the Six Days War, 76–78, 86, 101
Supreme Court of, 42
Italy, 5

Keynes, John Maynard, 130
Korean War, 38, 100, 175–176
Kosovo, 14, 56–57, 65, 97, 148
Kretzmer, David, 142–143, 178

law of armed conflict, 60
and additional protocols, 2
and compliance, 17, 31, 61
and consent, 6, 8
and contractual model, 3
and Geneva Conventions, 2
origins of, 1–2
and regulatory model, 3, 11
and targeting, 118

Lebanon, 4
levels of war
and interaction, 124
and operational, 21, 36, 98, 123
and strategic, 21–22, 26, 36, 117, 122, 149–150, 159
and tactical, 21, 36, 55, 123, 151, 159
Libya, 4, 77
Lieber Code, 17n82, 38
Lincoln, Abraham, 127, 132
LOAC camp (school of thought), 10
Luban, David, 11
Luttwak, Edward, 100n142, 131, 138

maneuver, principle of, 93
Marten's Clause, 7, 33
McChrystal, Gen. Stanley, 164
Meron, Theodore, 7
military advantage, 145, 148–150, 167, 193
military camp (school of thought), 1, 12–13, 18, 213–214, 217

Nagasaki, 195
National Security Strategy (U.S.) (2002), 81–82
National Security Strategy (U.S.) (2006), 82
National Security Strategy (U.S.) (2010), 57
NATO, 14, 56–57, 65
necessity, rule of, 15, 29, 46, 213
ad bellum, 67, 169
in bello, 17, 47, 67, 159
as a constraint, 39, 60, 64, 119
military, 21, 32–33, 39, 43, 50, 60, 64, 66
as a hollow rule, 38–40
as a professional military requirement, 34
sequential, 161
and targeting, 139–140, 161
vertical, 168
Netherlands, 102
NGO, 11, 41–42, 67, 166, 214

Obama, Barack, 84
objective, principle of, 93
Operational Last Resort, 96, 100–103, 108–111
Osirak (Iraqi nuclear reactor), 77, 106–107

Pakistan, 176
Paris, 127
Pearl Harbor, 75, 78, 85, 101, 141, 204
persistent objector, 3
Poland, 141, 204
post-heroic era, 112, 138
Powell, Colin, 64, 133, 142, 194
preventive war, 70, 73–74, 83, 85, 98
professionalism, military, 21–22, 28, 43, 46, 214–216
and application, 114, 161
and command, 89–90
as a constraint, 23, 35
as legal norms, 41, 45, 217
as a profession, 88–89
and targeting, 48, 150
and variants, 87
proportionality, rule of, 15, 39, 118, 139, 215
ad bellum, 141, 150, 160, 168–169
in bello, 39, 53, 65, 97, 152n145
as a constraint, 140
and state practice, 149
and the strategic school, 149

Reagan, Ronald, 77
realpolitik, 15, 19, 143, 149, 163, 177, 197, 213, 216
regime change, 203–206
"reasonable commander" standard, 65, 97, 215
Reiter, Dån, 75

reprisals
and API, 7
belligerent, 4
defensive, 16
and deterrence, 178, 180
and the United States, 6
Republican Guards, 51
Responsibility, political, 55–57
Richmond (town), 132
Roberts, Andrew, 101, 205
Rome Statue, 147
Roosevelt, Franklin D., 205
Root, Elihu, 96

San Remo Manual, 153
Saudi Arabia, 4
Schachter, Oscar, 203
Schelling, Thomas, 177
Security Council, 13, 15, 83
security, principle of, 94
self-defense
and armed attack, 70, 72
collective, 80
and Israel, 77–78
and the prevailing law, 72
and timing, 81, 86, 96, 105, 215
and the UN Charter, 69, 74, 136
September 11 (9/11), 166
Sherman, Gen. William, 126, 128
state practice, 12–16, 18, 146, 149–150
Stoker, Bram, 126
St. Petersburg Declaration, 47, 143
strategic school (of targeting), 120, 145, 149
Strategy
American, 132
and Clausewitz, 120
role of, 117, 122
sustainability, principle of, 94
Syria, 4

tactical school (of targeting), 120, 145, 149
Tallinn Manual, 98
targeting, 48, 118, 146–148, 150, 161
terrorism, 22, 44, 49, 79–81, 105, 165, 203
Tiran, Straits of, 78
"tit for tat," 142, 185
Tolstoy, Lev, 89
torture, 42
total war, 44–45, 59, 64
and current view, 134–135, 144
dimensions of, 126
history of, 125
and horizontal nexus, 158
as a legal default, 117–118, 151
as opposed to limited, 143, 168
transparency, 29, 112, 155, 163–167, 209, 214
Tzu, Sun, 60, 64, 91, 129, 131

UN, 15
UN Charter, 14, 16
article 2, 13
article 42, 13
article 51, 13–14, 70, 73–74, 87, 108, 111, 113, 155, 178
unconditional surrender, 135, 205
United Kingdom, 5–6
United States, 5–6, 79

"vertical nexus," 121, 158–160, 168
Vietnam, 63, 132
von Clausewitz, Carl, 42n34, 44, 50, 59, 64–65, 88, 99
and deterrence, 175
and Sun Tzu, 129
and total war, 125–126, 151
von Moltke, Helmuth, 127–128

Walzer, Michael, 13, 194
war, aims of, 152, 155, 165
war, principles of, 36
warfare
asymmetric, 62, 81, 134, 192, 196
urban, 62

Watkin, Kenneth, 8n36, 9n41, 37n21, 117n2, 124, 145, 149, 158n170
Webster, Daniel, 76
WMD (weapons of mass destruction), 104, 134, 174–176, 195–196
World War I, 13, 63, 75, 130, 175
World War II, 13, 61, 63, 100–101, 135, 154, 175

Yemen, 4